KNOW THINE ENEMY

KNOW THINE ENEMY

A Spy's Journey into Revolutionary Iran

EDWARD SHIRLEY

Farrar, Straus and Giroux • New York

Farrar, Straus and Giroux
19 Union Square West
New York 10003

Copyright © 1997 by Edward Shirley
All rights reserved
Published simultaneously in Canada by HarperCollins*CanadaLtd*
Printed in the United States of America
Designed by Debbie Glasserman
First edition, 1997

Library of Congress Cataloging-in-Publication Data
Shirley, Edward, 1949-
    Know thine enemy : a spy's journey into revolutionary Iran / by
Edward Shirley. — 1st ed.
        p.   cm.
    ISBN 0-374-18219-1 (alk. paper)
    1. Iran—Description and travel.   2. Iran—Politics and
government—1979-   I. Title.
DS259.2.S53   1997
955.05'43—dc21   97-2842

For my grandmother,
my mother,
my wife,
&
my daughter

KNOW THINE ENEMY

1 THE TRENCHES

Istanbul, 1990

Unable to find a taxi, Ahmad had hobbled from his hotel. His destination, the American consulate, isolated by unmarked one-way and dead-end streets, was hard to find. He hadn't noticed the neighborhood's tired beauty—its belle epoque apartments and hotels a century in decline. The past had given way to congested streets, honking homicidal drivers, cracked concrete sidewalks, and belly-dancer joints with broken neon signs. When he saw the American flag, machine-gun-toting Turkish guards, pea-green walls, and a visa-information bulletin board in Persian, he saw the Promised Land.

Wet and dirty from the incessant, coal-laden Istanbul winter rain, Ahmad was visibly relieved to see me. He was not your usual Iranian Revolutionary Guardsman: having lost a leg, having lost hope, he wanted to immigrate to America.

When I guided him into my room and asked him in Persian to be seated, Ahmad knew he'd found the man he was looking for. My greeting had reassured him as my predecessors' had not. When Iranians meet an American who speaks Persian, they assume they're meeting the CIA. Among the Middle East's most devout conspirators, they believe that American intelligence is everywhere, all-knowing, and of course Persian-speaking.

Anyone who has crossed paths with the CIA knows the truth is nearly the opposite, but Ahmad's assumption about my employer, at least, was correct. I had come to Turkey to talk to Iranians on behalf of the United States government; I had also come to pursue my own quest to understand better the Muslim mind and soul, particularly its militant Shi'ite Iranian version. I wanted to peel the Persian onion—the obligatory appetizer that resembles the many-layered Persian character—down to its core.

The Revolutionary Guard Corps, or, as it is known in Persian, the *Sepah-e Pasdaran*, is the protector and military will of Iran's mollahs. I'd met several ex-*Pasdaran* in my three years in Istanbul. Most were from the cadre of short-term draftees. Ahmad, however, had been a professional, the hardest of the hard core. He'd traveled by bus from Tehran to Istanbul, a wearying 1,200-mile trip across Iranian Azarbaijan, Kurdistan, and the 700-mile Anatolian plateau. He'd come to Istanbul, like thousands before him, because Iranians do not need visas to cross the frontier. Istanbul—with its foreign consulates, visa forgers, and underground refugee railroads—offered dissident Iranians the chance of immigration to the West.

"What can I do for you?" I asked Ahmad as he slowly lowered himself into the chair directly facing mine. His worn black polyester suit and graying polyester shirt buttoned at the collar had become the unofficial civilian uniform of Iranian men in the Islamic Republic. When he sank into the heavily cushioned chair, unable to control his descent without his right leg, he grabbed the bulbous armrest hard to regain his balance. I glanced at his folded pants leg, collapsed like an accordion. Four heavy black hand-stitched knots in the corners of the last flap held it together.

He finally raised his face, averting his eyes from mine, a traditional Persian reflex before a foreigner. He had pale-brown skin; a thick, stubby black beard only slightly shorter than the hair on his head grew high on his cheeks. It was the face of a serious fundamentalist—everything paid homage to his eyes. However, Ahmad's eyes were not Khomeini's. They were tired, and they were almost kind.

"I want to see America," he said calmly.

I felt his anxious hope in his lowered eyes, not in his words. Outside my window, I could hear the afternoon visa applicants forming lines in the streets, Iranians and Turks shouting at each other, the former always angry at the latter's quicker entrée.

"I like America. I am a friend of America."

"Am I the first American you've ever met?" I asked.

"My older brother knew many Americans before the revolution. He had many American friends, and he spoke English well. But you are *my* first American."

There is probably not a single Iranian who does not want to talk to America. The more militant, the stronger the desire for "the Great Satan." Iranians are more attracted to devils than to angels. They are fascinated by America's power, wealth, and optimistic, very un-Iranian dreams. They crave our recognition; our strong approval or our disapproval, or, most confusing, both at the same time. Fascinated by human faults, like their Zoroastrian forefathers they believe life is an open playing field, and Evil has at least an equal chance of winning. So much the better, then, to listen to what Evil has to say.

Ahmad had joined the Guard via the *Basij*, ragtag outfits of militarily untrained young and old men who backed up the slightly better trained Revolutionary Guard Corps during the eight years of the Iran–Iraq War (1980–88). *Basij* means "mobilization." Lightly armed except in faith, tens of thousands of *Basijis* became martyrs against Iraqi minefields, machine guns, tanks, and flaming oil pits. Ahmad became a *Basiji* and then a *Pasdar* because he wanted to die for Islam and Khomeini; he also joined up because he was bored.

Ahmad's Tehran—a vast peasant ghetto of uneducated young men alternately dreaming of women, wealth, and a new puritan Islamic order—offered few options. Serving God had seemed easily the most compelling and accessible. Ahmad was sixteen when he entered the *Basij*, nineteen when he entered the Guard. He had grown up near the Paradise of Zahra cemetery, famous for its martyrs' graves and a fountain that in the early war years spewed blood-red water in tribute to those who gave their lives in battle.

Ahmad had been too young to fight against the Shah or to occupy the American embassy in Tehran. If he'd been a few years older in 1979, when the revolutionaries seized the embassy for the second and last time, Ahmad definitely would have been there. He'd hated America, the Third World's worst oppressor and the backer of the Shah.

"Why do you want to see America?"

"My cousin lives there. In Austin, Texas." He pronounced the name reverently, then unconsciously touched his right hip a few inches above his stitched-up pants leg. "He told me the best doctors in the world are there. I want to walk again, and he told me I could find a new leg in America."

Ahmad's war memories were the keys to his mind. He had often dreamed of his grieving family visiting his grave, ululating as only the relatives of martyrs may. He kept volunteering for small-unit missions behind Iraqi lines. Yet, unlike most of his comrades, Ahmad kept coming back. As the war dragged on, more and more of his compatriots perished, "dying in pieces," as Ahmad put it—legs and feet ripped off by minefields; bellies, chests, and heads torn open by artillery.

The war defined Ahmad, gave him an identity and a community he never had in Tehran, where he was simply poor. His Shi'ite faith and his Iranian identity became more powerful as the war became more brutal. Then, on a routine night raid, a mine blew his right leg off. Crippled, no longer fighting for God, Ahmad returned home, honored but discarded. It was 1987, eight years after the revolution, four years since Ahmad had mobilized for martyrdom.

I wondered at what moment he'd begun to consider the idea of going to America.

"Are you willing to help me understand Iran, your Iran?" I asked. "If you help me understand your past, I will be indebted to you. You will have done *me* a great kindness, but you should know now that the United States government may *not* be thankful. You shouldn't talk to me if you believe by doing so you will get a visa to America. I don't give visas to make people talk. Talk to me because you want me to listen."

"I'd hoped I would find an American who would want to listen," Ahmad said evenly. "I have seen much that you should know about.

I want to talk to you, and I hope your government will appreciate what I have to say."

Iranians rarely tell linear stories, with a beginning, a middle, and an end. The Persian approach is circuitous; past and present can alternate rapidly, with subjects and objects intertwined, making it difficult to determine who really deserves praise, and who blame. It is thus virtually impossible to have a valuable short conversation with an Iranian. Hours are often required before the listener can know the primary players and get a vague idea of their interconnections, and much longer to assess the story's plot—usually the clash of Good and Evil.

Ahmad didn't plead. Unlike so many of his countrymen, he had not come to beg. Fate had been cruel to him; America, a just land, would want to right a wrong.

For Ahmad, as for most Iranians, things and people were viewed as essentially either good or bad. A change or nuance in character and action, whether for better or worse, would often be ascribed not to moral indecision or haphazard emotion but to deceit. It is a striking disposition in a people who excel at living in that shaded middle ground where an exceptionally kind act can be followed by the most repulsive cruelty. With each day's news about yet another discovered conspiracy or calamity—and there are always hundreds of conspiracies and calamities animating daily Iranian life and gossip—countries, politicians, and clerics are ever being reborn as devils or saints. When Ahmad lost his leg, his wartime identity, his brother, and in 1989 Khomeini, his understanding of the world became more fluid. Good and Evil kept reversing.

While he was with me, he was exactly what he said: my friend.

"Tell me what you want to know," he said calmly.

No matter what I answered, I knew very well that Ahmad would believe I could give him a visa. I could do anything. But I began with the truth, so that when we finished, Ahmad might realize I hadn't deceived him. One-legged leftovers of the Iran-Iraq War had little value to the CIA: Ahmad would never see America courtesy of Langley. Though some in the Agency disagree, deception and coercion are highly overrated tools. Efficient only in the short term, they quickly corrode all those involved. And Iranians often respond well to Americans because they cannot believe anyone can be so beguilingly, stupidly honest and open.

"What do you dream of?" I asked hesitantly. Such a question could strangle our conversation if Ahmad thought I was searching for a means to hurt him. But he did not seem to mind my curiosity—he indulged it.

"The war and women. But mostly women. For me the war is constant. I see it when I'm awake; I see it when I'm asleep. It's not really a dream or a nightmare anymore. It's just there."

Now twenty-three, Ahmad had never slept with a woman. He had never seen a grown woman nude. He had no firm idea of what a woman's genitalia looked like. He desperately wanted to have a woman to marry because his ignorance was exhausting him.

"When you think of America, do you think of women?"

"Yes," he replied, averting his eyes slightly. "Tell me, do American women hate Iranian men?"

"I've seen hundreds of Iranian men with American wives," I replied.

Ahmad smiled. According to State Department consular officers, every other blond in Southern California was marrying an Iranian.

For Muslim fundamentalists, the West's greatest crime is the way it individualizes women, inflaming their already narcissistic appetites that blind them to the role of motherhood, which requires dependence on men. Since medieval times, Islamic theologians have called a woman, because of her sex and her superior powers of entrapment, the most serious challenge to a man's fidelity to God. The veil hides and restrains a woman's passion, which perpetuates the species; take away the veil and the entire revolutionary order falls. Thus, the West encourages dangerous behavior in society's most vital, unstable element.

Islamic society has a highly fragile consciousness. This sensitivity can strike a Westerner as odd, given the unrivaled success of Islam's social order with vastly different peoples from Morocco to Java. But this success has made Muslims acutely conscious of threats to the binding essentials of their faith. Much of the violence, anger, and rabidly anti-Western language of Muslims arises from a concern for an ordered home—the birthright of every man. The militant senses in his own bridled lust the potential for disorder if the veil is lifted outside the home, if women and men act out their dreams—that is, if they behave like Americans.

"Do you still love Khomeini?" I asked Ahmad.

"No, not anymore. But I once loved him more than my father. Khomeini was the Imam, he was my Guide."

"Your guide to Islam? Weren't you a practicing Muslim before he became the Imam?"

"Khomeini taught me that a good life is a life of suffering. That the oppressed poor must not be scared of death. We are the true descendants of the Imams who gave their lives for Islam. WAR! WAR UNTIL FINAL VICTORY! is what I wore on my battle headbands. Khomeini taught me that purification could only come for me and my family through my death in war."

Despite his wounds, Ahmad did not flinch at those words. They briefly rejuvenated him—the fraternity and purpose, the warm comradeship of annihilation.

Ahmad, like most young revolutionaries, saw Khomeini as a personal interpreter of Shi'ism's glorious and bloody past, its early history of recurring pain and disappointment. With the violent death in 661 of Ali, the fourth caliph ("successor to") and nephew and son-in-law of the Prophet Muhammad, a mystical belief in the right of Ali's family to rule Islam was born. With the violent death of Ali's son Hosein, martyrdom became ingrained in Shi'ism, which exported the idea into the consciousness of the larger Sunni world.

For the revolution's true believers, Khomeini was a spiritual descendant of Ali, Hosein, and their ten successors—the dozen Imams who constitute the foundation of Twelver Shi'ism. The final Imam, the last rightful ruler of the world, "disappeared" in 874.

For many young Iranian men, Khomeini had surpassed his twelve predecessors. In a triumph of millenarian justice, he'd brought down an unrighteous *Shahanshah*, the King of all Kings, who no one thought could fall. And in Khomeini's war against the infidel Saddam Hussein, Iran's young men would redeem Ali's and Hosein's sacrifice of thirteen centuries before.

No less important, Khomeini was Ahmad's access to modernity: the oil wealth to make Iran a superpower and a new egalitarian order that would allow Ahmad to rise. Innumerable *things* available in the West would surely be made available and permissible in Iran by clerical rule.

Most crucially, Khomeini would give Ahmad access to women. As odd as it may sound to a Westerner, Khomeini was seen by Ahmad, and many other young men, as a divinely ordained matchmaker. Thoughts of women begin early in the Middle East; the separation of the sexes ensures precocious thoughts of marriage. Ahmad, between his death-wish dreams, burned with desire for women. Veils and combat increased the desire. Offering a share in his victory and rule, Khomeini had promised Ahmad and his compatriots enough status to marry beautiful women—the type Ahmad imagined ayatollahs wed. Ahmad had dreamed that the revolution would bring him nonstop licit sex, and as many children as he wanted. He would be what his father never was: a proud man, a virile warrior whose sons would follow him into the millennium.

"And after all that you have seen, what does it mean to you to be a Muslim?" I asked. "Can a Muslim be an American?"

He did not reply. He crossed his hands at his hips and moved his eyes off mine, waiting.

"The clerics," I said, "constantly talk about how 'we Muslims' must do this or that in order to protect Islam from the West. It appears that anti-Americanism has become a new pillar of the faith."

Ahmad winced at the mention of this. The rules of *ta'arrof* and *gozasht* encourage Iranians to behave well, to prefer a hundred indirect questions and answers over possibly offensive direct ones.

Ta'arrof has no adequate English translation. "Etiquette" captures some of its ceremony and tact but little of its depth and hold over the Persian mind and language. *Gozasht* is tolerance, a generous disposition toward the failings of others, particularly foreigners. Both concepts have been battered by a revolution that finds virtue in bad manners. But despite all the crudeness and violence in contemporary Iran, the two qualities remain strong, even in Revolutionary Guardsmen.

Setting politeness slightly aside, Ahmad tried to explain his faith. "Americans *can* be Muslims. Anyone can be a Muslim if he accepts Muhammad as his Prophet and the Qur'an as the Word of God. They believe the American government is anti-Islamic, not the American people. They believe the American government wants to deny the Prophet's mission and oppress the poor, to stop people from converting to Islam."

Ahmad once again began employing "they," the pronoun behind which Iranians always seek cover. But in this instance, "they" meant the clergy.

"Do you believe that?"

"I don't know."

"Well, is the West Christian?"

"Yes."

"Is the West also Jewish?"

"Of course. Jews are the world's oldest people. They're more clever and rich than Christians, so they run the West."

"Yet you want to move to America. Why would a Muslim want to live in a Judeo-Christian land with so few mosques?"

I expected another wince. Instead, he sidestepped me. "I know America gives visas to Muslims. You don't have to become a Christian to live in America, do you?" Ahmad asked anxiously.

Millions of Muslims live in the West. Four million in France, three million in Germany, two million in Great Britain, perhaps as many as eight million in the United States. Most came for economic reasons, but the migration has not been easy intellectually. Islam, unlike Christianity, is not essentially a matter of conscience or spiritual acrobatics. The Qur'an, the literal Word of God, reads in many passages like an administrative manual. Its divine inspiration, like that of the Jewish Talmud, is legalistic, explicitly aimed at building a community through law. Even the most irreligious Muslim immigrant can feel guilt in a secular foreign land where the muezzin's call is muffled by public ordinances that protect the tranquility of non-Muslim souls.

"Of course you don't have to convert to live in America," I said. "I just wanted to know whether you would feel comfortable living in a non-Muslim land."

Ahmad dropped his eyes to the floor. "I don't care."

Ahmad was a practicing Muslim. Somewhere there had to be guilt, so I searched. "You've grown up in a Muslim land. Your family, your friends are all Muslims. Your words, your jokes, your memories are touched by Islam. You dream of non-Muslim American women, yet you want your American wife to be Muslim, with the same values as your sisters. You'll find none of your ethical order in America. So why do you want to go to a land that will rob your children of their grandparents' faith?"

Ahmad's eyes told me I would now get a longer response. They weren't angry. They were moving backward in time. "I don't need mollahs anymore. I know when you look at me you don't see a soldier. You probably think I have exaggerated my past because you see in front of you the 'dropping of a dog.' But I was once the best of the *Pasdaran*. I burned to die for Khomeini and for my country. They promised us a better life. They promised us God's grace after death.

"Well, I am alive, and my family weeps for me. My mother and my sisters coddle me like a child. My mother can't look at me without lowering her head because she hurts so much inside. Do you know what it is like to see your mother cry for you every day?

"I was a *Pasdar* and now I often soil myself when I go to the bathroom. I can barely walk to the park five blocks away without puffing like an old man. Every night in my dreams I see myself whole, and I still sometimes try to rise at night or in the morning, forgetting about my missing parts. But I don't rise. I just flop or fall. I once killed four Iraqis on a single mission, one of them with only my hands. Now a child could beat me and I could not resist. I am supposed to take care of my mother, not the other way around. Look at me. I am everything an Iranian man should not be."

Ahmad's voice cracked and he turned his face away.

Once again, I felt uneasy. I'd become a confessor—but I inflicted pain without absolution. My questions left Ahmad in worse shape than before. I kept asking myself: How do you peel an onion without tears?

.   .   .

What is a Muslim? If Ahmad had still been a revolutionary, he would have answered the question differently. He would have spoken of power and social conscience. To a radical, Islam means pure, unstoppable power. It is absolute Good in a battle to the death with absolute Evil, the West. It is the ennobling of the poor, history's truest Muslims, and the merciless punishment of the sacrilegious rich; it is Justice. It means a reversal of history, the restoration of the Muslim spirit and community as they were before the Ottomans lost power and allowed the Christians, the Jews, and their treasonous Muslim agents to rule the Middle East.

The Iran–Iraq War and its afterlife had drained Ahmad of contemporary ideology and language. What remained were traditional roots. One is a Muslim, period. Islam is the last stop in man's religious evolution.

Ahmad no longer wanted to be on Iran's brutal front line of politics and faith. He'd left Iran because so many questions no longer made sense. With his faith no longer under siege, a certain serenity had returned. However incongruously, an older understanding of Islam remained, like America, a means of hope.

My conversations with Ahmad had taken me where my former university teachers had not. Every time he winced, digressed, or averted his eyes to the floor, I put down a marker. Without such a map, I could never have dreamed of going to his country.

A twisted irony: Ahmad wanted to go to America to escape the revolutionary problems that were pulling me toward Iran. I wanted nothing more than to live in his hometown, he in mine.

Curious Midwestern boys always dream of escaping home. From an early age, I'd wanted to travel and to live abroad. My mother and grandmother had raised me to leave the nest. My father had given me three thousand 35 mm slides of his early-1950s around-the-world motorcycle ride. An uncle who'd grown up in an Eastern European Jewish ghetto had fascinated me with the remnants of his many languages. Another uncle, a sea captain, had sailed everywhere it was warm.

By high school, I desperately needed to wander and my father's slides had given me an idea. The veiled women, mosques, and bazaars of the Middle East had captured my curiosity more than the castles, palaces, and sculptured gardens of Europe or the costumes, temples, and wars of the Far East. Being Jewish, I thought the Islamic world, which traced its faith to Abraham, was a natural choice. Arabs, Persians, and Turks—three different peoples united by Islam—had built the Muslim Middle East. In college, I decided to start with the Arabs, the Prophet Muhammad's first holy warriors, and work my way forward through the Persians and Turks.

"Does your cousin in America help your family financially?" I asked Ahmad when he told me of his decision to return to Tehran.

It had been several days since we first met, and Ahmad had failed to obtain a U.S. visa from a consular officer. According to American immigration law, a consular officer cannot give a tourist visa to an intending immigrant; all who apply are guilty until they prove their innocence. Even if Ahmad had tried to deceive an officer about his intentions, a one-legged, unemployed, twenty-three-year-old Iranian male could never overcome the presumption that he wanted to immigrate. And Ahmad had not tried to deceive. Without immediate family or a needed skill—and Ahmad had neither—he had no chance at a right of passage.

I could do nothing for him. The CIA was interested in whole Iranians, active-duty Guardsmen who wanted to return to the Islamic Republic. It cared not at all about the casualties of war. A lengthy debriefing should be done. Some financial compensation, perhaps. No more.

I didn't do a debriefing. Though Ahmad was an existential gold mine, he had no current information about the Guard Corps. The Agency, an incurious, bureaucratic institution with a very short attention span, wants information no older than yesterday with as few subjective distractions as possible. Ahmad's insights into the revolutionary Persian mind would have little currency among clandestine operatives and analysts, who strongly prefer answers to *who? what? when?* and *where?* over *why?*

With a visa out of reach, Ahmad could try the "Iranian Express." But he had neither the money nor the physical strength to travel by Istanbul's underground refugee railroad to the United States. The going price was twelve thousand dollars and the difficult voyage would take two weeks. From Istanbul to Madrid, where he would change planes for Havana—Castro ran "rest stop" hotels for Iranians illegally on their way to America—then by boat to Florida or by plane to Mexico. Or, alternatively, direct by air from Madrid to Mexico City, a "tour bus" to the border, then into the Promised Land on crutches at night. Even if he'd had the twelve thousand dollars, Ahmad did not want to hobble his way surreptitiously into the States.

He also did not want to stay any longer in Istanbul. The Turks scared him, and there was no honor and little sympathy for a crippled Persian. I imagined what his days were like: trying to navigate the trenches that had once been the streets of Beyoğlu, the Istanbul neighborhood where Ahmad had found a cheap hotel room five days earlier. The city government was tearing up the streets, laying pipelines for the Russian gas that would—according to theory and everybody's hopes—diminish Istanbul's lethal coal pollution in winter. To a crippled Ahmad, the familiar chaotic streets of Tehran, where thousands die every year in traffic accidents, seemed far safer.

"Yes, my American cousin sends us money," he admitted, when I pressed him about his livelihood. "The family would have a harder life without his help."

"How many years has your cousin been in America?"

"Many. He left before the revolution."

"Was your cousin for or against the Shah?"

"He was against. Everybody in my family was against the Shah."

"But he has not returned to Iran since the revolution?"

"No."

Again short answers. I'd obviously hit a nerve, so I waited.

"My cousin left to go to university. He protested in America against the Shah. But he did not come home when the Shah fell. He had to finish his studies."

"Was he worried about the mollahs? Did he associate with anticlerical as well as anti-Shah groups in America? Did he—"

Ahmad interrupted. "He is *not* scared of the mollahs. He has no reason to be scared. He loves us, but he has his own business, in computers."

"Iranians are never too busy for their families, are they? I'm sure he spends far more on telephone calls than he would on an airline ticket. Why hasn't he come home to see his family and you?"

"I don't know."

Ahmad again moved his hand across to his right hip.

I knew Ahmad couldn't explain his cousin's behavior. He didn't understand it. His cousin was another lost hero. Not dead like his older brother, but equally out of reach.

"Is he ashamed? Ashamed of having studied in America while his cousins and friends fought in the war?"

Ahmad lifted his eyes from the floor. "He was a committed revolutionary. He was never a coward. I know some of my cousin's former friends at Tehran University. They went wild when the revolution came, but they've suffered since. Many are dead. Those that are not hang out all day, talking about how things have gone wrong. How the revolution was betrayed."

"Do you still talk to them, Ahmad?"

"Before I joined the *Basij* they used to come and see me, but once I volunteered they stopped. They looked down on the *Basij.* Too many peasants without brains."

"Who are your friends now?" I asked, fearing Ahmad's reply.

"No one comes to see me now. Except Mehdi, my cousin's closest friend. He told me that America and England sent Khomeini to destroy the Shah in order to let loose Islam against the Soviets. But he thought America had tired of the clerics, and without American support the clerics could not last." He paused. "My cousin thinks that, too. Maybe he will come home if the clerics fall."

Most Iranians believe in conspiracy almost as much as they believe in God and poetry. Conspiracies, the more convoluted and illogical the better, are essential medicine for the perpetually unlucky.

"Have you told your cousin in America how difficult it is at home? Have you told him how much you miss him?"

"No. He knows how much he means to us. He calls and writes regularly. I can tell he is homesick. I often dream of him in America. Of the big house where he lives." Ahmad smiled. "With a swimming pool."

I spoke to Ahmad all afternoon that last day. He didn't want to let go of me and the last-minute hope that America would forgive him his sins and let him in. I knew I was stealing his time and giving him virtually nothing in return, but I couldn't stop asking questions, listening to Ahmad zigzag through his life as he'd once zigzagged through the Iraqi front lines.

Oddly enough, Ahmad didn't blame me for his visa problem. Iranians expect very little happiness in life—one reason they zealously seek refuge in poetry and physical pleasure. Fate had simply intervened cruelly, as it had always done.

I'd kept my Guardsman far too long. Istanbul, a Balkan city, grows dark early during winter. And Beyoğlu's dug-up streets were poorly lit. Ahmad could easily break his neck in the darkness and, for obvious reasons, I couldn't walk him home. So I ended our conversation.

For the last time, Ahmad rose slowly from his chair. For the last time, I extended my hand when he faltered. And as each time before, he politely refused it.

When we were at the door, he handed me a small package, wrapped in a brightly colored Turkish newspaper.

"It is not a bomb," he murmured, to break my hesitation.

I opened the package and found a bag of very large pistachios.

"They're Iranian, not Turkish," Ahmad quickly noted.

I smiled. "Thank God."

I thanked him several times for the gift, shook his hand, and opened the door. Ahmad pivoted and swung on his one crutch down the corridor. As he opened the street door, he turned and said for the last time, "May God protect you." *Khoda hafez*, Persian for goodbye.

He then walked out, back into the trenches.

No point on earth is farther away from Tehran than small-town Mid-America, where I was born. Among my childhood neighbors and friends, first impressions were accurate impressions. Truths were simple and clear; struggles between Good and Evil were rare in daily life.

Our desert has no bound, and our hearts and souls no rest.
World within world has taken Form's image; which of these images
  is ours?
When you see a severed head in the path rolling toward our field,
Ask of it, ask of it, the secrets of the heart: for you will learn from
  it our hidden mystery.

—*Rumi*

Iran's classical culture had seduced Alexander the Great, the Arabs, the Mongols, the Turks, and even the British; when I was an undergraduate, studying medieval history, she got me. Iran seduces through contradiction, through her ugliness as much as her beauty. Heaven is married to Hell. Isfahan and Tehran. Rumi and Khomeini.

And Iran's deepest contradictions are also Islam's. Since the eighth century, Persia has been the laboratory of the Islamic mind. All the energy and listlessness, the glory and decay, of the Middle East can be found in their purest forms in Iran. Unravel these contradictions and we begin to understand why Islam slides so easily into subterfuge and violence.

Espionage is an intimate endeavor, almost as intimate as love. You must get under a man's skin and inside his head to understand what he knows, to learn how much you can trust him, to persuade him to confide in a stranger more than in his family, and perhaps even to convince him to commit treason. Espionage is cultural surgery—exposing, stimulating, and calming foreign nerves. It is a very unacademic way of learning.

University history and poetry gave me the outline of Persian civilization. And two Iranian girlfriends supplied details professors could not. But at school I realized I could not follow the twists and turns of the Iranian mind—when truth swerves sharply into fiction—unless I got much, much closer.

When I first began my work in the CIA, I'd thought a clandestine operative must respect, if not love, his target country. Without some admiration, how do you draw close to a foreigner, how do you ask him to risk his life? Curiosity and friendship—not money—begin, and sustain, espionage. Most prospective foreign agents *want* to commit treason, and an intelligence officer must know exactly how to discover and cultivate the desire.

But without an understanding of an Iranian's language, history, and emotions, how can a case officer even take aim? Espionage is about redefining Good and Evil, the violable and the sacrosanct. Without background, how can an officer know whether his agents are good or bad, their information truth or fiction? How can he protect his agents? How can he protect himself?

This was all academic to the CIA. "Latin Americans, Iranians, Arabs, Russians, or Chinese, they're all the same," I was told by the Iran desk chief. "A good officer can go anywhere at any time. Language is not that important. The best ones speak English, anyway." When the American embassy was taken over in 1979, not a single Agency officer in Tehran spoke Persian. Almost all their sources had spoken English, a few French.

Case officers rise in the clandestine hierarchy by collecting "scalps." The number of agents recruited, not the quality of information collected, determines a reputation. Eclectic officers with languages and foreign passions, who love the world they prey on, have all but disappeared. Langley's suburban spies had won the bureaucratic wars. Mediocre information easily gets upgraded to state secrets in poorly written intelligence cables.

Still, I'd thought I could make my home in the Operations Directorate. After all, I'd joined the Agency to be among foreigners, not friends. And to Iranians the Agency offered access, a powerful, irresistible illusion. It also offered gifts. Expensive books of Persian poetry to men whose lives revolved around poems, medical care for children wounded in the war. Even, occasionally, airline tickets and visas to the Promised Land.

The Iranian community in Istanbul had given me—the rumor of me—a nickname: *the Angel.* They were too generous and quick in their praise. Angels save souls for free. The contradiction between my nickname and my profession did not disturb me at first. We were all free agents; I neither coerced nor blackmailed. Nor did I ever downplay the danger. On the contrary, I underscored the risks.

But accidents happen, and right and wrong can shift. My superiors wanted me to recruit as they recruited, to report as they reported, to turn over agents at risk to colleagues whom I neither knew nor trusted. "Recruit a man to report on lamb prices and gossip in Tehran." Turn over an Iranian who knew no English to an American who knew no Persian; I was assured that with time they could work it out.

When I left Istanbul, I no longer really believed in the CIA. Yet inertia moved me to another post. I knew, and slowly so did my bosses, that I could no longer play the game. I'd stopped attending office parties and seriously started thinking again about the Turkish-Iranian border.

In the autumns of 1992 and 1993, I briefly returned to Istanbul and the districts that form the heart of Little Tehran. Through the winding side streets of Laleli, where itinerant Iranian merchants had massed and made their own bazaar. To the currency-exchange shops of Aksaray, where women in black chadors sold wads of green and brown Iranian riyals for dollars. Through the basement fleshpot nightclubs off Taksim Square, where blond German and high-cheekboned Yugoslav dancers and Persian-speaking doormen had once tempted Iranian diplomats to forget their faith. Through the red-light districts of Topkapi, where Iranian hookers had taken refuge from the Revolutionary Guard. Through Beyoğlu and the linoleum-floor hotels where thousands of Iranians had waited their turn before godlike vice-consuls who occasionally issued visas to the West.

It had all changed. Istanbul was no longer Little Tehran, a 200,000-plus version of the Persian megalopolis back home. Except for Los Angeles, which has an immigrant Iranian population of perhaps half a million, Istanbul in the 1980s had had more Iranians than any other city outside Iran. And while Los Angeles's Persians came largely from prerevolutionary Iran's middle and upper classes, Istanbul's Iranians had been varied. Following the revolution and the beginning of the Iran–Iraq War, Istanbul became a magnet for political and economic refugees, draft dodgers, merchants, soldiers, spies, diplomats, clerics, and ordinary Iranian tourists. The poor outnumbered the rich, and traditional, peasant Muslims the secularized elite. But now Turkish was replacing Persian as the language of the streets. Iranians remained, but the neighborhood enclaves had vanished. Central Asian Kazakhs, Uzbeks, Uighurs, and Turkmens, Russians, Bulgarians, Romanians, and Poles had moved in. The Ottoman Empire was being resurrected. A few PERSIAN SPOKEN HERE signs in hotels and shops were all that remained to mark the former frontiers of Little Tehran.

I realized that if the whole Iranian refugee world was changing, the country, too, must be in flux. The hookers had at last gone to practice their trade at home. In Tehran, they could survive once again, if not prosper. Old habits were rebounding: the revolutionary mollahs could still crack the whip, but the stroke was far less sure.

During the 1980s, the Agency had known aspects of revolutionary Iran's activities abroad but virtually nothing about the country itself. Mesmerized by the clergy's assassination teams in Europe and the Middle East, the clandestine service hadn't seen what became obvious to me in Istanbul: <u>Iran's holy war was lost</u>.

U.S. blindness to Iran is not surprising. No other country has been so contemptuous of U.S. power, principles, and personnel and got away with it. Washington even allied with Saddam Hussein to take vengeance on Tehran. In U.S. officials' eyes, clerical Iran is more devious, her message more seductive and insidious, than her neighborhood rivals'. Iran may well be responsible for less state terrorism than Syria and less missionary mischief than Saudi Arabia, but Syria and Arabia are not self-proclaimed radical moral beacons to the Muslim world.

For more than eighteen years, ever since the Islamic revolution, the Iranian–American confrontation has been defined by a jumble of provocative images. A sea of men, women, and children screaming "Death to America!" Blindfolded American diplomats. Teenage girls in black chadors with assault rifles on their shoulders. Oliver North defending a misguided policy before Congress. Charred, spit-upon corpses of U.S. soldiers who had been sent by helicopter to rescue hostages in Tehran. Khomeini's merciless black eyes.

In 1953, the CIA helped overthrow an Iranian government; in 1979, Khomeini more than got even. And the undeclared war between the United States and Iran, between the West and radical Islam, goes on.

Each day muezzins in every mosque in the world summon the

faithful with the same Arabic call to prayer: *La ilaha illallah, Muhammad rasuluhu*, "There is no God but Allah and Muhammad is his Prophet." Historically, a Muslim within earshot knew he was protected by God's Holy Law. The words revealed the essential truth and strength of Islam: that politics and religion are one, and Muhammad was both Prophet and Caesar. For thirteen centuries, his successors—the caliphs, sultans, and emirs who ruled Islam's numerous dynasties—never threatened in principle the unity of the Prophet's mission.

But the Westernizing rulers of the modern Middle East—the colonels, presidents, prime ministers, and shahs—replaced God's law and the accumulated wisdom of the Islamic community with imported European legal codes and socialist thought. The fundamentalist, who insisted on preserving the political content of his faith, took aim.

His weapons are formidable. He, not the modernist, owns Islam's past, its golden age. He can pick and choose his heroes from a thousand years of Muslim triumph and conquest. His ancestors drove the Crusaders into the Mediterranean Sea; his indignation over a betrayed or unfulfilled faith has sent forth soldiers repeatedly in Islam's fourteen centuries. Each time, however, the radical faith has failed to anchor itself in the Muslim community, its reborn energy eventually withering.

If men burn too brightly, they cannot burn long. On February 16, 1990, Iran's radical faith sputtered out. In the West, no one seemed to notice. By the standards of Iran's hottest revolutionary period—1978 to 1982—when tens of thousands of Iranians regularly demonstrated and fought one another in the city's streets, the February riot was not large; probably a few thousand demonstrators participated. Nor was the damage that significant in people or property. At most, a few hundred were injured, several buildings and cars looted or burned. Nor was this riot as premeditated or ideologically defined as the violent demonstrations a decade earlier, when opposing sides—Khomeini against the Shah and then Khomeini against Westernized liberals, Communists, and the Muslim–Marxist *Mojahedin-e Khalq*—pitched articulate, organized forces against each other. The February 1990 riot was spontaneous, totally without a leader or manifesto, and scarcely mentioned in the international press.

The reason for the two-hour rampage? Youth discontent over the unexpected cancellation of a soccer match at the Amjadieh Stadium, only a few hundred yards from the former American embassy. Amjadieh matches mainly drew their spectators from south Tehran, the capital's most populous and volatile quarter, which had largely made the revolution and supplied most of the city's volunteers in the war against Iraq. The rioters were young men full of soccer passion. On hearing that the match had been canceled, they stormed through Tehran's streets screaming "Down with Rafsanjani!" and "Long live the *Taj!*" the prerevolutionary name of one team.

But *Taj* also means "the Crown" in Persian. Their pun meant everything.

Though it is perhaps too neat to pick a day's event to signify a turning point in history, the reasons behind the riot make a strong case for marking it as the end of the Islamic revolution. What the riot revealed publicly for the first time, and what became ever more apparent to me in Turkey, was how totally Iran's revolutionary clerics had lost the hearts and minds of Tehran's youth, as well as of the thousands of one-legged Ahmads. The mollahs could no longer assume that the poor were faithful to the clergy. Until the later years of the war with Iraq, Iran's clergy could count on the loyalty of most lower-class men. That loyalty subsided as Iranian casualties mounted and the clergy's constant declarations of "War! War until Final Victory!" seemed ever more perverse. It ebbed every time newly wealthy mollah-bureaucrats preached virtue to the poor. Shocked by the riot, the revolutionary clergy turned the *Basij* into domestic police and created a special urban riot-control Guard Corps unit.

Following Khomeini's death in June 1989, and the wild public mourning at his funeral, loyalty to the clerical regime started to unravel. In the February riot, Ahmad's disappointed friends in Tehran—many of whom no doubt were at the Ayatollah's graveside and appeared to Western observers as among the revolution's ardent faithful—announced that popular hysteria and spiritual allegiance were not transferable to Khomeini's successors.

The Iranian nation as a whole had reached for Islam as a means of grappling with—not rejecting—modernity. The revolutionary mollahs, in between their death wishes and attacks on the Indian-born British writer Salman Rushdie, had intertwined Islam with the Western idea of material progress. But with prosperity now an ever-more-distant memory, politics and faith were coming apart in the minds of many who not long ago had referred every daily act to God. The clerics lived in constant fear that some unexpected shock would unleash an avalanche of discontent. On that last visit to Istanbul in 1993, I realized the bloody war years with Iraq would soon be viewed as the Islamic Republic's first and only golden age.

It was in an unlikely setting—Neauphle-le-Château, a village north of Paris on the road to Normandy—that the Islamic revolution began. In 1978, Ayatollah Ruhollah al-Musavi al-Khomeini arrived there from Najaf, Iraq, the first Imam's burial place and Khomeini's home-in-exile for thirteen years. In one of the great miscalculations of the century, the Shah of Iran had asked Saddam Hussein to boot Khomeini from Iraq to France so the Ayatollah would be farther from home. Once installed in his French country house, Khomeini provoked a revolution through mass-produced cassettes and direct-dial telephone calls to Iran.

I visited Neauphle-le-Château in February 1993, fourteen years to the day after Khomeini boarded an Air France flight to Tehran. Surprisingly, Khomeini's home had not become a monument to the revolution. Neither real estate agents nor the mayor's office knew exactly where it was. Somewhere up on the hill, either a nineteenth-century high-windowed stone home or a prefabricated concrete 1950s blockhouse—"one of the two must be it." "No," a local bartender later told me, "some developer recently had it knocked down." All agreed: the Iranian government had not purchased it, and few Iranians visited. Because Iran is a land of shrines and Iranians will go on pilgrimage to absolutely anywhere, I'd expected to find Neauphle-le-Château sanctified somehow. But it appeared forgotten by friend and foe alike.

I never really saw Khomeini in the thousands of Persians I'd met.

Junior and senior clerics, Guardsmen, and *Basij* all bore aspects of him. But for every Khomeini-like quality, I'd always found the opposite expressed as powerfully.

Through the Ayatollah, Iranians had hoped to obliterate their own enfeebling contradictions: To deny how much they dislike hardship and sacrifice. To deny how much they dislike one another, how much they love life and cheat it for every riyal. In a mystical trance, they'd thrown themselves into the endeavor, through minefields, burning oil pits, and artillery fire.

Khomeini had understood the harder, vengeful side of the religious impulse. But life's misfortunes can also soften, not harden, a person's faith. Iran's innumerable shrines are all dedicated to poets and saints, not ruling clerics, soldiers, or shahs. What Khomeini never grasped was that a poet could beat a cleric in competition for a soul.

Standing on Khomeini's hillside under wet gray skies, I scrutinized the Islamic evolution of my life. A few slides, poems, and one thin book of history had hooked me. Then larger histories and more poetry. Qur'an classes in Cairo and my two Iranian girlfriends. The CIA and Istanbul. The revolution and I had developed simultaneously, joined at the waist.

And yet I'd never been to Iran. I'd tracked, measured, and battled it. I'd asked other men to go in my place. But no matter how I thought I loved Iran, or tried to pry loose its secrets, it remained just beyond my reach. One day, I told myself, after returning from Khomeini's tomb I would complete my Iranian odyssey. Then, and only then, could I stop hearing Ahmad confess his sins, and atone for a few of my own.

2 THE BORDER
Winter 1994

Hosein had promised me the crossing would be quick. He'd done it hundreds of times, he said, dozens with Iranians in my hiding spot. If people-smuggling went without a hitch from east to west, certainly going in the other direction should be no worse. And during winter the Iranian-Turkish frontier was frigid. Border guards and customs agents wouldn't want to inspect a truck for long. My Turkish friend Celal, an expert in Iranian-Turkish import-export, had assured me that on the border the Turks would be more difficult than the Persians. They searched for drugs and Kurds, while the Iranians sniffed only for ordinary contraband. And the drug trade went from Iran to Turkey, never in reverse. Kurdish separatists naturally could go both ways, but that was really a problem across frontiers farther south, where Turkey, Iraq, Syria, and Iran form what many people—not only cartographers—call Kurdistan.

Lying on my left side behind and slightly beneath Hosein's seat, I heard sounds better from below me than from above. With my right ear lightly pressed against the side of my wooden box, I tried to make out a conversation in the melding noises. But the low, gearshift grind of diesel-truck engines deadened the voices. I clearly heard Hosein, my driver, talking with the border guard, but I could pick up only disconnected words. *Kheli, khub, khedmat,* all beginning with the guttural *kh,* sliced through the engine sounds and the buffering of my box. For a moment, fear gave way to a Persian anagram. I put the three words together: "Very good service."

If the Turks caught me hiding, they'd just throw me in jail. And since I was an American, and once a CIA officer in their country, they'd be reasonably well behaved. Turkish Intelligence, like foreign intelligence services everywhere, identifies fairly quickly CIA case officers serving under diplomatic cover. Officially, Langley likes to believe otherwise, but everyone overseas knows the truth. Within a few days, Celal would bring my passport and other ID, and the Turks would release me. If things got really hairy, I could always call old friends at the U.S. embassy in Ankara. Eagerly, or reluctantly, they'd quietly get me out.

Of course, if the Iranians caught me, I'd get thrown in prison and interrogated around the clock. If I were lucky, they'd merely beat me for weeks, and then let me rot. In ten to twenty years, I might see America again.

Despite my heart-pounding fear of the Iranian border check, the odds of being caught in an inspection by an overly thorough official were, according to my friends, very small. Such searches happened, of course, but the Iranians hadn't really been nosy since the end of the Iran–Iraq War in 1988.

Once upon a time, smugglers were athletic Kurdish and Azarbaijani freebooters. Khomeini's Revolutionary Guards used to care very actively about "counterrevolutionary traitors, criminals, and draft dodgers" escaping over the frontier. Now more responsible men who didn't like to mountain-climb controlled the untaxed cross-border trade. With the rapid deterioration of clerical Iran's centrally planned economy in the 1990s, the border guards had become noticeably more corrupt, making illicit crossings more expensive but far less dangerous affairs.

Going over and coming back by truck would be easy, Celal predicted. "It's staying out of trouble once over—that's the danger, my friend. For that you will need an Azari. Someone to tell you what to do, where to go, and when to speak. In Hosein's hands, *inshallah*, you should have no trouble."

I knew Celal was right. Even in the worst years of the Islamic revolution and the war, when hundreds of thousands of Iranians were fleeing their homeland, border crossings from Iran to Turkey were not that difficult. I'd met hundreds of Iranians in Istanbul who'd made it clandestinely over the frontier—single young men stashed away in transport trucks; families (via enterprising mercenary Kurds) using horses, trucks, and goats; and deserting Persian soldiers who'd simply walked through the mountains until they found a Turkish road sign. The old gendarmerie of the Shah had never tried hard to stop Iranians who didn't like the revolution from leaving home. And the much-feared Revolutionary Guard weren't numerous along the northern part of the Iranian-Turkish border. The Iran–Iraq War and rebellious Iranian Kurds farther south drew most of the Guard's resources and attention.

Under no circumstances was I going to take the traditional mountain routes into Iran. Honorable and noble as they might be, I didn't want anything to do with the Kurds—nor with horseback riding, snowdrifts, or Revolutionary Guard foot patrols. I wanted a controlled, heated environment, where I could put my trust in only one man. As Celal had said, the crossing wouldn't be the primary challenge. Movement, lodgings, and food in Iran would be my biggest problems. With the right guardian and truck, all those difficulties could be managed. Islamic Iran is not, and never has been, like the former Soviet Union. Foreigners, even Americans, do not immediately provoke concern or an identity check. The clerical government never banned U.S. citizens from Iran. My greatest worry was not a police patrol but invitations to tea. I could get enmeshed by ordinary Persians who wouldn't let a Westerner, particularly an American, go. Gossip travels at light-speed in Persia, and I didn't want gossip getting ahead of me.

I needed to be able to choose the time and place for my outings, to control my conversations as best I could, and to have protective friends around me at night. Everything I'd learned from years of hovering about Persian borders told me I could go in under the mollahs' noses as long as I kept moving quickly in the company of friends.

Language could be a problem, since I didn't know Azari, a form of Turkish heavy in Persian words, the primary language of Iran's northwest province. Every educated Azarbaijani knows Persian well, and most Azarbaijanis know enough Persian to get by. But I needed to listen more than to speak. Your average Azarbaijani, like Hosein, could flip quickly into his native tongue if there were no highbrow Azarbaijanis or proper Iranians around. In such a setting, I couldn't eavesdrop without Hosein at my side. Hosein had advised me to butt in on any conversation I wanted to understand. "Even the worst Azari peasant will try to speak Persian if you speak Persian to him. Our Turkishness doesn't stop us from loving Iran. You must understand, we are much more Iranian than Turkish."

But butting in wasn't an option from my hidden box. And Hosein and the border guard weren't speaking Persian anymore. Given their conversation's speed and my hearing difficulties, I couldn't even pull out Azari Persian words. I could hear tones, changes of volume, and the rhythm in their speech—enough to know they'd changed from a Persian to a Turkish language. I kept listening, trying to rewind sounds in my mind, trying to find a Persian noun and glue it to a proper Turkish verb.

Suddenly the conversation flipped backed into Persian. Had a higher-ranking officer or customs official joined them? My ears still weren't good enough to overcome the distance, buffering, and surrounding noise. I could hear only the chaos of three Middle Eastern men talking simultaneously.

But noise and argument are normal in the Middle East, signs of healthy chaos in a give-and-take bazaari world. Disagreement and hustling meant state power hadn't become merciless and unchallengeable, officials could be bribed, and rich and poor alike still had the right to whine. As long as I could hear Hosein give as well as take, everything was going according to plan. He'd told me the crossing could take a couple of hours, and Hosein seemed precise for a Persian. Still, I translated a "couple" as anywhere between two and five.

"If you don't hear my voice for four hours," Hosein had warned,

"I'm probably in trouble and you're on your own. Stay in the truck until early morning, then get out and run home."

Run home? Trouble? My anxiety changed when someone slammed something in the cabin. With my right hand and my right knee, I applied pressure to the two wooden hooks that clamped shut the lid of my box. The hooks were already very tight, but the more pressure I applied, the less likely a blow from above might startle me.

My hiding spot was not terribly clever, assuming someone was hunting for a stowaway. But he'd have to work to find me, pulling out a tightly squeezed slender mattress from behind the cabin seats, then ripping out another sewn to a thick plywood base that was in turn screwed tight to the lid of my box. Except to a very sharp eye, matching the depth of the cot with the depth of the cabin would reveal no hidden chambers. A strong man could strike the mattress with all his might and neither hear an echo nor feel a void. If he was just snooping about, the layout of the small cabin, with its well-used battered cot and miscellany of clothes and personal effects, would easily convince him to pry no further. Even to a suspicious, unfriendly Persian official, the space behind the seats was too small and narrow for really interesting contraband.

Hosein had made a convincing case that the obvious, if cleverly concealed, always worked best. Even more convincing to me: if I were discovered, Hosein's fate would be at least as painful as mine.

I slowed my breath, shut my eyes, and listened for the compression of seat springs. Nothing. I only could hear truck noises—engines starting and pneumatic brakes being released and pumped. On the Turkish side of the border, I'd seen one truck in front of us and two behind. With luck, there were dozens more, each one thinning the attention and curiosity of the customs officials and border guards freezing in Iranian Azarbaijan's wind-whipped cold.

As the truck noises ebbed, I heard three or four male voices. This time I couldn't tell if they were speaking Persian, Azari, or Turkish. They were too far away.

Why the slamming? Perhaps Hosein had returned, opened the glove compartment to retrieve forgotten papers detailing his truck and freight, and slammed it shut, relieving a little frustration.

Though Celal had thought I was crazy to travel in eastern Turkey and northwestern Iran in winter, when the snows can paralyze the roads for weeks and the cold reaches Gulag extremes, Hosein and I felt differently. The border crossing, and the possibly more dangerous security checkpoints later, would be far easier if Revolutionary Guards were frozen and half asleep.

Behind my back, steel hit steel. Involuntarily, I jerked, hit my head against a wooden band protruding from the roof of my box, and bit my tongue. Miraculously, my reflex made no sound. Short-burst conversations echoed off the ground underneath the truck. Azari? Persian? Turkish? Without long sentences, I couldn't hear the flow and intonation, differentiate Persian highs and lows from a Turkish monotone. I turned my head and pressed my right ear against the box. Somewhere near us, another semi restarted its engines and released its brakes. It was heading into Turkey, not Iran.

I shut my eyes again. I could hardly move and what movement I could make, I shouldn't. Someone might be in the cabin and a bump of my boots, knees, elbows, or head might penetrate. I realized I'd made a stupid mistake in not asking Hosein to get into the box before the crossing and talk, kick, toss, and scream, so I'd have an idea of how sounds carried. If the crossing really took four hours, Hosein would have to haul me out of the box. From my knees down, my legs were going numb. In a few hours, I wouldn't be able to walk.

During my CIA training, I'd been put into hot and cold boxes and denied food, water, sleep, speech, and warmth for two December days. In the hot box, which would have cramped a small dog, the plywood bled burning resin on my skin; in the cold box, which was simply a larger wooden container with better ventilation, I shook uncontrollably. On the floors of unheated solitary cells, my bare feet went numb within hours, sending waves of fever up and down my spine. Mercifully, my mind eventually shut down the sensations between head and toes.

Hooded, without sight or light, and surrounded by continuous electronic static noise, I'd concentrate on interlocking memories offering protection against sound and pain. Visualizing shallow green Caribbean waters, hot blinding sands, white-tipped sharks, green moray eels, palm trees, known and unknown nude women, I could send my consciousness away from the ugly swamps of Virginia.

When the visions finally gave way to the cold, I'd recited everything I'd ever memorized, trying to pace it to have an accurate idea of passing time. "The Charge of the Light Brigade" took two minutes a run. A few paragraphs from the last chapter of J. B. Kelly's *Arabia, the Gulf, and the West*; two minutes to describe the collapse of the British Empire. And always back to verses of Saʿdi, a thirteenth-century Persian poet:

> *If a relation of the enemy be friendly to thee,*
> *Beware; be not secure of craftiness.*
>
> *Because his heart becomes torn for vengeance against thee.*
> *When memory of the love of his own relation comes to him.*
>
> *Consider not the sweet words of an enemy;*
> *For, it is possible, there is poison in the honey.*
>
> *That one took his life safe from the trouble of the enemy,*
> *Who reckoned friends as enemies.*
>
> *That knave preserves the pearl in his purse,*
> *Who considers all people purse-thieves.*
>
> *The soldier, who is an offender against the Amir,*
> *So long as thou canst, take not into service.*
>
> *Make long the tether of the aspirant;*
> *Break it not, lest thou shouldst not see him again.*
>
> *Essay with deliberation battle with the enemy;*
> *Reflect on counsel; and, conceal thy resolution.*
>
> *Reveal not the secret to everyone;*
> *For, I have seen many a cup-sharer, a spy.*

Do the poem thirty times slowly in Persian and you could kill two hours. Splice together a little Gibbon, Churchill, *The Wizard of*

Oz, favorite TV tunes, Aretha Franklin, the Rolling Stones, odd verses of the Qur'an, and Edgar Allan Poe and you'd lost two hours more. But the static noise and cold were always waiting for you to slip and lose a vision or a line. Mentally short-circuited, you'd quickly return to the swamps.

Although my fear was far greater now, it was easier in Hosein's box. Trucks and voices came and went—echoes to measure time. Also, I had a glowing push-button watch. However, the soul-searching was the same. I tried to remember the first Persian I'd ever met and whether it was love at first sight, and then the thousands of Iranians who'd followed. Fear, darkness, cramps, and thick air were robbing my memory of precision and faces. Istanbul, Ankara, Frankfurt, Munich, London, Paris, Geneva, New York, Washington, D.C., all the places I'd gone to meet Persians started to free-fall into the vortex of my box. Everything I'd learned in my studies and my work boiled down to its essence: Hosein.

He and I were headed for Tabriz, the capital of Iranian Azarbaijan, where in 1501 the Turkish-speaking fourteen-year-old Shah Ismail Safavi (1487–1524), the most successful radical in Islamic history, raised his sword and declared Iran a Shiʿite state. By the time his dynasty fell in 1732, the Safavids spoke Persian and Iran had become *the* Shiʿite stronghold. The most creative people in the Middle East had forsaken nine hundred years of loyalty to Sunnism, the orthodoxy within Islam, in favor of the exclusive right of the semi-divine descendants of Ali, the nephew and son-in-law of the Prophet Muhammad, to command the Islamic world. The ruling status quo—the Sunni sultans, emirs, and clerics, who thought power bestowed legitimacy—were challenged by warriors with martyrs' dreams. Persian exceptionalism, an unwillingness to be wholly absorbed into the Arabized Islamic community, had finally found its religious home.

From Tabriz, Hosein and I would go to mountainous Ardabil, the coldest city in Persia and the birthplace of Safavid power. And then southeast to Tehran, where radical Shiʿism in 1979 again overturned a dynasty and convulsed the Middle East.

In Tehran, I planned to visit a Revolutionary Guard bookstore outside the bannered walls of the former American embassy. I'd sent several Iranian friends there over the years to buy me books, in particular dark volumes of *The Nest of Spies*, a collection of classified Central Intelligence Agency and State Department cable traffic. The cables, chronicling America's complicated love affair with the Shah, were shredded just before the embassy was seized. Within a year, Iranian revolutionaries had devotedly reassembled the paper strips for sale. I intended to buy myself the missing volumes from my collection, and thereby pay a final homage to my former life.

The trailer's doors closed three hours and forty-one minutes after they'd opened. That whole time, I'd heard voices from the rear only twice. Five semis had come and gone, three on their way to Turkey, two to Iran. Several cars and smaller trucks like ours had also crossed the border. Hosein had warned me he'd neither signal nor speak to me the entire time we were stopped unless he was alone, and it had been over four hours since I'd clearly made out his voice.

The box was now wounding me seriously at the ankles, knees, hips, elbows, shoulders, and neck. Fortunately, I was heavily dressed and still fairly warm, except at my left hip and shoulder, where my weight pressed on the plywood and steel-conducted cold bored through my clothing.

Suddenly there was an explosion of voices alongside the truck. Several men screamed at one another, one cursing voice carrying above all the rest. *"Bilagh! Bilagh!"* the Persian equivalent of "Fuck you!" rang out.

I was terrified. Iranians curse often, regularly casting imprecations upon their enemies and distant friends, but there are rules. *Bilagh* is rarely used; it has the force of its English equivalent circa 1950. Whoever shouted it, if not an official, could expect the worst. At a minimum, the exchange would sour the mood of everyone around.

"My goods have cleared customs!" a man screamed in Persian. In rapid sequence, I heard the thud of someone mounting our truck's running board, the door slamming shut, and the engine grinding on. The truck started to roll in the direction of Iran. If Hosein was driving, we'd made it through the Pearly Gates. If not, I was in hell. I thought about my family, and especially about my wife, and wondered what I was doing.

. . .

He waited for ten minutes before he thumped the cot three times and yelled, "Hey, American, get out! You're in Iran."

Popping the box's lid was excruciating: my entire left arm had gone numb and was useless, and with my right hand alone I had insufficient force to hammer open the wooden hooks. But I persevered: once locked, the box could be opened only from the inside.

"Did you think I'd forgotten you?" Hosein asked as soon as I lifted the lid and rejoined the living.

"As a matter of fact, I had."

If I'd been able to move, I'd have kissed Hosein. But the box had rendered me a cripple, and fear reinforced my feebleness. I wasn't sure I wanted out. With my legs tingling from my crotch to my toes, I stayed where I was, my right arm holding the lid, waiting for my nerves to return.

"What idiot yelled *'Bilagh'*?" I asked.

"I don't know. I didn't ask." Hosein glanced back at me. "There were two Iranian truckers arguing with the officials. I'm sure the officials wanted more money than they were willing to pay."

"Did you have the same problem?"

Hosein glanced at me again, this time smiling. "Yes."

"What did you do?"

"I paid—but not what they asked. These men are blatant thieves, you can't give them what they want. All Iranians have become thieves, but *they* are real dog shit."

The revolution unhinged Iranians: with it, exquisitely developed Persian arts like bribery and deceit had become outright theft. I'd known many honest Iranians abroad, but you could never assume good intentions. At home, Iranians live in a vicious zero-sum world: if one man has, another doesn't. Any Iranian not protected by family and friends is open game. In a lifetime, nearly everyone gets screwed.

"Should I get out of the box?" I asked Hosein, fearing the ballsy Azarbaijani might even ask me to drive. "If you think we're going to hit a security check soon, I'll stay in. My legs aren't working well, and we can't see beyond the headlights."

"No security checks for at least an hour, probably two. But I'd stay back there for another thirty or forty minutes, until we get close to a turnoff for Kho'y. I'll pull off onto a small road so you can take a walk and taste Iranian snow. It's much better than the Turkish kind."

Actually, Hosein liked the Turks, an uncommon affection even among Turkish-speaking Azarbaijanis. He had distant family in Turkey whom he visited occasionally. "Stupid and stubborn, but more honest and much kinder than we are" was how he described them. "They're good Muslims, but the mollahs call them atheists and Western puppets. But there are more mosques in Turkey than in Iran. Most Turks I know go to mosque far more than we do."

Based on my experience, Hosein was more right than wrong. Of course, the Westernized Turks living in Istanbul along the Bosporus, in Ankara's elite Çankaya quarter, and in Izmir's posher neighborhoods were secular to the bone, ignorant of even the most basic Muslim prayers and practices. Since the abolition of the Turkish Ottoman caliphate by Kemal Atatürk in 1924, no other non-European ruling class has tried so hard to be European, changing its language's script and erasing, reworking, and reinventing its history to earn entry into a reluctant West.

Although they'd secularized themselves far more than Arabs or Persians, the vast majority of Turks still had a rock-solid Islamic core. To be a Turk was to be a Muslim, no exceptions made. And even among the Ivy League–educated, who wore Italian and English suits, drank Johnnie Walker Black, spent their nights in Bosporus discotheques, and bemoaned the death of Istanbul's Greek community, you could find prickly religious sentiments. The difficult cultural grafting hadn't yet securely taken hold. Scratch a Turk at Bankers Trust, or in an Anatolian village, and you still felt the seriousness, stubbornness, and confidence of a Muslim soldier race. The Ottomans had built their mosques out of unadorned stone; modern Turks built theirs out of undecorated concrete.

I'd never felt this Islamic solidity among Persians. Even Iranian holy warriors could have a lightness in their spirit and gesticulations—a joke, a laugh, a little blasphemy waiting behind a thirty-minute confession of ardent faith. Westernized expatriate Persians could, chameleonlike, disappear in the cultures of their exile homes. Find a Turk abroad, in thirty minutes you know what you have. Find an Iranian, it's a more involved guessing game. Iranian Shi'ites see history as a long, ugly, deceitful enterprise; Islamic history is, after all, full of Shi'ite, not Sunni, martyrs. Cheated repeatedly, Iranians cheat back. Persians have an age-old tradition of wine, women, and song, yet under Khomeini they destroyed their vineyards, hanged their whores, and stopped singing. Thus, *now you see us, now you don't*—that's what terrified me about Persians.

"We're not behind schedule, are we? We're still going to spend the night in the same spot?" I asked, looking at the back of Hosein's head. I was worried Hosein might have planned unrealistically on buzzing through customs and the border check.

"We're on time," he said. "What about your legs? Think you could outrun a Revolutionary Guard?"

I enjoyed Hosein's relaxed dark wit. We were going to spend two weeks together in close quarters, and I was glad he wasn't someone who would amplify my fear with pointless talk or silence.

And he had other virtues. He wasn't particularly macho, a serious Middle Eastern male malady, and for a Persian he was careful with his words. Misfortunes didn't become tragedies, good luck wasn't proof of genius. He was neither young nor middle-aged. He'd seen a bit of the world in quick visits to Turkey and Pakistan and was a real-world autodidact. Born in Tabriz, raised in Tehran, he'd driven his truck across the entire country. "When you have to bribe people in your daily work, you get to know them very well." And he'd fought in the Iran–Iraq War and survived. He hadn't had an easy life, but unlike most Persians, he preferred not to whine about it.

In 1979, he'd worshiped Khomeini because the Ayatollah had overthrown the Shah, kicked out the United States, and brought him closer to God. But the fervor didn't hold. With too much education to be a peasant, and too little to be a dreamer, he hadn't become a death-wish Persian, a radical true-believing youth who lived only to die for Khomeini, God, and Islam. After encountering Iraqi artillery in 1983, he totally gave up the idea of martyrdom.

I said, "Don't worry, I could easily outrun a Revolutionary Guard. Only God makes them run, not fear." An awkward try at quick repartee in Persian.

"You won't need to run as long as you do what I tell you." Hosein smiled firmly. This was the first time he'd ever had the chance to order an American around—every Iranian's dream. But the role reversal had been the border's price. It didn't bother me: it was the ideal U.S.–Iranian relationship. If either one of us screwed up, both went down.

"I ran from a Guardsman once in Tabriz." Hosein cut his chuckle as he downshifted to brake as the truck rounded a sharp turn. "I was just walking with friends, and we didn't get out of the way of three Guards quick enough.

"At the time, I actually admired how they'd forced us off the sidewalk. But that was before I'd served in the army. The Guards aren't so tough anymore. They're too busy and tired making extra money to support their families to actually run after anyone. If you don't bother them, they don't bother you. It's the *Basij*, they're the problem—teenagers with no discipline and no education."

"The *Basij* don't bother you on the highway, do they? Aren't they only city creatures?" I was trying to straighten and then bend my knees in the box.

"No, they're everywhere. Like hungry mice. When you find a Guardsman commanding them, it's safer. The Guards are usually older and better disciplined. When the *Basij* are alone, prowling for 'moral offenders,' people they can hit up for money, they're dangerous. They used to pick only on the rich; now they'll target anyone better off, anyone with a job. The worst thing about the *Basij* is you can't always spot them. If they're carrying guns, it's easy. If not, they can look like any other Iranian. The Guards are easier to spot. If you see someone who looks like a sloppy soldier in a military uniform, he's probably a Guardsman."

I immediately thought about Ahmad hopping about on one leg.

Hosein was politely reminding me again not to walk in a neighborhood without his permission. As a general rule, Hosein thought a *Basiji* would back off from a foreigner or, like any other Iranian, start asking innumerable questions about abroad. "Be polite and thank everyone a hundred times" was the first line of defense. "I've seen Europeans all over Iran. Not many, but enough," Hosein had told me. "In the bigger towns, Iranians aren't surprised to see foreigners and they're always pleased. If you're recognized as a foreigner, you probably won't attract a crowd walking down the street." With Hosein in tow, it would appear I had an official minder. Even the more independent-minded and suspicious *Basiji* or Guardsman would probably leave us alone. We'd do our damnedest to avoid trouble, but I shouldn't panic if one saw me. "Don't stare and keep walking" was Hosein's constant advice.

It was snowing harder outside. At sixty kilometers per hour, we were slow and safe. Other trucks and cars were passing us at speeds exceeding the reach of their headlights and brakes. Hosein had warned me that Iranian driving habits were awful, worse even than in Turkey, where they believe that turned-off headlights save gas. Persians have half the discipline and patience of Turks, far fewer forms of entertainment, cheaper cars, and much cheaper gas. Driving insanely would be one of the few licit ways a young man could have fun.

I was still sprawled out behind Hosein. Feeling had returned to my legs and I wanted out of the truck. We were hurrying; Mount Ararat was probably already out of sight. Six years earlier, on a wall of Ishakpasha, a ruined Ottoman hilltop palace in Turkey not far from Ararat, I'd seen a rainbow leap the mountains that divide Turkey from Iran. Wide awake but as if in a dream, I saw the arc land just beyond the pebbled, broken-rock courtyard, the red and yellow beams igniting the mountains' barren terra-cotta rock and disappearing finally in the valley's grass. The yellow of Persia's imperial lion and the green and red of the Islamic Republic celestially bound together: I'd wondered then how long it would be before I followed the rainbow into Iran.

The highway traffic had picked up, truck after truck moving toward Turkey. Hosein had insisted we couldn't just turn around if I lost my nerve. He went back and forth several times each month, and he didn't want to break his schedule unless there was an emergency. We had to stick to his itinerary. Hosein needn't have worried. I hadn't planned for months, traveled thousands of miles, and studied and dreamed of Iran for years to take a quick joyride.

I was happily aware that I was reversing the voyage of Shah Ismail Safavi. In the cause of religious conquest, he'd gone from Ardabil to Tabriz to Chaldiran, a dirt-road, open-sewer Turkish town about fifty kilometers from where we were and the site of a great battle. On its plains in 1514, Ismail's cavalry collided with the forces of the Ottoman Sultan Selim the Grim, the father of Suleiman the Magnificent. Ismail had intended to ride over Selim and convert his Turkish tribal auxiliaries to the Safavid holy-warrior faith. A victory would have had Ismail at the gates of Istanbul and an Islamic empire of Alexandrian proportions—in the sixteenth century, Muslim Turks of one tribe or another ruled much of the world, from North Africa north to the Danube and east to the Ganges and the borders of China.

In the eyes of his soldiers, Ismail was a messenger of God, if not God himself. At Chaldiran, waves of Ismail's fanatical red-turbaned cavalry rode against Selim's Janissaries, his chain-linked war wagons, and his artillery, then the finest in the world. Volleys of cannonballs, grapeshot, and mini-balls from long-barreled Ottoman musketry dropped thousands. By day's end, Ismail had led his faithful to within a sword's reach of breaking the Ottoman line and perhaps rewriting the spiritual map of the Middle East. A victorious Turkish-born Shi'ite contagion could have reduced Sunni orthodoxy from the faith of sultans, emirs, and khans to that of Arab peasants.

But the Ottoman line held. Within a year Ismail lost Kurdistan, Diyarbakr, Baghdad, and most of Azarbaijan. Worse for the Safavid family, the reversal of radical faith had begun. By the time his son and successor Shah Tahmasp died in 1576, Safavid horsemen no longer viewed their king as a demigod.

I was praying the same itinerary reversed wouldn't lead to defeat. I'd challenge no one. I wanted to be invisible, quietly moving through space and time.

We'd reached Maku, a sprawling Kurdish mountain town of pale stone and cracked concrete nestled in a broad mountain gorge. Through a truck window by night, it seemed quaint, illuminated by bare bulbs in a hundred windows. I saw a sign for a hotel; no doubt the clientele were travelers psychologically destroyed by customs officials.

Hosein snorted when I asked what there was to see in Maku. "I never stop here unless I need fuel. Also, there are often Guardsmen about."

Not far outside Maku the mountains ended and we descended onto a rolling snow-covered plain. A sparse but steady stream of traffic kept coming toward us. I pitied them: they'd hit the border late at night and be frozen stiff before escaping Iranian and Turkish officialdom the next morning. They'd find the Turkish side had more to offer; at Dogubeyazit there was the Hotel Isfahan with its first-rate raki, Turkish pastis, and decent beer, as well as an odd assortment of well-worn women.

Hosein turned off the main paved road onto a dirt one and drove on. When the truck finally stopped, I managed to roll across the passenger seat. Before I got my hand on the door lever, Hosein had opened my door from the outside and had me firmly by the arm. Before jumping off the running board, I looked into the oblong side-view mirror. My light-brown complexion had become puffy, oily white. In a black turtleneck, a green army coat, and a thick black cotton ski cap pulled down to my ears, I looked like a POW in solitary.

"What an ugly sight you are. The Iranians I took to Turkey looked much better than you," Hosein remarked once I'd made the two-foot jump to the ground. After eight years in the Central Intelligence Agency hunting Iranians in Europe and the Middle East and seventeen years of reading about this country, I'd finally set foot in Iran.

"Are you sick? Or just scared?"

We were on a rolling plain, just beyond the Zagros Mountains. The snow-covered road lay a few inches deep under my feet. With the truck lights off, the whiteness of the land extended several meters, then faded immediately into darkness. A gray-black sky bled a little light on the mountains, enough to separate one peak from another, and snow-covered rises in the ground gleamed dully.

"Terrified," I said. "But feeling better."

Hosein laughed and let go of my upper arm. Despite his schedule, I was sure he'd break the run and immediately return me to Turkey if he thought I was cracking. First and foremost, because his own neck was on the line. He'd also do it because he was kind. I looked into Hosein's face to see if I could discern any fear. But his brown eyes were shock-free, his tan-olive hue unchanged, and his cheeks and forehead without a trace of the nervous oil sweat that was all over mine. Celal had counseled me well. When I got back to Turkey, I'd give him the biggest dinner of his life.

Why had Hosein wanted so badly to take me on this trip? Unlike most Iranians I'd led into danger, he was much more than volunteer, a recruit. It wasn't just money—he needed it, but not badly enough to haul me to Tehran. Was it the thrill? Even very measured, good men can in the right circumstances become adrenaline addicts. Or was he taking his own private revenge on the past?

He'd run through a few allegiances in his life. As a child and a young man, he'd stuck by his father's side. When his father died, he awoke politically and adopted the Shah. Then the Shah lost his luster and he switched to Khomeini. Fighting in the army against Iraq, he'd briefly worshiped his commanding officers, as well as the Ayatollah. But after the army lost battles it should have won and Khomeini described defeats as martyrs' victories, Hosein abandoned his plans for a military career, went home to Tabriz, and started hauling freight and people over the Iranian-Turkish frontier.

Persians don't take long to build allegiances. They can come fast and furious, then dissipate before your eyes. Hosein had followed Khomeini because he'd thrown out the Americans, and now he was taking an American to Khomeini's tomb. The progression made perfect sense.

"Do you get a lot of snow here in winter?" I turned my frightened face away from Hosein down toward my feet.

"Sometimes yes, sometimes no. Near the mountains, you'll get snow. Leave the mountains, head south toward Zanjan, the snow diminishes quickly. But toward Ardabil, it can get deep. The storms strike quickly."

Hosein hadn't been thrilled about going to Ardabil in the winter. Though he actually had family and work there, he'd have preferred to skip it. "Too cold, too snowy, the roads aren't great, and my family always asks for money."

But I'd insisted. Unless the roads were closed because of weather or Hosein told me it was too dangerous because of omnipresent Guardsmen or *Basijis*—and he hadn't—we were going.

"How far are we from our truck stop?" I asked. With my body unfolded and walking, I suddenly realized I was hungry.

"Not far. We have to get back on the main road and we'll get there quickly." There was irritation in his voice. "Why?"

"I'd just like to eat something warm. But I can wait."

I could easily wait. Food meant more Iranians and perhaps another spell in the box.

"We'll walk a little more. I want you in the front seat so everything looks normal when we arrive. Don't worry, we'll be among friends."

My hunger vanished. Over and over again, this would happen. All the years of study and work reduced to nerve-racking blind dates. In the Agency, maintaining my cover had been a game, sometimes tense, sometimes silly. Now I had no fake offices, title, or ID. Just Hosein and a truck stood between me and prison. Staring back at the mountains, I reminded myself this was exactly what I'd wanted.

Hosein jumped quickly into the truck, rummaging loudly. Then he hit the ground like a leopard, flashlight in hand.

"Follow me, I want to show you something," Hosein said, as he darted past me down the road.

We hurried away, paralleling snow-covered clumps of trees on the plain. Losing sight of the truck behind a rise crowned with a serrated rocky knoll, we suddenly left the main road.

"Where in God's name are we going?" I yelled, hoping my question might slow Hosein's gallop.

"You wanted to see Iran. I am showing you Iran."

After three hundred yards, we walked up a long wave in the ground to another dirt road. Deep tire grooves were covered with untouched snow. Hosein was still ahead of me, though I was gaining.

Trying to slow him, I yelled, "You're a Kurd! Only a Kurd would take me sight-seeing in the middle of nowhere at midnight in winter."

Hosein kept walking, though he turned back to look at me. "There are no Revolutionary Guards out here. Just us and God."

"It's not the Guards, it's the ground that scares me. I can't see anything if you walk too far in front. How'd you like to carry an American with a broken leg?"

Hosein pivoted and shot the beam of light directly in front of me. From then on, we walked side by side.

"You obviously know this area very well," I said, trying to lessen the hurt on Hosein's face.

"I know it well. Better by day than at night." His frown disappeared as quickly as it'd formed.

"It wasn't just the beauty that brought you here. Was it?"

"In the old days, when the border was more difficult and you had more Guards crawling about, this was perfectly in the middle of the tight security zones. I needed a good rest stop on the road to Turkey. Going the other way, things could be very difficult around Marand and Maku. And after Maku, you could get stopped anytime. It was impossible to keep someone in the box all the way from Tabriz to the border."

"That's about a three-hundred-kilometer drive, right?"

"Yes, but it could take almost two days, depending on customs and security. Between Marand and Maku, there's a long stretch with several safe places to pull off the main road. People picnic there in summer."

"Did you ever haul people all the way from Tehran?" I asked, intensely curious about his logistics.

"A few times. I'd do it now, but I didn't like doing it then. Too far, too dangerous. You need more people to do that well, and more money. Tehran's a very big place where many things can go wrong. Cross-border traveling from there is a full-time business. I'm not that kind of a businessman. I helped mainly deserters and ex-soldiers from Azarbaijan, Tabriz mostly, who couldn't get passports because they'd been blacklisted by the regime. And getting to Tabriz from Tehran was never a problem. Even someone who'd deserted could travel from Tehran to Tabriz with a little planning. The Guards are mean but not efficient. I never had anyone arrested at a security check between Tehran and Tabriz. Questioned yes, arrested no."

"But how did these men find you?"

"Through a network of friends. You make friends when you go to war. Friends you can trust."

"You never felt you would be betrayed accidentally by an ex-soldier who said one word too many?"

"Oh, yes. But I'd made up my mind to do this, knowing the risks. After the war, it didn't seem that dangerous. If you have good friends and take precautions, you can get past the Revolutionary Guards. It's not like I've been working in enemy territory. Everyone here has hated the mollahs for years."

Hosein turned abruptly. "Over there," he shouted. He scurried down the dirt road's embankment, flashlight bobbing. Reluctantly, I jumped a small drift of snow by the road and followed him down the slope into knee-high, crystallized snow. Unless I fell into a boulder or down a well, I wasn't going to hurt myself.

Several hundred feet from the dirt road, the flashlight halted. I made out large shrublike trees, the outline of a small house. As I came closer I realized that the one-story structure was abandoned, a stone wall and part of the roof caved in, its windows without glass.

"This is it!" Hosein yelled. "I knew I could find it."

"Is this your rest stop?"

"My favorite. Haven't used it in a few years. You can't tell at night, but it's beautiful here in the daytime. In the spring, this whole valley is covered in the greenest grass. A perfect place for a picnic."

Hosein walked round the house and then stuck his head and the flashlight in under a squared beam that was once above a short front door. When he withdrew his head, he was smiling ear to ear, like a little boy who'd found a lost toy.

"It hasn't changed," he murmured. He ambled over to take a closer look at the collapsed wall.

I realized I was standing on holy ground. Iran is covered in pilgrimage sites where Persians pray that Good might just once triumph over Evil. Most are local, assuaging the pain of a particular tribe, town, or region. They are one of the few constants in Iranian lives, which are unceasingly convulsed by political and religious mayhem, economic uncertainty, and betrayal. While I was complaining about wandering nowhere in the cold, Hosein was paying me the highest compliment imaginable: he was leading me to his personal shrine.

In the sixth century B.C., on the west coast of a dead freshwater lake fifty kilometers away, Zarathustra was reputedly born. Zoroaster to the Greeks, Zardosht to modern Persians, he became the Iranian prophet of religious dualism—the eternal conflict between Good and Evil, Truth and the Lie. Zoroastrianism remained the Persian religion for a thousand years, until the coming of Islam. Then the Persians abandoned their fire temples and exchanged gods: Allah for Ahura Mazda, Satan for Ahriman.

That dualism still ran through every Persian. For years, I'd tried to separate the Good from the Bad: the honest from the dishonest, those with valuable secrets from those with lies, those who were pro-American from the Khomeiniites. Most of my former colleagues had given up trying and called in polygraphers and modern technology to straighten out the infuriating twists and turns of the Persian mind. But lie detectors and Persians are centuries apart. No Iranian I'd ever met believed the truth would set you free. Truth depended upon family, time and place, advantages gained and compromises struck. No Iranian I'd ever met felt guilty because he'd lied to a stranger.

I'd given up the black-and-white world of polygraph machines and operational files and gone on pilgrimage to a forbidden land I'd devoted my life to. I wanted to reverse roles and send myself where I'd sent others, assuaging my conscience as I privately tweaked Langley's and the ayatollahs' noses.

Years before in Istanbul, I'd seen radical Islam cracking in Iran and the gradual return of normalcy to Persian lives. I wanted finally to see firsthand what remained of the relationship between God and man after fifteen years of revolutionary rectitude. With Hosein as my guide, I was going to make it to the center of the Iranian mind and then back across the Turkish frontier. In two weeks, back at Ishakpasha, my own pilgrimage would be over, and I'd be happily drinking whiskey once again with Turks. All I had to do was avoid the roadblocks, *Basijis*, Revolutionary Guards, traffic cops, and Iranians from my past.

Inside the ruined house, the flashlight revealed no footprints but ours. Snow-powdered rusted cans and shreds of plastic sacks lay strewn along a wall. Hosein's clandestine cargo had no doubt thought this was the last stop before freedom. They'd probably prayed here that they'd find someone to listen to their suffering, someone from the Promised Land to stop the pain. Hosein's "safe house" was a temple: inside its crumbling walls, Good had held Evil at bay.

The odds were decent I'd met more than one of Hosein's broken yet hopeful soldiers. Met and forgotten among the thousands.

3 A PRIOR CROSSING
Hamburg, 1993

As I climbed the steps, my apprehension intensified. A camera bolted above the consulate's front door stared straight down at my head and the scarf-clad heads of three women standing beside me. Once in, I couldn't just walk out. Nor could I call the German police if I got into trouble. There were no public telephones inside. If I ran into an Iranian official I knew from the past, I could conceivably end up in a back room answering questions. My well-laid plans to arrive in Tehran via Mehrabad airport escorted by protective friends would be in ruins. I might have to endure the type of questioning that I'd occasionally inflicted upon suspicious Iranians. It could turn out to be a very unpleasant morning.

I pushed the front-door buzzer; the women, cursing as their scarves and faces became wet from the drizzle, pushed harder. When the wood-facade steel door was buzzed open, the women crowded past, not giving me the chance to invite them to go first. A few feet beyond the threshold, the camera operator, short and bald with a scruffy salt-and-pepper beard, stood behind a tinted window. He nodded his approval at each of us as we moved through another door into a white-walled, rectangular waiting room with a television suspended from the ceiling. He looked at me only a bit longer than he'd looked at the women.

My nervousness eased. The security procedures were not tight. My shoulder bag hadn't been checked. One interior camera watched the waiting room, but given the number of people and the camera's locked position—eye level just above the visa windows—detailed observation of the large room would be difficult.

A sweet and sour smell, body odor mixing with fresh paint, permeated the room. On the far wall, a large sign in flowing black *nastaliq* Persian script caught my eye: BROTHERS AND SISTERS WELCOME BACK TO THE ISLAMIC REPUBLIC! Legally speaking, the sign was of course accurate: after the threshold, I was in clerical Iran.

Because I couldn't find a seat, I went to the rear of the room next to the barred windows—the farthest point from the camera. I looked through the crowd, and especially at the Iranian officials behind the consular windows, to see if by chance I could recognize someone—or someone could recognize me—from the past. Happily, everyone seemed a stranger.

I wasn't the only Westerner in the room. Or the only American: the loud, twanging voices of two businessmen cut through the singsong Persian chatter. I also spotted two blond women standing together in an Iranians-only queue, their German chatter rising above the rest. With scarves partly over their hair, raincoats over their dresses, and leather pumps on their feet, they looked like most of the female expatriates in the room. They'd no doubt married Persians, which made them citizens according to Iranian law.

The one consular window reserved for foreigners was "temporarily closed." Instinctively, I scanned the room for Iranians a CIA officer might want to meet. I wasn't—and never would be again—a case officer who recruits foreigners into espionage. But I kept looking at the world as a spy, endlessly guessing whether a foreigner, stranger, acquaintance, or friend might for principle, profit, anger, or love illicitly ally with an American.

The curiosity had become indiscriminate in me: Frenchmen, Germans, Brits, Persians, Turks, Israelis, Arabs, or Americans—all provoked questions about the bonds that tie individuals to their countries. Though I had studied and traveled among Arabs first, and actually lived with the Italians, French, British, and Turks, I didn't feel I could quickly and accurately anticipate them. Only with Persians could I usually guess a man's emotions, reflexes, and sins. I felt I could properly ask a Persian to commit treason, though I'd never been to Iran.

In the waiting room, the standing men and seated scarf-clad women appeared depressed, at first glance. Much against Persian character, Iranians of the Islamic Republic have abandoned individualism and vanity in their dress. Color, a hallmark of Islamic and particularly Persian architecture, has nearly disappeared from their clothes—the decadent, fun-loving Iranian character hidden by gray, black, and brown.

But you should always look several times for exploitable hints. The quality of an Iranian's suit, his shoes, the whiteness of his tieless shirts may hint about his class. Language helps immensely: pronunciation usually gives away class, though class, even in a poor man's revolution, doesn't necessarily incline one toward treason. Foreign education always leaves linguistic marks; many of Iran's most extreme revolutionaries have been educated abroad.

Islamic sensibility expresses itself quickly in Persian. Revolutionary formulas and informality compete against more nuanced, traditional conventions. This balance can reveal a man's preferences and dislikes.

An Iranian's eyes, and how quickly he averts them, can indicate if he is native born and bred, socially more comfortable as an inferior, or disturbed by a violation of decorum.

How an Iranian moves his hands, whether he holds them still, puts them near his knees, or moves them out of sight, can betray his social status, a religious or secular education, or even the depth of his Shi'ite Muslim faith.

Walking slowly through the room, I found three men who interested me. They seemed slightly Westernized, but not educated outside Iran. They were not timid; they led the conversations they were in. They laughed just a little in a room where virtually no one smiled. I guessed they were all in their thirties—time enough to have brought down the Shah and had their revolutionary enthusiasm dampened by the eight-year Iran–Iraq War. Time enough for a wife and several children to refocus their lives.

When I was a spy, I could never make up my mind whether I preferred to recruit single or married Iranians. Bachelors would more quickly take risks, but married men needed more money and, more importantly, hated with greater constancy. An Iranian can scream "Death to America!" one moment and ask you sincerely a minute later to help his sister get a visa to the States, a land they both adore. These feelings are not contradictory; they are sequential. Commitments come and go, then return. I had found married men less volatile, less likely to forgive an offense or a disappointment that might incline them toward treason. Once agents, they gave me fewer doubts about their loyalty.

Were these men around me now married or single? I couldn't tell. Sometimes married Iranian men wear wedding rings, sometimes not. Their age, and the fact they were abroad, strongly suggested these men were husbands. In general, Iranian men are devoted to matrimony, though not necessarily to their wives. An Iranian man can't have a child out of wedlock without being socially ostracized or murdered, and every Iranian man wants a son. If you have money, you have a wife. And if a Persian could persuade a suspicious German consular officer to give him a visa, then purchase a round-trip airline ticket to Germany, he had enough money to marry. Since I didn't see young women near any of the three, I guessed they'd left their wives in Iran. Traveling without a spouse, they could more easily convince a consular officer of their intent to return, and more easily find Western women with whom to act out their sexual dreams.

Their possible professions? I doubted they represented the Iranian government: none had the appearance of an Iranian functionary overseas, that unkempt, four- or five-day-bearded look, a dark turtle-neck more often than a decent suit. Iran has had only occasional diplomat-dandies (Iranian foreign minister Ali Velayati comes to mind), much-traveled bureaucrats on the European model who look kind, at ease, and well trimmed.

These men all spoke confidently, without prompting or concern about superiors possibly listening. Their pressed dark suits indicated free enterprise: in my experience, officials weren't wrinkle-free. And their heavily starched shirt collars flared noticeably, suggesting they had recently worn ties. Though I'd once seen Iranian officials furtively and joyously sporting ties in Istanbul's Dedeman Hotel bar, this was extremely uncommon. A *kravat* was strictly forbidden Western attire for the representatives of Islamic Iran.

Business for the government, for themselves, or for both was more likely. Or, perhaps, they were Iranian representatives of European or American companies. Even possibly new-generation bazaaris, Persian merchants who have bought and sold through the ages and, since the revolution, have become ever closer in appearance to modern businessmen with portable telephones, laptops, and fax modems. All might be in the consulate for lost passports or identity papers, notarizations, or official commercial assistance, which in Iran is often, unless you're well connected, more a hindrance than a help.

The three might even know a lot about U.S. companies circumventing Washington's restrictions on commerce with Iran. They could certainly help me to understand better Iran's collapsing economy, its maze of bureaucratic corruption, and the corrosive contradictions between public poverty and private wealth. They might offer helpful tidbits about clerics who spend more time doing business than reading the Qur'an. Were they the kind of Iranians who, within their own consulate, would joke with an American?

I started wondering how I might encounter them outside the consulate, imagining scenarios where we might "accidentally" meet. Were they my favorite kind of Persian, who would talk to me more than I'd have to talk to them?

I glanced at the coffee tables next to two of them, hunting for pocket litter disgorged. When visiting the West, Persians are like vacuum cleaners: they suck up matchbooks, brochures, pens, plastic cigarette lighters, paper pads—anything with a label that will show later where they visited, stayed, or dined. More than once, I'd learned where a chain-smoking Iranian was staying by a glimpse of a hotel matchbook or a disposable plastic lighter.

My attention drifted away from the businessmen. Three diplomats had caught my eye. Two were behind the consular windows, but one was now kneeling in the waiting room, talking to two seated elderly women. The women both wore black chadors, the body-enveloping thin fabric that can give mobile women the appearance of walking black bowling pins. As the chadors were open at the face, I saw a family resemblance: they were quite likely sisters and widows, abroad to visit or live with elder sons. This was a common recourse for widowed mothers even with younger sons in Iran. One was crying, a stream of tears winding down a deep wrinkled channel that cut her cheek.

I moved closer.

I knew the kneeling gentleman was an official because I'd seen him walk through an open door behind the camera operator's security post. Surprising to see him on this side of the glass: in a consulate, Iranian officials, like their American counterparts, almost never get close to their own citizens. To maintain authority and security, you stay behind the thick applicant windows. And Iranian consulates and embassies had been attacked several times since the revolution by the *Mojahedin-e Khalq*, the People's Holy Warriors, revolutionary friends-turned-enemies of the mollahs. With the *Mojahedin* about, Iranian diplomats were rightfully worried about the peaceful intentions of their citizens abroad.

This consular official had crossed the glass dividing line. A small and perhaps telling transgression. I doubted that many other colleagues had ever done the same. Courtesy is what you should expect and demand of a Persian, whose ancient culture commands respect for the old. But revolutionary Muslims had made war on Persia's rules of politeness, hierarchy, etiquette, and charm. Iranian consular officials, showpieces of a new fundamentalist Islamic order, had become particularly unkind.

Others in the room had noted that this official hadn't forgotten the age-old rules. Young men in particular were staring. I wondered whether this young diplomat had ever waged war against the conventions and customs, insouciance, cynicism, and moral generosity of his Persian past. Had he ever cast it aside to become one of Khomeini's holy warriors who hated their tolerant, good-natured, obsequious village fathers and grandfathers as much as they hated the West? I wondered if he still viewed Khomeini's victorious return from exile, from Paris to Tehran in 1979, as the annus mirabilis of his faith. Was he a proud and gentle Persian who would never have beaten a blindfolded State Department hostage inside the U.S. embassy compound in Tehran?

Because I couldn't hear the conversation between the diplomat and the old woman, I moved forward slowly along the right-hand wall until I was about six feet away. I could hear their conversation, but not clearly. I could tell the woman who was not crying was pleading with the official to help the woman who was.

How often had I heard Iranians beg me in this manner? How often had I heard old women tearfully implore me to give them visas so they could see sons, daughters, and grandchildren one more time before they died? How often had I stretched U.S. visa regulations, imagining my own grandmother in their shoes? How often had I followed the rules, denying visas according to 214B, the "guilty until proven innocent" subsection of the U.S. Immigration Code? To give a tourist visa to a widowed Iranian woman to see a Stateside, green-card–holding son or daughter *was*, after all, an invitation for illegal immigration: for what Iranian son or daughter would allow his or her mother to go home and die alone?

The old woman repeated tearfully, *"Ested'a mikonam, ested'a mikonam. Lutfan, khahesh mikonam, lotfi konin,"* "I beseech you, I beseech you, please, I beg you, do me a kindness." I had so often heard the same words. From old women, persecuted Baha'is, and Persian Jews, from young secularized women trapped in a world they loathed, from young men evading the Iran–Iraq War, from ordinary Muslim Iranians wanting to reach the Promised Land. These words were always the preface to horrendous stories of suffering in revolution and war. They were also often the introduction to heartrending tales of invented agony and lost loved ones, the masterly histrionics of duplicitous, visa-hungry souls.

The Iranian official, down on one knee, didn't think the old women were lying. Repeatedly wrinkling his brow, he seemed committed to the crying woman's cause. His umber eyes didn't look away. With his short obsidian hair and beard, gray-black turtleneck, and gold-buckled black shoes, he seemed more a New Age shaman than a diplomat of an Islamic-law state.

Then he broke *another* rule. He touched the old woman. Persian men usually don't touch women who aren't members of their family, even if the women are very old. He was holding one of her hands in both of his. He spoke too softly for me to follow, trying to assuage her fears. I wanted to hear his Persian; I imagined it formal but warm.

When Persians speak well, they enrapture. Turkish Ottoman princes forbade their sons to study Persian, the diplomatic language of the medieval Islamic world, before they were fifteen years old, fearing the beauty of the language would convert their Sunni Muslim sons to Iran's heretical Shi'ite faith. The Persian language, rich in repeated long vowels and hard consonants, can make everyday speech sound like an epic poem.

I could hear the diplomat slowing his speech for the old woman, comforting her with repeated promises of help. If I'd still been in the CIA, I would have locked on to this man. I would have tried to convince the chief of the local CIA station to give me the time and money to follow and assess him. He would have been worth a year or two of my life.

I would have wanted to know where he lived, whether he walked to work alone or with others. Whether he ever prayed at a local mosque. Whether he, like most Iranians, believed emphatically in leisure. Was he a family man, or did he prefer the company of other men?

I would have wanted to know when and where he'd gone to grade school, lycée, and university. Degrees received or left unfinished? Who were his professors? Did he go to bookstores and what kind? Did he know the local representatives of Iranian Radio and Television, the accessible, loose-lipped journalist-spies of every Persian community abroad?

Was he that odd Iranian diplomat who had the inclination and courage to have Western friends? Did he ever cross the divide between the official and expatriate Iranian communities to see separated family or friends? Or, perhaps, to run a little import-export business on the side? Most importantly, I would have wanted to know his wife, her habits, and her friends. Did she stay at home or did she, like many wives outside of Iran, go wild in the freedom, zealously moving about town, children in tow, to discover the truth about the West?

As other Iranians noticed the restrained but emotional scene, the diplomat tensed, realizing he'd become the center of attention. The conversation was closing between the women and my man. He rose, surprising me by his height. Over six foot, I estimated. Tall for an Iranian, but not rare. Compared to Arabs, even Turks, Persians aren't short. Briefly, we made eye contact, but nothing more.

After a slow goodbye of many thank-yous, the diplomat left. Feeling cheated, I glanced over at the closed foreigners-only line. I moved to the rear of the room next to the windows and tried to find the other two officials who'd attracted my attention, but they'd abandoned their chairs. The Iranian applicants, however, remained steadfast in line. They were no happier than the Westerners, just more patient. I kept thinking about the recently departed diplomat and my gut feeling that in a different time and place, with considerable luck, I could have had a recruitment, a soul mate, someone to teach me about Iran.

Such operations are feast or famine. Sometimes you meet the right people, most often you don't. Rarely, very rarely, do you find a prospective jewel—once, maybe twice, in an espionage career. Many officers never find one. The rest is downtime, "operational make-believe," when case officers pretend to be defending the frontiers of freedom, recruiting valuable agents, and collecting important intelligence. They're really only paying their mortgages, eating out on Uncle Sam, and repeating the clandestine-service mantra about being the chosen few. C/O careers can't be made on prospective jewels; they come too rarely, require too much expertise and luck, and take too much time. Flimflam is easier, possible everywhere, and has always been a more reliable basis for Agency promotion.

Now all the windows but one were "temporarily closed." The Iranians started forming small groups in and out of line. The ones nearest me were complaining. About the unbearable burdens that Iranians bear every day. About how Persians had been born to suffer. How no one in recorded history had ever suffered more. About the cost of airline tickets, jewelry, and food overseas. And about officials: how much dumber they were in the Islamic Republic than under the Shah, but not as dumb this year as the year before. Last but not least, a stunning Hermès-scarfed Iranian beauty, with cheek-bones higher than heaven, complained about the stench of native Iranians abroad.

Those who weren't complaining were reading. *Kayhan, Ettel'at, Abrar, Resalat,* and even *Salam,* one of the more independent and iconoclastic revolutionary papers of Tehran. The consulate apparently provided the popular newspapers from back home. They were everywhere, stacked on small tables or thrown on the floor. The 1979 revolution had provoked an explosion of opinion in print—a reaction to the Shah's stifling twenty-five-year censorship of the press. Within a year of their victory, the mollahs too began to rein in free speech; some maneuvering room still existed, because mollahs weren't the same ideologically. Many supported a centralized, planned economy; many did not. There were those who strongly supported the export of the revolution, and those who didn't; those who viewed the United States as Evil Incarnate, and those who only bashed the United States for pleasure or political need. This clerical diversity kept Iran's press again from becoming simply a mouthpiece for an authoritarian regime. Read critically, the newspapers revealed considerable information about the internecine quarrels within Iran, about who was up and who was down. More importantly, they confessed, often by screaming the opposite, the failings of revolutionary Islam.

These newspapers had been untapped resources at the CIA. With rare exceptions, nobody read them. I'd known the Iran desks of both sides of my intelligence world—in the Directorate of Operations and Intelligence, the Agency's analytical wing—and in each the newspapers were stacked in cubbyholes reserved for Persian "paraphernalia." Not a single analyst and only two case officers besides me even read Persian, and the two C/Os, an Iranian-American man and woman, generally avoided Persian culture or prose. Neither one, I was sure, had ever read a paper, magazine, or book from the Islamic Republic in the years that I'd known them. Both were very sensitive about their origins and wanted to seem as American as they could—a wise choice in the white-bread, foreigner-hostile, Middle America bastion of the CIA. Only an Armenian-Iranian-American woman

who stacked the Persian newspapers ever ventured into the DO cubbyhole, a six-foot-square sanctuary where I walked daily from headquarters into Iran.

I forgot about newspapers when a large Sony color television suspended from the ceiling snapped on. An obsequious Iranian TV
journalist was questioning Hojjat ol-Eslam Ali Akbar Hashemi-
Rafsanjani, the cleric who ran the Persian side of the late CIA director William Casey's Iran–Contra affair. Rafsanjani, who'd been
elected Iran's president in 1989 and reelected in 1993, was listing
his successes: an improving economy; better relations with the newly
independent, ex-Soviet Muslim republics of Central Asia and Iran's
Arab neighbors; an increase in Iran's oil production. I stopped listening. The Persians around me had also stopped—or probably had
never even started.

For Western-educated Iranian expatriates—and from their bet-
ter-quality clothes, confident faces, and Persian heavily peppered
with foreign words, I guessed about half of the seventy-odd people
in the room were expatriates—Rafsanjani had extended the hope
that the worst was over. The eight-year, World War I–style conflict
with Iraq had ended in 1988; Khomeini had died in 1989. Rafsanjani, the *gorbeh*, the clever cat, the cleric who couldn't grow a beard,
would bury once and for all the revolutionary madness, the utopian
streak in the Persian Muslim character that during the Iran–Iraq
War sent fourteen-year-olds across minefields on motorcycles. With
a little luck, Rafsanjani might even deliver what every expatriate and
probably many officials in that visa room prayed for—restored relations with the United States.

Rafsanjani had tried. The war had ended—and Rafsanjani more
than anyone deserved credit for convincing a reluctant Ayatollah
Khomeini to end a losing holy cause—and the revolutionary fever
ebbed. DEATH TO AMERICA headbands and banners had become
fewer in Iran. The government was even trying to encourage Western-educated and affluent expatriates, former "traitors and criminals," to come home and help rebuild the country, guaranteeing
them their safety, if not their property, on their return.

But not enough had changed. The economy was still awful despite Rafsanjani's free-market efforts, far worse than when the rev-

olution erupted in 1978. And young men, faithful toughs in the Urban Morals Police Force, could still hassle or arrest a woman for exposing a lock of hair. The regime imprisoned or killed without warning or explanation. Christian Iranian priests, Baha'is, and even revolution-loyal army counterintelligence chiefs could disappear or die, killed anonymously by a knife or car. Prominent Persian Jews, if they didn't behave and publicly denounce their Holy Land, could find themselves charged with sexual molestation of children or other capital crimes. And Iranian terrorists were still active overseas, their targets usually unforgiven Iranian expatriates. Iran was still isolated, its passports viewed contemptuously and suspiciously in virtually every consulate in the world. America, the mollahs' Great Satan, the land most Iranians love more than they hate, lay no closer than before. Rafsanjani, white-turbaned, white-shirted, wrapped in an immaculate dark-brown camel's-hair cleric's cloak, bored many of his countrymen. He was not, in the end, as so many expatriates surreally hoped, a new pro-Western shah camouflaged in mollah's clothing.

Intensely shamed by the ugliness and violence of the revolution, Iranians abroad often tried to camouflage their homeland as Persia, not Iran, hoping a Western listener didn't know both words meant the same country. With luck, an American would associate Persia with miniatures, carpets, and caviar, not hostages, Muslim zealots, and Khomeini. The millions of Iranians in exile kept hoping that someone somehow would turn back the clock and return to them their homes and comfortable prerevolutionary lives. Despite Rafsanjani's betrayal, they hadn't given up the dream. Perhaps another soldier-shah would arrive or, better, Washington would awaken and unleash the CIA. After all, they told themselves, Mohammad Reza Pahlavi (1919–80), the *Shahanshah*, the Shah of Shahs, King of Kings, surely wouldn't have fallen to lowly clerics if the United States hadn't taken their side. The Shah had brought on Washington's ill will by becoming too strong and too independent, forming alliances in 1971 and 1973 with Muammar Qaddafi and the Saudis to jack up the price of oil.

I'd never had the heart or the patience, in conversations with Iranians, to sink their conspiracies or their dreams. Professionally, it had always worked to my advantage to render Iranian myth and conspiratorial madness into U.S. power. Why should I tell Iranians that the CIA-backed 1953 coup d'état against the oil-nationalizing left-wing prime minister Mohammad Mosaddeq had been only a lucky exception, not the rule?

Rafsanjani himself might fear the CIA, but we who'd worked at Langley knew better.

Bored with Rafsanjani, I searched the room for anti-U.S. slogan-eering. I'd seen it regularly on the walls of Iranian embassies and consulates around the world: anti-U.S posters and translated Persian newspaper editorials side by side with pictures of Iran's wounded in the Iran–Iraq War. In many Iranian eyes, Washington had un-leashed Saddam Hussein against the Islamic Republic in September 1980 in punishment for the fall of the Shah and the hostage-taking in Tehran. I'd always derived great pleasure from listening to the same Iranians damn the United States for supporting Khomeini's war against the Shah.

I couldn't see a single anti-U.S. poster or manifesto on the waiting room's walls. They were full of legalistic bulletins, official state-ments, and framed quotations from Khomeini, great Persian poets, and the Qur'an. On a side wall hung the obligatory pictures of a gelid, black-eyed Khomeini and his limp, less earthshaking successor, Ali Khameneh'i. The walls' collage of paper, poems, and pictures seemed more chaotic than threatening. Except for Khomeini's pic-ture and the BROTHERS AND SISTERS WELCOME BACK HOME sign, which had a distinctly Orwellian touch, nothing on the walls looked hostile. Happily, America seemed ignored.

I started eyeing more carefully the taped-up typing-paper bulle-tins closest to me. I wasn't looking for small-print anti-U.S. com-mentary; I was actually looking for U.S.–Iranian bureaucratic parallels. I wanted to see how their bulletins about passport-renewal applications were similar to or different from ours. I was curious to see if in the boring details I could find an "Islamic" imprint, some-thing in language or theme from traditional Islamic law. The *Shari'at*, like the Jewish Halakhah but unlike the Christian canon, can theoretically touch virtually every aspect of life—the way you eat, make love, urinate, speak, buy a home, start a business, pay taxes, travel, shake hands, or make war. The list is nearly endless, reflecting the creativity, profound faith, and iron logic of Muslim jurists, who have applied God's Qur'anic dictates and the inspired seventh-century example of the Prophet Muhammad to nearly fourteen hundred years of Islamic history. As church and state are one in Islam, no realm of human activity (in theory) is immune from religious supervision and inspiration.

But theory is not practice, and I wanted to see whether I could find God's handiwork in posted instructions for renewing Iranian identity papers. I wasn't sure what I was looking for, but I felt certain I'd recognize it if I saw it. So I started perusing the Persian fine print.

A voice from behind my right shoulder interrupted me. *"Farsi baladin?"*

Stupidly, I turned.

A short, balding middle-aged man in a glistening fake-silk, silver-lead suit stood just behind me. I'd not intended anyone in the consulate to know that I both spoke and read Persian. It could provoke too many questions and oblige me to violate Rule One: Never talk to Iranians more than they talk to me. If an Iranian discovered I knew Persian, I'd probably have to talk about my former Persian instructors, the universities I'd attended, the origins of my Persian curiosity, past and present Iranian friends—who, where, and how much they earn. All my answers would of course be innocent, and mostly true. But truth and falsehoods don't matter as much as impressions. Iranians think all Westerners, and most of their fellow Iranians, are spies. Before even getting to the visa window, I could be the subject of a lively, good-natured group interrogation.

I'd thought endlessly about this issue before risking the consulate. In general, being suspected of espionage didn't paralyze me with fear: all foreigners are assumed guilty and remain guilty thereafter. But with so much company, there's a certain anonymity. And Persians have a very hard time blistering you well on one subject before galloping off to another. Also, spies have a certain allure and hidden power, and in the shifting alliances and conspiratorial insanity that rule Iran, spooky suspicions can reinforce, not undermine, a protective mystique.

Revolutionary Iranians would deal with Satan for the right reasons, as Khomeini and Rafsanjani proved in 1985 when they welcomed Bud McFarlane's and Oliver North's little mixed band of American and Israeli officials bearing missiles and pastries to Tehran. Most in Iran would assume that an American or European in their midst had an Iranian guardian angel. The suspicion might land you in jail one moment but get you invited to dinner the next. It all depended on time, place, and the people involved.

Nonetheless, I wanted to appear less, not more, of a spy to my Iranian beholder: friendly, curious, somewhat tutored, but not particularly well schooled. I didn't want to give an Iranian extraordinary reasons to be suspicious, to linger on me more than your average foreigner-cum-spy.

"Excuse me," I replied in English, trying to recoup orally what I had lost through reflex.

"You read Persian, don't you?" he said in Persian. "Do you need help?" At my feigned consternation, he repeated this in English and added, "Do you have an Iranian wife?"

I took a good look at him. He wasn't an expatriate: such a tacky Middle Eastern suit would have been discarded with the first full-time Western job. Similarly, the pseudo-silk sheen was what most diplomats of the Islamic Republic would wear if they could; but they couldn't. Too shiny for paragons of a joyless faith.

I quickly relaxed as common sense took hold. Iranian diplomats were neither *that* curious nor *that* courteous.

"No, I don't read Persian," I lied. "I know a little of the alphabet, but I can barely recognize the letters in this sheet of paper."

The paper taped to the wall was in fact difficult to read. It was handwritten in *nastaliq*, the classic swirling script that exists in Persian but not in Arabic. Derived from the Arabic word meaning "to hang," *nastaliq*, when well done, frictionlessly and harmoniously fills a space, as if a calculus equation had been used to determine the ideal balance between black and white. Though I'd been tutored in *nastaliq*, I still found it time-consuming. And this was not first-rate *nastaliq*. It was more *shekasteh*, an individualistic, rule-free bastardization of proper Persian script that Iranians prefer when writing quickly. *Shekasteh* means "broken" in Persian, which is how I felt whenever I tried to read it. Iranians know that *nastaliq-shekasteh* can be a bitch to read, so my questioner might buy the response and keep his distance.

"They're awful here," he said. "Look at this consulate, it's a mess. I can't get anything done and I'm an Iranian. Do they treat you any better?"

Iranians rightly assume their officials favor foreigners over their own. Though Iranians naturally make extra efforts for foreigners, many dislike *seeing* foreigners receive preferential treatment. It reminds them that for hundreds of years it's been a one-way street—how seldom they have been able to lord it over the other guy. I was cheered that this gentleman was jealous, because when I looked at the Iranian officials behind the consular windows, at their surly, disheveled, constipated revolutionary faces, I couldn't see a foreigner's advantage.

"No, they don't treat me better," I said. "They won't even open up my window."

My questioner seemed relieved. "You are learning Persian? Are you an American? Are you German? Why do you want to learn Persian? Do you have an Iranian wife? You have been to Iran? Do you do business in Iran? Most people want to leave Iran. Why do you want to go?"

Maintaining Rule One would be hard. Too many questions too quickly. Iranians often use questions as shields, an active defense against questions coming their way. They want as much information as possible as quickly as possible to see whether they can expose a slice of their true feelings. Iranians know instinctively that the American admonition to tell the truth is nonsense in the Middle East, like playing draw poker with your cards face forward. The more you lie, the more questions you ask, the greater the distance between you and the other guy. Deceptions and lies are extensions of the high walls surrounding Persian homes.

Still, in a world full of potential enemies, Persians desperately want friends. Thus, they're drawn to foreigners, who they hope will be more friend than foe, an outsider innocent and ignorant of their power games or, much better, a possible trump against their Persian enemies.

Though my questioner appeared to be one of those Iranians

(partly Westernized, partly peasant) who speak English for hours about the price of rice in Tehran, I had the feeling he might go personal, telling me more about himself and his family than I wanted to know. If the foreigners-only line didn't open—and I was beginning to believe that "temporarily closed" might mean open one hour once a week when you're not looking—I could be deluged by this man's problems, held hostage with stories of daily travails, life-threatening political intrigue, and perhaps a we-are-good-friends, halvah-sweet request for a favor.

I tried turning back politely toward the window and the sunlight, hoping he'd let me off with a few words. Then I'd furtively return to my *nastaliq-shekasteh* bulletins on the wall.

"I want to see Isfahan." I avoided his other questions. "I've heard it's nice."

Isfahan was once one of the loveliest cities in the world. The seventeenth-century capital of Persia's great Safavid Islamic kings, Isfahan is often referred to as *Esfahan nesf-e Jahan*, "Isfahan is half the World," a city of turquoise-tiled fountains, palaces, mosques, and polo fields. Few other cities declaim architecturally such an unrequited national passion for water, a rare resource in arid Iran. Of no other Persian city are Iranians so proud. Only the ruins at Persepolis, the capital of the Achaemenian shahs, the Persian kings whom Alexander the Great dethroned, show equally the power, excess, and beauty of Iran. But Persepolis was pre-Islamic; Isfahan, though built by card-playing, wine-loving, slave-girl-sated kings, is also a monument to Iran's devotion to Islam. No devout Muslim has ever built a more beautiful mosque than the least beautiful of Isfahan. I was hoping my silver-suited friend would reel off the city's past glories and then leave me be.

"I have gone to Isfahan several times. I prefer Shiraz, but Isfahan is more beautiful. You should visit both. I am Shirazi—we are so much nicer than Isfahanis. They are very difficult people. They were bad before the revolution, they are worse now. See Isfahan, but don't stay long. For fun, Tehran and Shiraz are much better."

Known for their brusque, dishonest, and homosexual manners before the revolution, Isfahanis in 1978–79 became known for their revolutionary zeal, rising in insurrection even before Tehranis did.

The city's incomparable mosques became home to many of Iran's most vicious mollahs.

Given the number of Iranian cities, I began to think I could keep my tour adviser busy until my window opened. Even if he hadn't been to a city—most Persians travel little within Iran—he'd still tell me its pros and cons. After five or six cities he might want to escape a foreigner with so many questions.

"I also want to go to Mashhad," I added. "I've heard it's the holiest city in Iran. Don't all Iranians do a pilgrimage to Mashhad at least once in their lives? I heard you can feel both the emptiness of Central Asia and the mountains of Afghanistan in Mashhad."

God only knew if you really could feel both Turkmenistan's vastness and Herat's mountain ranges. If Mashhad was like most Middle Eastern cities, neither its history nor its geography would strike you first. Pollution and traffic would take precedence. And Mashhad is the primary bottling plant for the Iranian subsidiary of Coca-Cola, with transport trucks running in and out of town. I'd heard one immediately felt that Iran's preeminent pilgrim site was the gateway to soda-pop heaven, not God's grace.

"Mashhad is not as beautiful as Isfahan, but more beautiful than Shiraz," said my new friend. "Our Imam Reza is buried in Mashhad. After Ali and his son Hosein, he is the greatest of our Imams. I went to Mashhad twice—not for pilgrimage, I have never gone on pilgrimage. As a tourist. To see the *haram-e motahhar*, the sacred grounds, and the mosque of Gohar Shad. Yes, you must definitely see Mashhad. Very different from Tehran or Shiraz, even Isfahan. The people of Mashhad are very religious, not fanatics the way they are in Isfahan or Tehran or Qom. They are good people who believe in God and his Imams."

Soda pop notwithstanding, Mashhad remains Iran's most revered city, containing the country's holiest site, the shrine of Imam Reza (d. 817)—the eighth of the twelve Imams who form the historical and mystical inspiration behind Twelver Shi'ism, the primary Muslim faith of Iran, Iraq, and Lebanon. Located in the northeast corner of the country near the borders of both Turkmenistan and Afghanistan, Mashhad was Iran's historic gateway to Central Asia and Persian-speaking Bukhara and Samarkand, two of the medieval world's most glorious cities. Since the Soviet invasion of Afghanistan in 1980, Mashhad had also become a haven for Persian-speaking Afghan refugees.

No matter what he said, I was willing to bet that my friend *had* gone to Mashhad on *ziyarat*, on pilgrimage. An Iranian going to Mashhad twice as a tourist! That was like a devout Catholic saying he'd gone twice to Lourdes for the shops. I could see he was ready to pivot and fire questions at me. So I fired first.

"Would a man go on pilgrimage because he has sinned? Would a woman go because she can't have children?" I asked, corking him just as he started to speak. Sex, children, pilgrimage, poetry, God, and America—somewhere in their cross-stitching I'd been able to open up most Iranian men.

"Yes, Iranians go to Mashhad because they have done wrong. But they also go for hope. To thank God they have survived great pain. Mashhad is a peaceful place. It has more good Muslims than bad. The mollahs do not scream in the mosques. Neither do the people. Mashhad was built by the love of Islam, good Islam. But how do you know about Mashhad? Do you have an Iranian wife?"

Women and Islam. Impossible to talk about one without talking about the other. Women are at the center of the Muslim mind. Arguably, the greatest strength of Islam is its promise of fraternity and family solace in a world with few brothers and little hope. Every Muslim man knows that at least within his home there is order, that even the humblest have been vouchsafed a place to rule and conceive.

My friend's question about a Persian wife was also a rear-door way of inquiring about my faith. He was not an upper-class Westernized Iranian who spent as much time overseas as at home. Even among them, eyebrows could be raised when a Shi'ite Persian woman married a Western man. If I had an Iranian wife, then I might well be a Muslim, since Iranian Muslim women aren't supposed to marry non-Muslim men. On the other hand, Iranian Muslim men, like all Muslim men, may have non-Muslim wives.

Of course, in the West, expatriates may do whatever they please, but no Iranian woman would dare take her non-Muslim husband back to Iran without at least nominal conversion. That is, he should know how to say the Shi'ite *shahadat*, the confession of faith in Arabic, if asked: *Ashadu an la ilaha illallah Mohammad rasulullah va Aliyun valillah*, "I testify that there is no god but Allah, Mohammad is the Messenger of God and Ali is His Deputy." These words, if uttered freely, with intent, make one a Shi'ite Muslim. No more is required, and no Shi'ite Muslim may challenge the depth of another Shi'ite Muslim's faith.

If I had an Iranian wife, my silver-suited friend would wonder whether my conversion could in fact be real. Whether I might have been a Muslim before I married—that Islam had drawn me to my Iranian wife, and not the reverse. Or, alternatively, had my conversion become profound, transcending the initial pull of love or sex? Even the most Westernized Muslim can feel especially proud when a Westerner joins his faith, astonishingly embracing a religion that hasn't won a war in centuries. Still, conversion raises doubts. Even the most devout radical Muslims, who loudly proclaim the evident superiority and inevitable victory of Islam, are suspicious of Western changes of faith.

Muslims were born to victory. For nearly a thousand years of holy war against the infidel, they won more than they lost. But this millennium's confidence weakened after the Polish cavalry broke the Ottoman line at Vienna in 1683. Thereafter, Muslims, God's battle-chosen people, rarely, inexplicably, could hold their own against infidels. Muslims, unlike Christians, see neither virtue in weakness nor benefit in suffering. The Holy Law envisions Muslims as rulers, not subjects.

Though most Muslims still assume the obvious superiority of their religion, they are often puzzled to find white Western males reaching the same conclusion. If you have taken the world, why change your faith? Aren't battlefield victories, aircraft carriers, and ICBMs the most convincing proof that God has chosen your side?

Deceit, love of a woman, or divine insight—each could be an acceptable explanation for my Shi'ite conversion. Most Iranians would probably give me the benefit of the doubt.

But for getting Iranians talking, being a Muslim would not *nec-*

essarily be more advantageous. Some Iranians, even very faithful ones, believe Christians and Jews are more trustworthy than Muslims. As an American spy, I'd regularly been in the odd position of listening to Iranians who desperately wanted to confess their sins and, even more enthusiastically, their neighbors'.

The Near East Division within the CIA has never really understood the confessional possibilities in Muslim/non-Muslim dialogues. Yes, every Middle Easterner wants to talk to an American official—that was gospel at Langley. And in the Muslim world this *is* true more often than not. But Agency understanding always remained secular. It wasn't just a question of power—the weak desperately wanting to give secret counsel to the strong; it was a question of faith.

For many, contact with the CIA can verge on a religious experience. A pilgrimage to the Forbidden Land for devout Muslims who might have recurring doubts—who can't quite believe their side has been losing for so long. It is a chance to see, talk to, and touch the devils who have successfully denied God's promise; an opportunity to explore the possibility, however remote, that God has temporarily changed sides. Muslims, whose not too distant ancestors called all Christians "Romans" or "Franks," have become exceptionally curious about infidels. And the more provocative the *kafir*, the greater the Muslim curiosity.

Hence, the unappreciated importance of Western women in espionage against Muslim men. When I was a case officer, the CIA never valued female C/Os in the Middle East. Most men in the Directorate of Operations' Senior Intelligence Service, the dons who run U.S. espionage, were uncomfortable with female colleagues anywhere, let alone in the male-dominated Middle East. You could find female C/Os here and there in the Arab world, but they were usually tokens, posted more for the Equal Opportunity balance sheet than for their innate power over Muslim men.

But Western women can often loosen the lips, if not gain the confidence, of even devout Muslim males more quickly than Western men. Journalists like the *Los Angeles Times* reporter Robin Wright, the *New York Times*'s Elaine Sciolino, the *Wall Street Journal*'s Geraldine Brooks, or CNN's Christiane Amanpour, women not scared to project their femininity in the company of Muslim men, can gain impressive access in Iran and throughout the Muslim world. Talent aside, that access is in part due to their sex. They would very likely not be allowed as deep inside a Muslim man's mind as an equally talented male observer, but they'd get through the heavily guarded front gate more quickly than even the most intrepid, clever, or duplicitous male colleague.

I'd always thought women C/Os should be used against Muslim volunteers, men who would offer their services at U.S. embassies and consulates abroad. Such walk-ins put a high priority on time: the C/O has to make up his mind quickly whether he's got the real thing, a provocation, a poseur, or a combination of all three. Walk-ins can be fickle, mutating before your eyes. One moment a volunteer, the next a hostile witness who'd rather be miles away from you and the Marine guards outside your interview-room door. A case officer has to obtain as much information as quickly as possible. He must listen and, if appropriate, pounce. He must assuage and confess fears. He must suggest that Muslim dreams about the West are in part reality, that survival rules learned from birth are suspended so long as he is in the company of his C/O. A Western woman can turn a Muslim man topsy-turvy by her walk, hair, dress, and lips, while doing virtually nothing. The sensual stimulation can cause him to believe his words with a dreamworld woman don't really count. Perhaps for the first time in his life, he can tell the truth without penalty. What a woman C/O lacks in authority—and no woman, no matter how strong or ugly, can command the physical authority of any man in a Muslim's eyes—she makes up for through disorienting allure.

I never thought this female magic had a long life: the more contact between a Muslim and a Western female, the more the rules returned. And even if an American woman C/O did her best to act like a man, a sense of embarrassment would still start to replace the thrill in a protracted nonsexual relationship with an all-powerful Western woman. But as a general rule, if an Islamic fundamentalist walked into a U.S. embassy, I'd rather have a five-foot-ten Arabic-speaking blond debrief him than one of the Near East Division's ex-military khaki-clad Arabists.

To be a Muslim, or not to be? I still couldn't make up my mind which was more advantageous with my new friend. I could experiment and tell him I was a Muslim. Though I wasn't married to an Iranian woman, I'd often thought about converting to Islam, of crossing civilization lines to learn in reverse what so many Iranians and other Muslims had learned by living in the West. Although a hopeless rationalist, I could come close to faith. All I had to say was "I testify that there is no god but Allah and Muhammad is His Prophet," which would make me a Sunni, and add "Ali is His Deputy," which would make me a Shi'ite.

The rest would be between me and Allah.

"No, I don't have an Iranian wife," I said. "But I've had Iranian girlfriends. They've told me how important Mashhad is."

I'd seen women pray in mosques in Cairo, Khartoum, Rabat, Alexandria, Jerusalem, Katmandu, Trabzon, and Istanbul. Except at Eyup in Istanbul, Turkey's holiest Sunni site, where thousands of barren women and cripples come to ask God for mercy, I'd never seen women pray with the fervor Muslim males exhibit.

The Qur'anic vision of paradise is distinctly masculine. Virtuous Muslims are rewarded by endless days and nights with houris: beautiful, renewable virgins. Do Muslim women in the afterlife become houris? Do they become men? I'd once asked an accomplished professor of Islamic law where virtuous Muslim women went after death. "To heaven, I'm sure. But what they do once they get there isn't quite clear."

It was an important theological question without relevance to everyday Muslim life. Yet I kept wondering how Muslim women worship God. Once upon a time I'd wondered whether a Muslim woman might be more apt to betray her community than a Muslim man would be.

I'd asked my two Iranian girlfriends about female prayers in Islam. Did women pray in the same manner, with the same rituals, as men? Were there certain suras in the Qur'an that women always knew and men didn't? My girlfriends had all stopped believing in the Almighty. Islam still shadowed them wherever they went, but the

sensations were no longer inspirational. These women felt only respect, hatred, or fear.

My questions about God, man, and Mashhad hadn't tweaked my
friend's curiosity, but my girlfriends had. If you want a Muslim man
interested in you, suggest that you, a Westerner, have slept with a
Muslim woman who is not your wife. Go further and suggest you
have slept with more than one and you supercharge his curiosity,
revulsion, or envy. I didn't know what his reaction would be, but I
didn't think he'd rat on me with one of the nasty-looking consular
officials. Nor did I think he'd be angry. By the way his light-brown
eyes popped and a little grin appeared, he seemed envious of how
I'd succeeded where he'd failed.

"You're lucky you don't have an Iranian wife. They are very painful. They demand much, much more than Western women. They
stay at home and make Iranian men miserable. Don't believe all this
talk about women suffering in Iran. They are very powerful. They
don't respect men like they used to."

"This wasn't my experience," I said.

He paused, shot his eyes left, then right, and moved closer to
me. "Iranian women don't like to make love. Not like Western
women. Not like Russian women. Iranian women want to control
you, they don't want to please you. We are lucky Iranian women
must wear long dresses or chadors, or we would have to look at
them. They are very fat, you know."

"I don't believe that."

"Yes, they are fatter now than before the revolution. Why? Because they control men more. They don't have to please men the
way they did when I was young."

"I've always liked Iranian women."

"You *like* Iranian women? You are lucky. Where do you meet
these Iranian women who told you about Mashhad? Here? You are
American or *Britisshhhh?*"

I'd misjudged my friend. I was sure he'd slept with both Western
and Russian women. And given his ugliness, and perhaps his pre-
dilections, I imagined he'd paid for the pleasure. Persians aren't
prudes. Iranians of the same sex can become sexually frank in conversation quite quickly. Given his intention—for me to elaborate

what I'd implied, that I, too, could compare the lovemaking skills of Iranian and Western women—he'd actually been almost polite.

My friend was beginning to let down his guard. So was I. If we kept talking only about sex, a favorite Persian pastime, I could hardly get into trouble. Was he an average curious, horny Iranian? Was he more? What did he do for a living? Why was he here? Had he ever been to the States? Where else in Europe? How often and when? What was his name? Who was his father? What languages did he speak? Had he risen with the revolution or fallen, or was he holding his own? How large was his hard-currency account in Dubai? Most Persians who regularly traveled abroad had bank accounts there. Did he have credit cards? If so, issued by whom and paid in what currencies? Bank accounts and credit cards can sometimes indicate residency permits. What kinds of cachets and stamps were in his passport? Did he have special Persian stamps that might indicate he was abroad to work on an Iranian government contract or mission—stamps the CIA always thought too pedantic, time-consuming, and pointless to read? Did he pray? Abroad or only at home? Did he drink? Did he eat pork, always the last Muslim dietary restriction to fall? What kind of whores did he prefer? Fat, skinny, or tall; blond, brunet, or black; Americans, Yugoslavs, Filipinos, or Russians? Did he have a son? If so, how old? If eighteen, was he studying abroad?

All the practical questions necessary to interpret the answers to larger Persian questions about God and man came back to me. I decided to stay on the subject of women.

"I once thought about marrying an Iranian woman." I glanced around to make sure no one overheard. "However, this woman had been married once before, and once was enough. Incredibly beautiful. The oldest daughter of a fairly senior military officer."

My friend's light-brown eyes popped again. Divorced women are worth their weight in gold in the Middle East. They are sexually open game. They no longer have *namus* in Persian (*ʿird* in Arabic), the family honor that only chaste unmarried females possess and their fathers and brothers must defend. Once a woman is married, her honor is no longer the responsibility of her male kin. Once she is divorced, *namus* vanishes. A certain family pride will remain—no Muslim man wants to have a female relation with a loose reputation—but the tie between daughter/sister and father/brother is no longer electrified. If a divorced Iranian woman wants to play around discreetly—and Iranian men believe divorced women are the most voracious sexual predators—her father and brothers are probably not going to stop her. Saying I'd had a divorced Iranian woman as a friend meant that I'd had incredible good fortune. That she was also beautiful and from an upper-class prerevolution family—loosest of the loose—only added fat to the fire.

"This officer's daughter, is she the one who told you about Mashhad? Is she from Mashhad?"

"No."

"You have been a lucky man to meet such a woman. An Iranian woman who wanted to make you happy! Did you meet her here, in America, where? Our women like to marry American men because you spoil them. So many Iranian women in Europe and America, and they all marry foreigners. Why go to Mashhad if you can find such women here?"

My friend, of course, had it in reverse. I had to go to Iran because I'd found such women in Europe and the States. Afsaneh had been captivating. Tall, lithe, with thick brown hair down her back. Perfect bronze skin and high cheekbones, almond-shaped brown eyes.

Though dedicated to learning the philosophy and methodology of her new country, regularly shaming me with her grasp and appreciation of American literature and the obvious virtues of U.S. life, Afsaneh couldn't change her Persian reflexes. Her movements were always halfhearted: she did nothing she couldn't retract. When most rebellious, she remained profoundly conservative. Sexually experienced and aggressive, at the point of contact she was timid. She hated Islam and its long history of four wives and innumerable concubines; yet when I absentmindedly placed my Arabic–English Qur'an toward the bottom of a stack of books, she quietly rescued it by placing it back on the bookshelf.

"I think Iran is full of such women," I said to my friend. "Women who are strong but want to please. Perhaps it's hard to find them under the chadors."

Before I'd finished the word "chadors," he shot both black eyebrows upward and made a loud tongue-against-the-teeth click—a

Middle Eastern way of saying no. And eyebrow clicking can mean *no* or *no-bloody-way-no*. I guessed by the volume more than the jerk that he meant a polite *hell-no*.

"When you go to Iran, you will see. The best women are not there. Your friend, she lives outside Iran? Her father was a general for the Shah? Did he escape during the revolution, or did he die? The ones who got away were rich or had foreigners as friends. Trust me, if you married this girl, you wouldn't be happy. Your friend lives in Los Angeles, I'm sure. The lucky part of Iran lives in Los Angeles. Go there instead. There are no mollahs in California, are there? I tried to visit the United States, but I couldn't get a visa. You're not German, are you? You spoke to me in English. And you are not *Britisshhhh*. Why would an American want to go to Iran?"

He stopped and eyed the Iranian man on the other side of the window, who had thrown us obvious looks. The fellow, dressed in a double-breasted olive-green suit and a bloodred tie, was surveying everybody in the room, one by one.

"There are many Germans in Iran, but not many Americans. Everybody wants to see more, but the mollahs are afraid. You know, Iranians are a great people who have bad luck. Things are awful, but it's a very beautiful country."

I wondered how I should respond. I didn't see the point in lying. Iranians are drawn to Americans, not to Germans.

"You're right, I'm an American."

He drew nearer while glancing behind with two quick, barely furtive twists.

"I love America. All Iranians do. You shouldn't believe all that mollah-shouting. All those people who yelled "Death to America! Death to America!" really liked America. The *akhunds* did all that. Iranians have always loved America. We have had problems with the American government, but we love the American people. Personally, I like the government, too. Look what we have. I'd rather have yours than mine. America saved us from Russia. We will never forget that."

In my experience, Iranians had almost always forgotten this, a casualty of the revolutionary impulse to deny the United States any positive role in Persian history. In 1946, when the British and the

Americans withdrew from Iran, the Soviets, who had invaded northern Iran when the British occupied the south in 1941, did not withdraw—until Harry Truman told Stalin that not to do so could bring a confrontation with the U.S..

But as the *akhunds* (a derogatory word for mollahs) were losing ground in Iran, history was being rewritten again, this time in our favor. I couldn't tell whether my friendly inquisitor had ever hated America; most Iranians had at least flirted with the emotion. I took him at his word that he didn't now.

He glanced around again, a little more furtively, and moved closer. He was short, antsy, hyperactive, and squat. A muscular man who ate too much lamb kebab. Sweat speckled his balding, heavily creased head.

"Americans should help us. Your secretary of state was spit upon by Khomeini. He calls Iran the most evil state in the world, but he does nothing. Unless you want Iranians thinking that you like the mollahs, you should bring them down. The British put them in, and America should drive them out. The young Shah, he is like his father, a coward. And the United States wastes money on him. Iranians don't want to fight anymore. They need a sign from America."

I checked to see if anyone was within earshot. Talking about sex with my friend had been safer. Iranians bitch endlessly about their government; I hadn't, however, expected to hear inside the Islamic Republic's consulate an appeal for U.S. covert action. I suspected my friend saw the world as a U.S. Monopoly board game.

"I'm not sure the American government wants to overthrow the Iranian government," I said. "Or even get involved. It did that once, didn't it? A lot of people blame us for destroying Mosaddeq and the beginnings of democracy." And, I thought, a parliament democratically elected might have been stronger against the clerics than the Shah proved to be. "Maybe America should just stay out of Iran's internal affairs. Maybe America shouldn't interfere in something it really doesn't understand."

My friend didn't like what I'd said. His thick black eyebrows slid together in the deep well above his nose as he murmured, as if to himself, "Mosaddeq."

The history and argument had been put too simply. But many

Iranians, and many U.S. Iran scholars, argued the CIA/MI6-organized coup d'état had short-circuited Iran's democratic development. According to them, Prime Minister Mohammad Mosaddeq (1880–1967), a left-wing aristocratic nationalist educated in France, would have been far more adept back in 1953 at engaging and outmaneuvering the Iranian left, particularly the Communists in the Tudeh party who completely dominated Iran's intellectual life. With the left corralled, they wouldn't have thrown themselves into violent opposition, transferring their energies and support to Khomeini and the clerics. And the clerics would have had a far harder time attacking a democratically elected Mosaddeq government, which, unlike the Shah's, could not have been easily portrayed as a lapdog of foreign powers. Mosaddeq, emotionally a live wire, had been unrivaled in his capacity to outrage Washington and London.

I always found this recast history a little too neat and clean, overestimating Mosaddeq's popularity and, perhaps, his democratic sentiment, his strength on the left, and the Shah's dictatorial rule as the most decisive element in the growth of Iranian Islamic radicalism. The Shah's autocracy, which worsened from 1963 through 1977, no doubt encouraged intellectuals and ordinary men to find solace and support in their faith and among their divines. In the Middle East, mosques are the last and best refuge, where even the most despotic secular rulers hesitate to intrude violently.

But would an Iranian democracy have been better able to neutralize the passion and frustration of young peasant men colliding with the modern world? Perhaps. Well enough to have survived the ideological currents and oil-fueled economic changes of the post–World War II years? Well enough to have prevented politicized clerics from summoning young men to battle the West and their secularized Muslim allies? The years 1953 to 1979 were awful years in the Middle East. After the collapse of Christian Europe's empires, Muslim hopes and testosterone levels were high.

Visions of socialism, nationalism, and rapid change displaced thousand-year-old traditional Muslim understandings about right and wrong, rich and poor, Muslims and non-Muslims, and male–female roles. Would Mosaddeq and his "democratic" successors have been any less enamored of the modern world than the Shah, any less determined to make Iran wealthy, powerful, and proud, any more capable of stopping semi-educated peasant men from abandoning the countryside for a cruel, polluted, concrete dream of Tehran?

The primary players who brought Mosaddeq down in 1953 had been clerics, not Cambridge- or Yale-educated spies. Without Ayatollahs Kashani and Behbahani giving orders to the mob, the coup d'état would not have happened. What the clerics did in 1953, they perhaps could have done in 1954, 1955, or 1956 without American or British assistance. Perhaps they might have won the elections and then declared future elections irreligious and unnecessary.

The 1953 aborted-democracy theory was appealing, but it was too convenient in its diabolization of the CIA and MI6, and too Persian in its determination to make someone else responsible for failure. Still, some Iranians believe in the theory passionately and hold a grudge. I didn't think my friend was one of these, but the question about Mosaddeq always helped me place a Persian: left or right, more or less religious, historically attentive and motivated or couldn't give a damn.

"Mosaddeq was a pig!" my friend snapped. "He and his kind are all pigs. They didn't understand Iran. Without Mosaddeq, Khomeini was not possible. Mosaddeq started it; Bazargan finished it. These left-wingers who thought they could remake Iran. Young men the Shah sent to university in the West—they came home and started the revolution. They're dead or back living in Europe or America. But *I* live in Iran with the mollahs! Bazargan thought Khomeini would bring freedom. What an idiot! Did Bazargan ever risk his life to stop Khomeini, to stop all the killing after the revolution? All those teenage thugs with German machine guns? Everybody likes Bazargan. 'A good man.' 'A kind man.' He was a pig and a coward."

I'd found a sore spot. Mehdi Bazargan (1907–95) had been the first prime minister of Iran after the Islamic revolution. A French-trained engineer and dedicated democrat, he'd been instrumental in founding political organizations free of the Shah. The Iran Party, the National Liberation Movement, and the most influential vehicle of political opposition to the Shah after World War II, the National Front, all owed their existence in part to Bazargan. A devout Muslim from a wealthy bazaari family, he had long-standing personal and professional ties to the clergy and was occasionally in prison, as many of them were under the Shah. By 1978, he'd become the premier lay oppositionist aligned with Ayatollah Khomeini. In 1979, after meeting in Algiers with President Carter's national security adviser Zbigniew Brzezinski, he fell from power, a victim of the revolution's hostage-taking hard core. Bazargan was an exquisitely civilized Islamic democrat who hadn't appreciated how difficult revolutions were to control. I thought my friend's commentary severe but not entirely unjust.

Though we were still standing by the window alone, the nearest person now several feet away, I'd noticed a few people turn toward us when my friend had loudly enunciated "Mosaddeq," "Bazargan," and "pig."

I decided to switch the conversation back to tourism. "I've heard it takes a lot of time to travel by road in Iran. And the hotels are few and far between. It's cheap, isn't it, to travel by plane?"

My friend shifted as quickly as I. "You like Iranians, don't you?" he said. "Most Americans hate Iran. They hate us for taking their diplomats and spies hostage. They think Iranians want to kill Jews, and America always protects the Jews. But we hate the mollahs more than you do, and only the mollahs want to kill Jews; Iranians always protect the Jews. The oldest Jewish community in the world is in Iran."

He was, mercifully, speaking less loudly than before. Say the word "Jew" in the Middle East and heads turn. Nearly everyone has an opinion about the Jews. For most, they are the cleverest, most stubborn, and tribal—most Middle Eastern—of all peoples, the infidels who are the easiest to love and hate. They are the public enemy number one whom privately everyone would like to have as a friend. The smallest of the three great monotheisms, which inexplicably keeps beating Islam, arguably the largest, on the battlefield.

Put a believing Jew and a devout Christian in a room with a faithful Muslim, and it will probably be to the Jew that the Muslim gravitates. Unencumbered by doctrines that turn man into God and the ideal mother into a virgin, Jews and Muslims have fewer philosophical obstacles between them. Both have devoted themselves to holy law, not theology and redemption. Also, both have repeatedly been on the receiving end of Christian violence. And in their similar, quick informality and ironic humor, Jews, Arabs, and Persians fall more quickly and easily into chitchat, the lifeblood of even the most serious Middle Eastern conversations.

I always thought it an operational pity that so many Near East Division CIA officers didn't want American Jews as colleagues, seeing them as potential Israeli fifth columnists. Yet these friend-of-the-Arab officers usually referred to Arabs as "rag heads." Not one had seen through the perfunctory Arab–Israeli polemics to the affinity between Muslim and Jew. Or seen the possibility that Jews might be more adept at leading Muslims into espionage.

For Persians no less than Arabs, Jews are a cornerstone of history. They are almost as old as time itself, the only Middle Eastern people to whom Iranians must pay their historical respects. At a greater distance from the Israeli–Arab conflict than most of the Arab world, less influenced by the pre–World War II anti-Semitic literature of Eastern and Central Europe that has become de rigueur in Arab circles, and generally more tolerant toward non-Muslims in their midst, Iranians can be very affectionate toward Jews. Even revolutionary clerics can look with pride on Persia's twenty-five-hundred-year-old tolerant treatment of the *Yahudiyan*.

For Persians, the creation of Israel complicated but did not annul the historical tie. Israel's many triumphs over the Arabs warmed most Persian hearts, even among radical Islamic fundamentalists, who would, if they could, destroy the Jewish state. Iran's Islamic revolutionaries have periodically harassed the Persian Jewish community, attacking their own Jews in lieu of the Jews in Israel and America whom they couldn't reach. Yet there have been clear limits. Twelve hundred years of residence in Baghdad, a city that was more than a third Jewish in 1900, guaranteed nothing to its Jewish residents when radical Arab nationalism began to boil after World War I. In Iran, two millennia of Jewish residence guaranteed that Iran's revolutionary mollahs would not countenance Persian Jews being slaughtered in the streets or driven from their houses. Unlike Arab radicals and fundamentalists in Iraq, Egypt, Syria, Libya, or Yemen, Iran's Shi'ites never suggested their Jews didn't have the same rights as Muslims to citizenship or to practice their faith in public.

I had a brief urge to correct my silver-suited friend: the oldest Jewish community in the world is in Israel, not Iran, but I didn't want to be provocative. Persians, with nostalgic justification, believe they have the oldest, biggest, and best of everything.

"Sure, I like Iranians. I wouldn't want to go to Iran if I hated them," I said reassuringly. "But you didn't tell me where I should go in Iran. I won't have much time, no more than three weeks. I've heard it can take a week just to get through a Tehran traffic jam. If you were me, where would you go?"

"I would go to Los Angeles."

"But I've been to *Tehrangeles*. I couldn't find a single Iranian woman in a chador. Los Angeles isn't Tehran. I want to see the real thing."

"Why? *Tehrangeles* is better. You go to Tehran, you will not like Iran anymore. The mollahs have made my beautiful country ugly." An elfin grin after *Tehrangeles* vanished when he said *mollahs*.

"Iran is an old country. She has seen worse than the mollahs. Are they really that bad? In 1979, didn't everybody support Khomeini?"

"You know Persian history? We have survived so much. We may not survive the *akhunds*. And please forgive me, you are wrong if you think everybody loved the mollahs. Most people thought the mollahs were dogs."

"Weren't there good mollahs?"

"Of course. But not many. We never loved them. We no longer respected the Shah. We did not think the Shah was a real Iranian. He was owned by the British and the Americans. He and his family were very *kasif*, very dirty. Personally, I don't know if the Shah was owned by the Americans, but he was weak. He did not kill the mollahs when the mollahs were weak."

Before he finished the last line, I saw another Iranian applicant move to the other side of the window, about five feet away. He was obviously trying to listen.

I'd often underestimated Iranian boldness. Collectively, they're lambs; individually, they're often lions. My friend's mollah-bashing with an American was perhaps the most fun he'd had in years. Probably half the people in the room were damning the clergy in their conversations, but they were Iranian, speaking to their fellow countrymen, and therefore entitled.

"Aren't people still loyal to Khomeini, to his memory, even though they may hate Khameneh'i, Rafsanjani, and all the rest? Would anyone in your family want to fight for the Islamic revolution, if not the mollahs?"

When I arrived at the Iran Desk in the Directorate of Operations, I was surprised to learn how little the CIA knew about the clergy. How little the officers cared about who was married to whom. What had been gospel to my professor of medieval Persian history—"the bedroom politics of the Islamic world"—interested no one enough to do the nuts-and-bolts work of building family trees or learning how to read foreign languages. To "action-oriented" spies, these were pedantic exercises best left to academics.

CIA attention was drawn to the headlines: Was Khomeini ill again and might he die soon? Would Iran's Karbala offensives finally break through Iraq's Basra lines? Did Iran have anything to do with the TWA hijacking that landed in Beirut in June 1985? Had the mollahs masterminded the terrorist offensive in Paris in 1986? Of course, these were all good questions, but they seemed premature and almost inappropriate for intelligence officers who didn't know the Persian word for God (*Khoda*).

If Agency officers didn't know how clerics or Revolutionary Guardsmen were formed, if they'd never once read anything Khomeini had written, if they'd never shot the breeze with Persians, listening to them dream and whine, how could they do their part in answering the larger questions about *whither Iran* after Khomeini died? The CIA wanted the big answers about the Islamic Republic without working its way up the Persian food chain. Yet spies are by definition bottom feeders, constantly searching for the elemental matter composing a man's mind.

My friend hadn't liked my question about his family and the revolution. He eyebrow-clicked me twice. I was fairly certain he'd been a revolutionary as a young man. By late 1979, after the Shah had been repeatedly intimidated by ever-larger demonstrations in the street, most thirty-year-old men in cities had joined the pro-Khomeini bandwagon. Had my friend once committed his heart and soul to radical Islam? Had the fire burned out, exhausted by war, worsening poverty, unbearable clerical hypocrisy, or simply middle age? Or were there still embers? One of the most historically minded peoples, Iranians had become averse to accurately remembering the past. Islamic revolutionary, Communist, constitutionalist, monar-chist—all wanted to hide their failure to make Iran glorious again. A happy Persian had to find someone else to blame the mistakes on.

"The Shah was dirty, but I did *not* support Khomeini," my friend replied defensively, his rising intonation suggesting more a question than a statement.

"*Khahesh mikonam mano bebakhshid,*" I said.

My friend's head jerked back.

"*Farsi harf mizanin! Goftin Farsi balad nistin!* See! See, you speak Persian! You told me you didn't speak Persian. I knew you spoke Persian." His accusations arrived with an immense smile.

"I know only a few phrases," I replied quickly. "My Persian girl-friend thought I was constantly insulting Iran. She made me say that every time I made her angry. I thought perhaps I'd made you angry."

I'd told him the truth. I'd used that line constantly with a one-time Muslim–Marxist, who, by the time I knew her in the mid-eighties, had abandoned the *Mojahedin-e Khalq,* divorced Marx from Muhammad, and become a supporter of the *Tudeh,* Iran's banned and nearly obliterated pro-Soviet Communist party. From our first date, we'd found it impossible to have a conversation without her damning me variously as an "Orientalist," an "imperialist," a "me-dievalist," a "mollah lover," an "Islam freak," or a "modern-day Crusader" who wanted to pillage, enslave, and embarrass the Third World. However, with daily Persian apologies, the relationship sur-vived a bit longer than expected. She was, like the lovely Afsaneh, powerfully drawn to a Westerner who'd spent a great deal of time reading books about a faith she'd abandoned but not escaped.

My friend's entire face had changed with those few words of Per-sian. Behind the grin were the particular pride and appreciation you so often encounter if you speak to formerly imperial Third Worlders in their native language. Frenchmen still expect you to speak French; Persians, who similarly see their language as their greatest treasure, don't expect you to speak it. Speak a little Persian to an Iranian, Turkish to a Turk, or Arabic to an Arab, and they'll forgive you innumerable shortcomings. Americans, who don't have a linguistic component to their pride, and probably wouldn't even if they were no longer a superpower, have a hard time understanding and exploiting linguistic politics.

If I'd said to my friend the literal English translation, "I ask you to forgive me," it would have sounded wrong. In English it would have been more like "Please don't take what I said seriously," or, "I didn't really mean to suggest you supported Khomeini." But the etiquette still wouldn't have been right. With the surprise Persian, I could beg his pardon and not retract a word.

"No, no, please, I was not angry. You know how the revolution has ruined our lives. We have suffered horribly since '79. Personally, my family has been lucky. I have two sons and both were too young to fight in the war. Business has been very hard for years. It has never really been good since the revolution, unless you have connections to the regime. I don't. I import automobile parts—mainly electronics, radios, batteries, and whatever else I can find and afford and get into Iran. I'm lucky, Iranians love their cars like Americans do. And cars always fall apart, especially in Iran. My sons can find work with me and are not lost on the streets."

"That's good to hear," I said quickly, not wanting to stop him.

"When I went to a mosque as a boy with my father—and we did not go often—I always left the mosque proud and happy. My father rewarded me every time I could recite another sura from the Qur'an. I didn't receive many rewards, because I'm afraid I never found it easy to memorize Arabic and Persian. You see, I'm not a good Iranian.

"I would not now take my sons to a mosque. I'm embarrassed. Imagine a Muslim embarrassed to go to a mosque! That is what the revolution has done. I hate the mollahs for taking from me what my father had. Khomeini told us Islam would make us stronger. We had lost Islam and the revolution would give it back. So we made the revolution, the war with Iraq is over, and all we do now is talk about Islam.

"It is good to live by the *Shar'iat*. But do the mollahs live by the *Shar'iat*? Do these officials behind the windows who treat me like a dog live by the *Shar'iat*? I don't think these officials know anything about Islam. Look at this room. Do you see the words from Hafez Shirazi, the greatest of Persian poets, hanging on the wall? These words praise God, but they don't praise mollahs. Do you know these other words, did your Iranian friends ever teach you these words? *"Va'izan kayn jelveh dar mehrabo membar mikonand/Chun be khalvat miravand an kar-e diger mikonand."*

"No, I don't know what that means." I lied. I knew them by heart.

"I translate for you." For a few seconds I watched his tongue, visible behind his smile, beating the translation out on the back of his yellowed, slightly twisted large front teeth. Raising his right forefinger—a distinctly Western, not a Persian gesture—he said, "In the mosque, mollahs tell us how to behave. In private, they break all the rules."

The quick translation cheated Hafez of some colorful description, particularly a libidinous allusion to the private homosexual behavior of clerics; but it accurately conveyed the poet's intent.

Gesturing toward the two Iranian consular officials who'd deigned to return to windows (though not mine), he snapped, "If Khomeini had bowed down before an idol I think these idiots would bow before it."

Lions and lambs. Persians were always one or the other; usually both at the same time. At heart, Iranian men are individualists. They all know they could be martyrs or heroes from an ancient Persian epic if fate would only give them half a chance. Their bravery, however, is usually thwarted by an acute dislike of pain. The common Western image of Persian men whipping themselves with chains during the religious ceremony of Ashura, the commemoration of the martyr of all martyrs, Ali's son Hosein, belies the deeper and more common strain in the Persian character: a resolute desire for self-preservation.

Iranians are consummate tacticians with their fingers always in the air. Regularly run over by Arab, Turkoman, Mongol, Uzbek, Afghan, Russian, and British armies, Iranians learned to bend in the wind. The Islamic revolution was in part an effort by Persians collectively to stand up straight, to check their reflex to compromise, absorb, and survive.

As a case officer, I'd never liked lions, preferring courageous lambs, men who quietly and steadfastly bore grudges. The strong silent type, fortunately a rare breed among Persians, scared me. You never knew what you had, and you usually had to violate Rule One—don't tell Persians more than they tell you—to find out. Quite quickly you could start wondering whether the roles had reversed: Who was the hunter and who the prey?

My friend had welcomed the revolution—that was certain. He was a practicing Muslim, but praying in a mosque does not lead to radical Islam; usually, I'd found just the opposite. In Iran, as elsewhere in the Muslim world, radical and traditional Islam are enemies, not friends. In Iran there are overlaps. Both hate Baha'ism, the nineteenth-century offshoot of Iranian Shi'ism that denies the finality of the Prophet Muhammad's mission and the supreme holiness of the Qur'an. And both fear foreign power—the oft repeated *tahojom-e farangi*, the Western cultural invasion. But their differences easily put them at odds. I seriously doubted my friend had ever been sympathetic to the Hezbollah, the fanatical young men who knew little about Islam and started to go to mosques only when Ayatollah Khomeini called. He'd been too old in 1979, thirty-something, with too many responsibilities and not enough energy to have thrown himself into the collective Iranian death wish that became a substitute for prayer during the war years. He'd perhaps been horrified to see the senior Iranian clergy, who traditionally kept their distance from politics, manhandled and silenced by Khomeini, the self-proclaimed vice-regent of God. My friend appeared a healthy Iranian: he had as many vices as virtues and no burning desire to remake the world. He wanted to raise his sons, keep them close, out of radical Islam's way.

"Do you think Iranian youth still read Hafez?" I asked.

"Iranians will never stop reading poetry. More than ever, Hafez is a hero in Iran."

"More than Khomeini?" I asked.

He didn't answer. Instead he said abruptly, "Do you believe in God?"

His question caught me off guard. I stared at him and then lied. "Yes, I do."

I'd had Muslims ask me whether I was a Muslim, a Christian, or a Jew. But never if I believed in God.

"How often have you heard God speak to you? I believe in God, and I've only heard God twice. Iranians are always listening for God but they never expect to hear him. *That* is why we go on pilgrimage to Mashhad. It is easier to hear God there. Many Iranians believed Khomeini had found God, and if we followed him, he would help us listen to him. You know, that was Khomeini's real strength. He told us to be hard on ourselves and we would find Allah."

My friend kept looking at the applicant lines. Four officials had now come to the Iranians-only windows and the lines were actually moving. My friend wanted to leave but was too polite to budge. It was for me to end the conversation, but as my window was still closed, I wanted him to stay. Another half hour and I might actually get him to talk about his family, where they came from, whom they'd married, and did any of them live abroad. Most of all, I could ask him about the two times he'd heard God.

"You never did tell me where I should go in Iran if I had only three weeks."

"Go anywhere. It's all the same. It's worse in Tehran, though."

"Should I travel in the spring, or should I wait for summer?"

"It's always best to travel between March and June. When it's not too hot. But anytime you go, you will be welcome. You will see, Iranians love Americans. You are our favorite people."

He turned toward the door and looked at the steady stream of Iranians leaving the consulate. Most were leaving as quickly as they could. Through the window, I could see two Iranian women on the sidewalk stripping off their raincoats and scarves and stuffing them into a plastic shopping bag. They were both dressed in pantsuits and décolleté blouses. The scene reminded me of the waiting lounge in Istanbul's international airport where Iran Air docked. Chador-covered women would go into the bathrooms; they would come out in miniskirts, lipstick, and rouge.

"They may love Americans in Iran, but I don't think they love them here. Look at your lines. Look at mine. Who will be out that door first? You or me?"

"You have to wait because the best consul serves you. You get the one man who is polite and therefore very busy. We get the others."

He was probably right. The officials at the Iranians-only lines looked very severe.

"You had better get into line or you'll lose your place. You wouldn't want your countrymen to think that things work quickly here."

"No, no, I don't need to rush," he said. "I have waited all morning."

"If you wait all afternoon, I'll still be here. Perhaps we can have a late lunch together, if my line ever opens. But you get in line before they decide to take a two-hour tea break."

"Lunch would be excellent. These idiots have made me very hungry. I know a very good Iranian restaurant not far from here. It has the best *chelokebab* and *khoresht-e bademjan*. Did your Iranian girlfriends teach you about Iranian food? You will be my guest. Even if lunch becomes dinner because of these idiots, I will take you there. *Shomaro mehmun mikonam.* You will be my guest," he insisted.

I already had dinner plans, but I liked *khoresht-e bademjan*, an eggplant and veal stew. Over food, I was sure, he'd tell me about the two times he'd heard God. We'd have to argue about who invited whom. According to Persian etiquette, I'd have to try at least three times to reverse the invitation—then I could surrender. In the old days, I would have tried desperately to pay the bill to ensure my friend was indebted. Now that I was no longer a spy, there was no long-term development, no concern about pushing an initial meeting into another. The rules of friendship and curiosity could now hold sway. I'd let him pay because to do otherwise would insult him.

Besides, if he paid I might get a look at his wallet and see if he had any credit cards. His *shenasnameh*, his identity papers, might come into view and discussion. Supported by eggplant, veal, grilled

lamb, and basmati rice, I also might learn whether he'd ever worshiped Khomeini. At least I'd learn his first name.

"Lunch or dinner sounds good. We'll discuss later who invites
whom. But you should take your place quickly."

"If they do not start your line, I will mention it when I get to
the window. They have no right to keep you waiting."

The lion was loose again. All I wanted to do was walk up to the
window, deposit my application and all my supporting documentation plus letters from Tehran, and walk away. Iranian consular
officials are not like their U.S. counterparts: they don't ask questions
unless provoked. They're poorly paid functionaries who sort, send,
and receive the mail. Anonymity and a low profile were all that was
required.

"No, please, don't worry about my case," I said. "I'm not in a
hurry. I can wait as long as they can. There are dozens of bulletins
on the wall for me to try to read. And I must confess, I like being
here. I don't visit Iranian consulates often," I added quickly, hoping
that my friend wasn't stubborn.

"It would be my pleasure to help you."

"There's no need to wait for me. If you finish first, I'll meet you
outside. There's a café a few blocks on your right. I'll meet you
there."

We both smiled and then he took a place in line, maybe fifteen
or twenty spots back from the front of window 4.

Of the thirty-eight people who remained in the room, I counted
four probable foreigners. I'd have to get ahead of them. Given Iranian efficiency, each foreigner might mean at least a half hour, even
for simply collecting documents. If the foreigners-only window ever
opened, I might have only an hour before it closed.

So I moved—around a near-empty row of plastic chairs and filthy
coffee tables, past a fat chador-clad old woman seated in the corner,
her hips rolling over the edges of her chair, past her standing white-
haired, willowy husband, who smelled like a wet gunnysack, and a
middle-aged man with a sweet-sour smell. Through a gauntlet of
well-dressed Persian expatriates, one beauty perhaps wearing Shali-
mar.

An hour later, when my Iranian friend was only five back from his window, a young official, no more than thirty-five, came to our window and sat down. Unlike the other consuls working, he had a kind, nearly clean-shaven face. A middle-aged, scarfed, white-faced woman leaped past me to the window.

"Do you speak . . ." I didn't hear her say "English." Her voice was small and she'd lowered her head so that it paralleled the small opening at the bottom of the window.

He did. I could hear neither her words nor his, but they both kept talking. A few seconds later she raised her head from the opening, pivoted in anger, and walked out. She'd not shown her passport; the only thing I had seen was the official smile.

I went forward, pulling all my papers from my briefcase. I slid them under the window as I lowered my head and murmured, "Hello."

He didn't reply but looked carefully through the papers, checking everything. He read my application twice slowly, using his right forefinger to trace the words. "Do you want to visit only Tehran?" He spoke in near-perfect American English.

"No, I've written down my travel plans on the reverse side where requested."

"You've written down Mashhad, Isfahan, and one other city I can't . . ."

"Shiraz. I'd like to see the tombs of Hafez and Saʿdi."

"Good choice," he said, giving me a short smile that disappeared as quickly as it formed. "Do you intend to travel anywhere else?"

"That would depend on how much time I have and how much time Tehran uses up. I've always wanted to see Tabriz."

He smiled again. He slid a piece of paper with a number on it under the window. "That's your case number. Don't lose it. Call or come back in a month. Your visa should be ready."

"Thank you. That was quick."

"We try to be."

I laughed. He didn't.

I turned around and went straight for the glass door. My friend was still fifth in line. He eyebrow-clicked me one last time. As I saw another man being buzzed out the front door, I darted past the camera operator through the open armored door. Five minutes later I was in the café, wondering when my Iranian friend would show.

Before the month was out, I'd received word from my friends in Iran. It was not the time to visit. In Tehran, the winds had changed. U.S.–Iranian relations had again taken a nasty turn. Now you see it, now you don't—that's what terrified me about Persians.

But I'd been a case officer too long to depend on only one set of friends. An alternate well-traveled route could take me to Tehran. Other friends had offered to help. For years, I'd played hide-and-seek with Iranians. I'd just have to play a little longer.

4 THE ROADSIDE

We turned off the main highway onto a country road with tire tracks already cut through the snow. It was snowing again, though too lightly to matter much. Looking out the passenger window, I could see the distant glow of a few headlights moving toward Turkey. Cracking my window, I heard the hiccuping roar of trucks or buses shifting gears.

I bent forward to look again into the side-view mirror. I still resembled a POW.

"You don't look so bad now," Hosein remarked, catching me. "To tell the truth, you look like a Revolutionary Guard. If your beard were grungier and you took off your cap, you could enlist. The first American Guardsman. With God's blessing, you'd go far."

I leaned forward again for a less furtive look. I'd known a few ex-Guards. They'd come in all sizes: tall, short, and crippled. One had a wild helter-skelter look, shaggy hair, a thick beard, a layer of oil-dirt sheen, and a filthy surplus U.S. Army coat. Another looked more like a subcontinental bouncer at a high-end London discotheque: black turtleneck, pants, and jacket; shoulder-length, neatly combed

India-ink hair set off by a permanent five-day growth. All seemed tired.

In the mirror, I could see parts of each: a dirty military coat, facial growth somewhere between stubble and a beard, and a wide stare born more of fear than of faith.

"Do you think they'd take me if I converted to Shi'ite Islam, declared my love for Khomeini, my loyalty to the revolution, and my hatred for the U.S. government? Seriously, think I'd have a chance?"

The prospect amused me. My former employer had always considered me a little un-American, not a true believer in the value and glory of U.S. espionage. Ending up in the Guard Corps, arguably the CIA's worst enemy since the collapse of the KGB, would therefore have a certain perverse appeal. A few former colleagues would surely believe I'd gone native and sold them out, but I doubted the Guard Corps would draw the same conclusion if they uncovered my past.

"If you paid them, they'd accept you," Hosein laughingly replied. "But if you pay them once, you'd have to keep paying. Your faith and your wallet would be the same in their eyes."

"Aren't there any true-believing radicals left?"

I spotted parked vehicles in the distance and felt my gut go tight.

"Sure, and they'd shoot you or throw you in Evin prison. They're always less open-minded than those who take money." Hosein downshifted the truck to a crawl.

Up ahead, silver and white sub-semi trucks. Also a dilapidated American pickup from the early sixties. Hosein parked a good distance past them on the opposite side.

"Stay in the truck until I see who's here. I only recognized one of them."

Before I could ask Hosein to leave the heat on, he'd turned the engine off, hit the lights, and jumped out the door.

I looked in Hosein's side-view mirror to see if I could spot the truckers. Only the pickup and the front window of one truck appeared. Through my front window, the mountains still dominated the horizon, though their snowy surfaces had dulled to a uniform navy-blue black. There were more trees here than at Hosein's "rest stop." Short, wide-bodied oaklike trees punctuated by more numerous needlepoint poplars or pines; their density suggested we were near a river.

I tried to think of an American parallel. The mountains were a little like the Rockies of the Southwest: jagged higher up, rounded farther down, no peak high or triangular enough to be magnificent. But the ground had too much of a voluptuous roll in it to be Arizona, Colorado, or New Mexico. It was more like the hilly parts of the Dakotas with a few more trees.

"They're cooking!" Hosein shouted as he snapped the driver's door open. "They've asked us to join them."

"Who's they?" I asked.

"Four men. That is, three men and a teenage son. I know one man well. He's a good friend. He came over the border tonight just before us."

"And the other three? Who are they?"

"Never seen them before. They've driven the pickup from Tehran. They live up north, near Jolfa, and decided to break here and eat."

"That's two trucks. What about the third?"

"The driver's already gone to sleep in his truck." Hosein's brow tightened.

"Option one or option two? What *exactly* did you tell them?"

"I have an American with me that I picked up at the border. The border guards wouldn't let you leave through Bazargan because you'd flown in through Tehran. So you were headed back to catch a flight. I gave you a lift because you were stranded and the guards wouldn't help."

"You didn't want to do the non-American routine? You feel safe this way?"

Hosein didn't like my questions; I didn't like questioning him. I didn't doubt his competence, his good intentions, or his commitment; we'd already reviewed thoroughly different encounters and confrontations. He'd probably made the right decision, but I wanted to be asked. It wasn't a question of control. I wanted him in control. Hosein was my advance-warning system, allowing me more time to prepare. But he was too clever, and I was too slow.

I wasn't sure Hosein realized how scared I was, and I wasn't sure I wanted him to catch on.

"Of course I do," Hosein replied firmly. "There's no problem here."

"Even with your friend?"

"Especially with my friend. Come. They are very excited to meet an American." Hosein reached under his seat to pull out two strips of cardboard.

"All right," I replied. There was no point in arguing.

My heart pounding more than at the border, I stepped onto the running board and jumped. When I hit, I stumbled, thrusting my gloved hands into the snow. Loose gravel or pebbles on top of frozen, uneven ground almost brought me down. After knocking the snow off my gloves, I slowly went round the rear of the trailer and noticed Hosein hadn't repadlocked the doors.

"This way," Hosein called, signaling also with his hand.

I followed him across the road and up a rise. Once on top, I saw them sitting near the trees. I smelled the food before I saw the charcoal grill.

"Come, please come, please come eat with us. We have plenty of food," one of them called out in Persian.

The standing Iranian had a lanky body and curly black hair. Thirtyish, with a toothy smile on his face. Behind his feet, I saw the grill full of golden coals.

"Welcome! Welcome! You and America welcome!" he added in English.

I quickly gave the universal Islamic greeting in Arabic, "Peace be upon you," and added in Persian, "Thank you very much for inviting me to eat with you."

A bigger smile exploded on the man's face, and the other three simultaneously grinned.

"By the blessing of God, you speak Persian! Hosein, you didn't tell me he spoke Persian! An American who speaks Persian! By the blessing of God!"

The other three were now also standing, the boy with snow on his knees.

"My name is Hamid. Please, please come eat with us. We have

only just started ourselves. Hosein told me what happened at the border. I'm very, very sorry. It's awful the way they treated you. But please sit with us and share my food."

Hamid's Azari accent was much stronger than Hosein's. His politeness was also more pronounced. Politeness should never be construed as good intentions in the Middle East, but its absence is always a bad sign. The slightest civility, however false, means all is not lost to politics or rigid faith. Trapped in a box for several hours listening to Iranians scream, I'd briefly feared the worst—that Persian charm flourished only outside revolutionary Iran. Hamid's manners restored my faith. Any one of these men might later cause me trouble, but at least this dinner would be among friends.

After Hamid, I greeted the other three. I shook the hands of the two older men, though not the boy's. The boy and the younger of the two men were standing next to each other and were obviously son and father.

The older man, who was maybe forty-five, had no facial resemblances to the other and stood a little aside. His dark wool overcoat had big black splotches, but his lace-up boots had some polish since they reflected a little light. The coats of the other two, both army surplus, were torn and stained. They both wore brownish-black pants—in the twilight it was impossible to distinguish an underlying color from the camouflage dirt—and rubber hunting boots, one man's nearly torn to his ankle.

Hosein threw the cardboard strips on the ground and, using the formal form of "you," asked me to sit. Till now, we'd used the informal. I had Hosein to my right, Hamid to my left, the other three in front, and the road behind. As I sat down, they sat, too.

Before I could take my gloves off and warm my hands over the coals, the older man from the pickup truck asked, "How long have you been in Iran? Do you like what you've seen?"

He wasn't an Azari. He had unaccented Persian, that is, he didn't have an accent I knew. I could spot Persians from the western periphery: Azaris and Iranian Kurds. I'd spoken to hundreds, if not thousands, when I'd worked in Turkey. I could spot Baluchis, the eastern Iranian people who border on Pakistan. Their accents were uniformly incomprehensible. I suspected I could quickly identify

Iranian Arabs—the world's most perfect oxymoron, who number 1.2 million in Iran—but since I'd never met one, I didn't know for sure. But an average Iranian, like this fellow, could come from Tehran, Qazvin, Kerman, Yazd, or Mashhad, and I wouldn't be able to place the accent for sure.

Hamid was an Azari peasant, and the pickup-truck Persian a city peasant with just a little more schooling. Given where they were, the company they kept, and their clothes, the other two were no doubt similar.

"I've been in Iran for two weeks, and what I've seen I've liked. Iran is a beautiful country and Iranians are very hospitable and kind. Only the border guards gave me the impression that America and Iran are at war."

I glanced over at Hosein. He was looking at the kebabs on the grill, not at me, but he'd cracked a smile.

"You don't hate Iran?" asked the pickup-truck Persian a split second after I'd finished speaking.

"No, I like Iran very much," I replied.

"Please, you should eat. You must be hungry," Hamid implored, cutting off the other Iranian. "It's not good, but it was the best meat I could find in Dogubeyazit across the border in Turkey. Hosein and I were there this morning."

I'd been inexcusably stupid. I hadn't thought to ask Hosein whether he'd briefly rendezvoused with his friend in Turkey. He could easily have seen me in Dogubeyazit as we passed through. It didn't appear that he had; then again if he was Hosein's friend, I wouldn't necessarily ever know. Hosein might tell him and not tell me, their older friendship preempting our "deal." But if he wasn't a "good" friend, he wouldn't mention it either, at least not now.

Hamid reached out and pulled a very well done kebab off the grill and placed it on a piece of brown paper. From a paper sack, he took an onion, sliced it with a pocketknife, and put both halves next to the meat.

"Please, please eat. Don't let it go cold," Hamid insisted as he handed me the kebab and onion.

I bit one of the onion halves and then slid a piece of lamb off the skewer into my right hand, then into my mouth. A moist core surrounded by a very well done thick crust, unexpectedly tangy. Iranian food is usually closer to bland Turkish than to spicy Indian or Pakistani.

"Very, very tasty. The best kebab I've had in Iran," I said truthfully, before swallowing the first piece. "Please, please, don't let me eat alone," I said, sliding off another strip into my hand.

Hamid immediately took a kebab from the grill and handed it to Hosein. The other three, already served, resumed eating their meat, probably already cold.

The older pickup-truck Persian resumed. "You speak nice Persian. Have you lived in Iran before?"

"No, never."

"Do you have an Iranian wife?" he asked in a curious, tense voice.

"No, I don't."

"You learned Persian in America?! By God, they actually teach Persian in America?! May God be praised!"

"Several universities teach Persian," I said. "There are large Iranian communities all over America now. California, especially. You can find Persian television, newspapers, and radio."

"But you're an American, not an Iranian, and you've learned Persian. By God," he said again, more quietly than before, "only once, before the revolution, did I meet an American who spoke Persian. He worked for some oil company in Tehran."

"Are you an American journalist?" asked the younger pickup-truck Iranian.

Journalist in Persian, as in most Middle Eastern languages, is a synonym for spy.

"A teacher. I teach Islamic history in America. I've never been to Iran before." Half lie, half truth, a reasonable proportion for my first day in Persia.

"Are you a Muslim?" Hamid asked. The love of asking strangers questions is another reason why Americans and Middle Easterners get along so well. In Europe, where I'd lived for years, even rudimentary personal questions can take ages to be asked. If Hamid hadn't asked this question, one of the others would have. Hosein already had. Every Muslim I'd ever known who hadn't been secularized by the West had asked. For a faithful Muslim, it was natural and not at all offensive. If a Westerner had taken the time and trouble to learn Islam's history, languages, and Holy Book (the Qur'an), he obviously wasn't a benighted infidel. The Truth should be evident to those intelligent enough to seek. Western power and ICBMs aside, conversion is the logical end for a well-informed non-Muslim mind. When I'd once spent a week with the devout family of a close Pakistani friend, I nearly broke his parents' hearts by reading a sura from the Qur'an and then telling them I was a Jew. To lessen their dismay and pain, I told them later I'd convert as soon as my parents died. As good Muslims, who rank parental authority next to God's, they understood and no face was lost on either side.

"No, I'm not a Muslim." In response, I got a quick facial tic from both Hamid and the older man.

"Does America want to make war on Iran? Does President Clinton want to bomb Iran the way Bush bombed Iraq?"

The jolting questions came from an unexpected, silent quarter: Hosein. He'd asked the questions clearly through a mouthful of lamb.

"I doubt President Clinton wants to bomb Iran. Do you think the mollahs want to bomb the U.S.?"

"The mollahs would love to bomb America. If the mollahs could eliminate America, who would bring them down? America is the only thing that can destroy the mollahs."

The older man immediately corrected Hosein. "The mollahs don't want to bomb America. They want to be left alone so they can rule and ruin this country."

"Yes, you are right!" Hamid interjected. "The mollahs are scared of America. In the beginning, they thought they could beat America. Our war with Iraq changed all that. They learned they can't even beat Arabs. But the Americans destroyed the Iraqis in days."

The younger man then jumped in. "America has destroyed all her enemies! One day she'll destroy Iran if the mollahs don't destroy it first!"

"No! No! The Americans don't want to destroy Iran. The Americans want to destroy the mollahs, but I think the mollahs will destroy Iran first," Hamid shot back.

"No! No! No! The mollahs don't want to destroy Iran, they want to keep it alive so they can feed off it. The mollahs are leeches! They can't live on their own," Hosein shouted, almost spitting out a chunk of lamb.

Waiting to see how long this exchange would go on, and suspecting it could go on forever, I stayed silent and ate. I also kept searching the woods and regularly glancing behind for company. Few and far between, Revolutionary Guards still did roving patrols. I reassured myself that in this weather they'd not come over open countryside through the woods. In the darkness, we wouldn't know a bad truck or car from a good one until it was right on top of us. I'd have a few minutes to prepare for the encounter.

"The mollahs have embarrassed Iran and they have betrayed Islam." The younger man's voice, unlike everybody else's, was calm, and his eyes, unlike Hosein's and Hamid's, weren't glowing from leaning too close to the grill. He sat on a folded kilim with frayed yellow and black edges while his son and the older man sat on very small pieces of dark pile rug.

"The mollahs are thieves," Hamid chimed in, after ensuring I had another kebab. "They are worse thieves than the Shah and his family because they are mollahs. They can hide more money in their robes than the Shah could hide in his tunic." Everyone but the boy laughed.

"Do you know any mollahs? Have you ever met one?" asked the younger man.

With the spirited round-robin mollah-bashing, I didn't at first realize the soft-spoken question was directed at me. A discreet tap from Hosein's boot brought me around. "No, I don't know any mollahs, and I've never met one face-to-face," I replied, upping my day's total of lies. I'd met mollahs, before I started to work for the U.S. government and after, and developed through the years on-again, off-again relationships with a few. Of course, I'd never confess to this to any Iranians. They'd immediately start asking *who*, *where*, and *why*. Mollahs who know Americans, let alone U.S. officials, would be the subjects of light-speed Persian gossip at home and abroad.

"Then you don't really know how bad they are. They promised to save our country but they're killing it. Do you know why Iranians don't hate America for blowing up our airplane in the Gulf?"

The man was referring to Iran Air Flight 655, a civilian passenger flight from the Iranian city of Bandar Abbas to Dubai; the plane was accidentally blown out of the sky by a missile from a U.S. Navy cruiser on July 3, 1988. The ship, the U.S.S. *Vincennes*, was part of a U.S. Navy task force dispatched to the Persian Gulf during the Iran–Iraq War to protect international sea-lanes and Kuwaiti oil tankers reflagged as U.S. ships. In the early summer of 1988, Iranian gunboats had been attacking Persian Gulf shipping, and on the morning of July 3, fatefully, a helicopter from the *Vincennes*. In response to this attack, the *Vincennes* and her companion ship, the U.S.S. *Elmer Montgomery*, sank two Revolutionary Guard gunboats and damaged a third. Mistaking the passenger plane for an Iranian fighter-bomber on a possible revenge attack run, the *Vincennes* fired on Flight 655, killing all 290 on board.

In the years since, I'd rarely met an Iranian who thought the shoot-down an accident. Most thought it an unmistakable U.S. signal: Washington had definitively, mercilessly, and indefatigably chosen sides. Rafsanjani, then speaker of Iran's parliament, and Khameneh'i, then Iran's president, interpreted the tragedy similarly. Already reeling from Iraqi gas attacks, Iran couldn't go on. Khomeini declared the holy war against the Iraqi invader over. The downing of 655 effectively ended the war: in a direct confrontation with the Great Satan, even the Ayatollah knew Allah's soldiers didn't have a chance.

"No, I don't know why Iranians aren't mad." Most of my expatriate friends had been furious, hoping Tehran would terror-bomb a U.S. plane in reprisal.

"Because we were thankful. America stopped the war with Iraq. Khomeini said that surrendering was like eating poison. And America made Khomeini eat poison. No one else could have made him do that. By God, America saved Iran from Khomeini and from the Iraqis."

"Then America saved the Islamic revolution?" I asked, noticing everybody had stopped eating.

"What is the Islamic revolution?" Hosein snapped. "We make women veil themselves and we have clerics ruling us instead of shahs. This is the Islamic revolution! In Turkey, some women wear the veil, some women don't. I'm sure fewer unveiled women in Turkey cheat on their husbands than veiled women in Iran. Who really lives by the *Shariat* in Iran? Only the poor, and they don't even know what it is. But things are changing. The poor see the mollahs have two Islams, one for them and one for everybody else. It's all a lie."

"I believe in the Islamic revolution," the older man cut in, his eyes squinting a bit in the direction of Hosein. "We needed to get rid of the Shah. We needed to recover our dignity. There was no justice in Iran. No one could speak freely. We were all scared of the Shah's spies. The Imam made us feel proud to be Iranian and Muslim. We all knew the Shah was a bad Muslim. We all knew his crimes. The Imam reminded us that we'd become bad Muslims by following him. The younger mollahs around him have ruined this country, not the Imam. The Imam never stole money. He always lived simply, like us."

"I'm very sorry, I can't agree with you," said the younger man quietly. "Khomeini had an evil spirit."

I'd heard Iranians abroad call Khomeini unpleasant things—the more Westernized they were, the harsher the comments. But to hear a lower-class man in Iran call Khomeini evil seemed more shocking. His one word by itself was a counterrevolution. For years, I'd known Khomeiniism was unraveling because of military, economic, and spiritual failures. And here I was finally in Iran, face to face with poor, hardworking Persians—the *mostazafin*, the poor and oppressed whom Khomeini had risen to defend—and they were damning the clergy and even the Ayatollah himself with language they'd once no doubt reserved for the enemies of Islam.

"He was a mean old man," said Hosein. "He slaughtered thousands of Iranians in a war he could have stopped. We'd beaten Saddam Hussein in 1982. We'd kicked him out of Iran and we could have made peace. But we didn't. We became martyrs for what? Our Shi'ite brothers fought against us in Iraq. Who were the true Muslims of Iraq if not the Iraqi Shi'a? We were fighting to liberate them while they were machine-gunning us."

Hosein had leapt back in, not giving the other man the chance to continue. I wanted to return to him, to see if he'd been a soldier like Hosein who'd lost his faith at the front. Or had he fallen away via another route?

He and Hosein were exhausted believers in an imploded faith. What I wondered was whether they were grassroots proof that Islam's historical union of religion and politics—a Muslim's obligation to follow God's will as written in the Qur'an and the Holy Law—was coming undone. Had the revolution turned into a religious black hole, destroying in under twenty years identities and loyalties built over fourteen hundred?

Islamic radicals everywhere and many Westerners had viewed Khomeini's triumph as the first victory in the inevitable fundamentalist conquest of the Middle East. The success of the Khomeini of Sudan, Hassan at-Turabi, in 1989 and the ever more popular and powerful fundamentalist movements in Egypt, Jordan, Saudi Arabia, Tunisia, Morocco, and Algeria appeared to reinforce the fundamentalist domino theory. But sitting with Hosein, Hamid, and the two other Persians, I wondered again whether we understood everything in reverse. The Iranian revolution, like fundamentalist movements elsewhere, was not a rebirth of spirit and faith—as Islamic activism developed under the Safavids—but the tremors of a dying body torn apart by modern life. Iran, always on the cutting edge of Islamic history, was perhaps taking Muslims where they'd never gone before—to a permanent rupture of church and state, that awkward division of heart and mind that becomes inevitable when God's earthly representatives demand, and promise, more than they can deliver.

Hamid, Hosein, and the pickup-truck Persians suggested again that something had gone very wrong. Iran's revolutionary clergy had pushed and pulled Islam into an uncomfortable modern ideology where the recitation of "Death to America!" had taken precedence over kinder Qur'anic verses as the preferred liturgy of Friday prayers. In traditional Islamic society, God's compassion and authority had not been tied to public health care, sewage systems, affordable public transportation, inflation, oil production, GNP, or other prosaic dreams. Caliphs and sultans hadn't promised their subjects ever more earthly goods; they applied the *Shariat* to others, and usually to themselves, made war on infidels when they could, and endowed mosques and religious schools. The duties and responsibilities of medieval sacred government did not extend much beyond that.

Though Khomeini had said that Islam transcended economics, his message to the Persian faithful, raised on Shah-inspired dreams of ever-greater modern glory, had unavoidable economic overtones. The Shi'ite title given to Khomeini, the Imam, suggested a link to the *Imam ol-Zaman*, "the Imam of all time," a mythical semidivine messenger, the last charismatic descendant of the Prophet Muhammad and his son-in-law Ali, whose arrival signaled the end of history and the beginning of paradise. But the Imam had arrived and almost everything had got worse.

The Ayatollah had come to power railing against the Shah for abandoning the Holy Law, giving thousands of American officials extraterritorial rights, allowing women to shame their families and ruin their virtue by wearing miniskirts and voting, and exiling religious jurisconsults like himself to write unread books in ever-poorer religious schools. For Khomeini, there was only one answer. In order to move forward, Muslims had to look inward and back in time for their strength and morals. "O believers, take not Jews and Christians as friends; they are the friends of each other. Whoso of you makes them his friends is one of them. God guides not the people of the evildoers." This Qur'anic injunction had become one of the principal anti-Western war cries of Islamic radicalism in Iran and elsewhere.

Yet, before me were three Iranian men, all (I suspected) once proud soldiers of the revolution, who'd taken an infidel quickly into their confidence, without any Persian elusiveness or timidity. As I'd learned in Istanbul, Iranians had grown tired of being faithful. They wanted once again to be Persians—imperfect Muslims without guilty consciences.

The crack-up of the Islamic revolution had become a boon to me.

All around, Persian walls were coming down. If not arrested at a security check or by a roving patrol, a Westerner could now go farther in Islamic Iran than he ever could have in the Shah's era.

After asking me three times whether I wanted to have the last kebab, Hamid passed it to the older pickup-truck Persian, who in turn asked me if I wouldn't reconsider and take it. Four times refused and a good deal colder, it was then passed to the father and his son, who in turn refused it several times, until the older man relented and ate it.

Looking at the younger man, I asked, "Do you think Khomeini has ruined Islam in Iran?" I looked around to see if anyone was flinching. "Is your faith, your feeling of being a Muslim, less now than before the revolution?"

"I'm a Muslim. We all are Muslims. Nothing can change that. But we're tired of the lies. Maybe there are a few mollahs who tell the truth, but who can hear them among the liars? We're without hope. That's why everybody steals. We steal for our families because that's the only thing left we believe in."

"We believe in the Line of the Imam!" Hamid shouted sarcastically. Hosein, Hamid, the father, and his son laughed; the older Persian and I didn't. An American laughing at Khomeini in Iran somehow seemed wrong. The "Line of the Imam" was a call sign for the hard core of the revolution, denoting those who followed the radical teachings of Khomeini. Its most famous use was by the "students" who'd seized the U.S. embassy in Tehran.

We were all getting cold. The charcoal was no longer glowing and the snow's chill had worked its way through my piece of cardboard, my pants, and into my thermal underwear. Cold quivers had probably penetrated farther against ripped rubber boots and worn-out army coats. But I didn't think they'd return to their trucks unless I did, and now I didn't want to. I'd finally put my paranoia to rest; neither the audience nor the woods concealed Revolutionary Guards.

"Do any of you have Iranian friends or family in America?" I asked. Though Iranian Americans had come largely from the pre-revolutionary upper and middle classes, in most cases they hadn't been affluent long. Most families have poor roots somewhere in Iran.

"I have a second cousin on my mother's side in America." The older man smiled. "But I don't really know him. He left Iran more than ten years ago and hasn't come back. I would like to visit him, but I have no passport or money. Or time to travel. And I don't think I could get a U.S. visa."

He was right: he had no chance of getting a visa.

"You know Iranians in America, don't you? Are they as rich as everybody says? The government always says they fled after stealing the nation's money. But my cousin went to America without any money and my family tells me even he's rich now."

"Many are rich, most aren't," I said. "But I don't know many Iranian Americans who are poor. The ones I've met work very hard. And do well."

"Americans aren't mean to Iranians because of all the troubles?" Hamid asked earnestly.

I shrugged. "I've never met an Iranian in America who felt scared or even lonely because he was an Iranian. The loudest complaint I've heard is that Americans often think Iranians are Arabs."

"I would rather have America bomb us than call us Arabs," Hamid muttered. He'd mockingly pronounced the first a of "Arabs" as an Arab would, a broad-mouth guttural that only comes from the compression of your windpipe and a blast of air. For a Persian, it's the least favorite of all Arabic sounds, and Hamid's "*Aaaarab*" caused everybody, including me, to laugh.

"Do Iranians in America care about Iran? Do they support the Shah's son or do they support the *Mojahedin-e Khalq*?"

The younger man's question surprised me. I'd rarely heard non-American Iranians ask about Reza Pahlavi, who called himself Reza Shah II and was called Baby Shah at the CIA. A friend of mine had once known him at Williams College, where the future Shah spent a year in between fighter-pilot schools. "A nice young man, not bright not dumb, who liked to play the drums." When the Shah fell, his son went with him into exile. Though Reza Pahlavi continued to dabble in exile politics and still had his sources in Iran, he'd kept his distance from serious in-country counterrevolutionary activity.

Which wasn't the case at all for the *Mojahedin-e Khalq*, the rabidly anti-American Muslim–Marxists who'd been the principal street fighters against the Shah. After Khomeini's triumph, the mollahs crushed these erstwhile allies in a yearlong bloody duel, leaving the *Mojahedin* exiled in Iraq, Europe, and the United States, permanently encamped in Washington on the Mall protesting the mollahs' never-ending horrors and trying to convince U.S. congressmen of their goodwill.

"Most Iranian-Americans I know aren't very political. I don't think they support either," I said. "They wish the mollahs would go away, but even if they did, I don't know how many would come home. They think about Iran all the time, but they have new lives and children who are often more American than Iranian. Why did you ask about the Shah's son and the *Mojahedin?*"

"Because the mollahs always say that we can't trust Iranians abroad. They are counterrevolutionaries who want to give power to the *Mojahedin* or the wealthy families who ruled us before."

"And whom do you prefer?" I asked.

"I'm neither for the *Mojahedin* nor for the Shah's son. The *Mojahedin* are traitors—they fought for Saddam. And the Shah's son will never come home because we don't want that family again. But the mollahs lie about everything else, maybe they're lying about Iranians in America. I don't have family or friends abroad, but I know they can't all be traitors. Don't they want to come back and help rebuild their country?"

"It doesn't matter what Iranians think, here or abroad!" Hamid burst in. As he leaned over the grill to warm his hands, I saw a black plastic digital Casio watch on his wrist. "It only matters what the Americans and the *Englissss* think. They hold the power. The *Englissss* have always had the clergy in their pockets."

"Fuck the *Englissss!* They've always screwed Iran!" Hosein barked.

Both Hamid and Hosein had elongated the s in *Englis*, as so many

Iranians do. England and Iran had a long and bittersweet history, a prelude to the American–Iranian confrontation. Rare are Iranians who neither admire nor hate the English. Most do both concurrently. Persians developed their fondness for conspiracies into a national hobby with the British in mind, whom they charge with two hundred years of wrongdoing. Depending on the Persian you listen to, the British have meddled in Iranian internal affairs without invitation, meddled with invitation but for the wrong side, or failed to meddle when they should have. They have repeatedly forced unfair treaties down Iranians' throats and failed to stand by signed treaties risking British lives. They have advocated liberty and democracy with one hand while stealing Iranian oil and buttressing autocratic shahs with the other. They have pledged honor and fair play yet lied and swindled as if they'd been born in the bazaar.

Many Iranians, even those immunized against Middle Eastern intrigue by distance and Western educations, still believe the British clandestinely run the world, bowing to no one, except possibly the Jews. I once showed an Iranian friend with a CalTech Ph.D. a book by Lyndon LaRouche, the left-now-right-wing high-tech American cuckoo who keeps running for the U.S. presidency. The book describes the queen of England as the real power behind the CIA, the KGB, Mossad, Henry Kissinger, and even the French Overseas Intelligence Service, the DGSE. It had been intended as a bizarre light read; my friend took it as the holy grail of international politics.

His prejudice went back centuries. After the British had taken control of the Indian subcontinent's Muslim Mogul Empire in the late eighteenth century, they quickly became the preeminent power of the Persian Gulf and south-central Asia. From the end of the eighteenth to the beginning of the twentieth century, Iran was caught in the Great Game, the competition pitting Russia (and occasionally Napoleonic France and Wilhelmine Germany) against Britain for control of the Central Asian marches to India, the linchpin of British power and wealth. Persia's kings tried to keep Iran free of foreigners by playing the Europeans against one another. But Iran was usually too weak and the foreigners too strong. In particular, Russian armies inexorably moved south and east, taking revenge on Tatar and Mongol hordes who for centuries had kept Russia in a Muslim yoke. In the process, Iranian land and trade fell to the Russians in the Caucasus and Central Asia.

As early as the seventeenth century, Safavid Iran saw Great Britain as a possible ally against the Ottoman Empire, then Iran's preeminent foe. Anthony and Robert Shirley, the English representatives-cum-mercenaries of Queen Elizabeth I, provided Shah Abbas the Great with helpful artillery hints on how to kill more Turkish troops. Robert Shirley eventually became Shah Abbas's ambassador to the English kings James I and Charles II.

As their own power waned and land-hungry Russians and marauding Afghans grew stronger, the Persians began to view the British Empire, now firmly established in India and similarly confronting aggressive Afghans and Russians, as the least dangerous of neighborhood devils. Naturally, the British encouraged this view. By the early twentieth century, Britain exercised significant, though not overwhelming, financial and political influence in Tehran and in the oil-rich southern provinces, where the Anglo–Persian Oil Company was rapidly developing Iran's immense oil resources. Particularly in the south, which after the 1907 Anglo–Russian accord was officially recognized as a British sphere of influence, His Majesty's Government was perceived, accurately or not, as having in its pocket the Shah's representatives, the tribal aristocracy, and a good deal of the clergy.

When in 1941 Reza Shah Pahlavi (1878–1944), the tough, often brutal peasant-soldier who founded the Pahlavi dynasty, made the mistake of expressing his sympathies for Nazi Germany once too often, the British invaded Iran to protect their oil and the military supply lines to their desperate Russian foes-turned-allies. At British and Soviet bayonet point, Reza Shah abdicated in favor of his son, Mohammad Reza Pahlavi; he died in 1944 in South African exile.

In 1946 the British and the Americans, who had followed the British into Iran, withdrew, allowing the young Shah to keep his throne and Iran's great landed families most of the political power. Even before the 1953 CIA/MI6 supported coup d'état against Prime Minister Mohammad Mosaddeq, most Iranians were convinced Britain was Persia's puppeteer. With the coup, Washington assumed London's role—though the British, in the eyes of many Iranians (including the Shah), never really withdrew from the region, preferring to supply English brainpower to American brawn behind the scenes.

The image of the United States in Iran became more contradictory than that of the British because it was vastly more popular. Only the Iranian elite could learn to love Great Britain; everybody else hated her. America, with her popular culture and egalitarian ideas, appealed to and hence was loathed by all. When Hamid and Hosein said *"Amrika,"* I could hear this dissonance between affection and awe. When they said *"Englissss,"* I felt certain I heard much more disdain—or perhaps the respect that accomplished thieves have for each other.

Praying my comment wouldn't ignite a thirty-minute oration on perfidious Albion, I said, "England is a small country with very little power. I don't think she can help or hurt you now." Wanting to see whether the Khomeini-damned British author of *The Satanic Verses* provoked any reaction, I quickly added, "The most dangerous thing the English have is Salman Rushdie."

"He's a bad man," replied the older Persian. "He shouldn't have attacked the Prophet and abandoned Islam. But I don't think we should try to kill him. He means nothing to us."

"Rushdie is a problem for you, not for us. Only the mollahs think about him, we don't," added the younger man.

"Rushdie! Rushdie! He's a very lucky man!" Hosein cut in. "The mollahs have made our country poor and they've made Rushdie famous. The mollahs are really killing us. They only want to kill him. Who has the better deal?"

"Rushdie insulted the Prophet; the mollahs insult the Prophet every day. They should both be punished the same," added Hamid. "We'll kill Rushdie, if you kill the mollahs."

We all laughed. I wondered whether Salman Rushdie appreciated Persian humor.

It was now early morning and we were all intermittently shivering in the cold. As the conversation had developed and my adrenaline-fear faded, my neck, shoulders, legs, and eyes reminded me how tired I was. For the first time since entering Iran, I was looking forward to the cot.

I looked at the boy again. His face was hairless and his skin innocent and unmarked. The Hezbollahi look, the nasty-eyed stare framed by dirty stubble, was at least a few years away. And as I was learning, "the look" might not arrive at all. He'd not have the Imam to guide him to manhood; he'd have only his father. And his father's faith was cold. Would he learn more from him or from teachers who still called Khomeini the Imam? Was there the slightest chance this boy could become a new-generation holy warrior, his faith rekindled by a new messenger?

I didn't think so. Persians can always flip on you, kind one moment, cruel the next. But after the Ayatollah, Iranians would be tired for a very long time. More than 450 years had passed between Shah Ismail's holy war and Khomeini's.

I gave Hosein a telling nod, and he surprised me by immediately rolling forward onto his feet and thanking Hamid profusely for the meal. I added a few superlatives, thanked the other three for their company, and expressed a wish that we might meet again. In reply, all invited me to visit them in their homes if I ever had the chance. I thanked them again and told them I would, God willing.

After shaking Hamid's hand, Hosein and I walked back to the truck. As we walked, the pickup-truck Persians gathered up their rugs. Hosein thought they'd probably spend the night in the pickup rather than risk the tricky mountain drive at night. I asked Hosein whether he thought they might offhandedly mention me to some security post. He chortled. "No one ever gossips to Revolutionary Guards."

I wanted to offer Hosein the cot since he'd be doing the driving. But I couldn't. If someone came knocking, I wouldn't be able to hide in the front seats. On the cot, I'd be invisible except to someone on the running boards peering in with a flashlight. If I had to, it wouldn't take me long to pop back into the box. So I rolled over the seats as Hosein turned the engine on to give us a few minutes of heat. I handed him a blanket and a pillow, then debated whether to take off my boots. I decided to leave them on.

My left shoulder started to ache as soon as it touched the mattress, but I stopped noticing when a wave of heat rolled through between the seats. Before I even put my head onto a small kilim pillow, I was moving back again in time to my first days in the Agency, to the first time I met Shahpur, my colloquial-language tutor. Unannounced, he'd walked into my office and asked in Persian when I wanted to start my lessons. I replied in halting, flawed university Persian, "As soon as possible." He agreed.

For months we worked together in classrooms and in one-on-one immersions at the Farm, the CIA's primary training facility near Williamsburg, Virginia. We played poker, backgammon, and chess together, and stayed up nights carousing in tacky Virginia bars. Drunk, I had to strip women in Persian in my mind. It's hard in a foreign language to harmonize alcohol, motion, and body parts. He taught me how to curse, cheat, and throw a temper tantrum in his language, and also how to tell jokes and laugh. He was one of only a handful of Iranians who'd made it to the brain center of the Great Satan, and, like me, he was surprised by what he'd found. Never trusted completely because of his undeniable Persianness, he remained outside the Agency brotherhood. Yet he honored both his nations' best interests even as he advanced his own.

As I fell asleep behind Hosein, I realized I owed Shahpur more than I could ever possibly repay. The time he'd spent on me—the endless conversations where he tried to knock the professor out of my Persian, the hangovers incurred, and his sly revelations of Iranian weaknesses—hadn't been for naught. Though he was only supposed to be my language instructor, he became my *pir*, my spiritual guide, who revealed secrets I'd not seen in Arabic and Persian books. He was the most valuable Iranian the Agency had ever employed and the finest of Persian friends. Without him, I could never have come to Iran.

5   TABRIZ

I was back in the box. Hosein had told me I wouldn't miss much—
except the security roadblock on the outskirts of town. Tabriz, the
capital of Azarbaijan, wasn't like most older Persian cities, where medieval central squares with turquoise-tiled mosques, seminaries, and
ablution pools were surrounded by urban-peasant sprawl and asphyx-
iating factories. Tabriz, with a population of over one million, was
more like Tehran: ugliness was uniform. Broad, potholed streets, traffic jams, and low-rise concrete buildings penetrated to its heart. Tabriz's past had largely disappeared or was in ruins. A visitor without
a history book to guide him wouldn't see the vanished splendor: a
capital for both the Mongol and the Safavid empires, a beautiful oasis
town rich with poplar trees, gardens, palaces, *hammams*, and mosques.

Unlike Mashhad and Isfahan—modern Iran's other large, historic
cities—Tabriz is situated in a treacherous geological zone. Azarbaijan's capital has been repeatedly shaken and burned by earthquakes
and fire. Cholera and various plagues have periodically struck the
city. Wars, too, have been unkind. Fifteenth-century Mongols and
Ottomans sacked and burned the town. After World War I, the
Soviets closed the northwestern frontier, shutting down much

of Iran's east-west commerce, which had made Tabriz the country's largest, richest, and most Westernized city. Though the former Soviet border was now open, Tabriz's withering, according to Hosein, hadn't stopped. Pahlavi Iran's numerous highways, airplanes, and trains had permanently made Tehran, half the size of Tabriz in 1900, the center of Persian commerce. And what earthquakes, fires, wars, diseases, and the Soviets hadn't diminished, modern tastes had. Tabrizis tore down many of the older stone and brick buildings, because they no longer appealed. In Third World countries chasing modern life, concrete is often a preference, not a low-cost necessity.

Stuck in the box, I imagined myself strolling leisurely down Tabriz's avenues. I'd start at the city's center, the Bazaar, one of Tabriz's few medieval glories left intact by time. I'd lose myself in its twisting, intersecting alleys, and then escape through a sunlit archway into a street lined with well-kept yellow brick buildings. I'd then wander south through the heart of Tabriz toward the ruins of the fifteenth-century Blue Mosque. Meandering in old cobblestone streets that hadn't been straightened or paved, I'd finally find the Citadel, the Mongol's thick-walled fortress. From the fourteenth to the late nineteenth century, Tabriz's rulers hurled religious deviates, spies, and common criminals from its ramparts. All along the way, I'd talk to shop owners, street vendors, and toothless, tobacco-stained old men in worn-out winter coats who could compare Reza Shah's pre-World War II Iran with Khomeini's. Most of all, I'd talk to young men or boys perpetually loafing or playing soccer in empty streets. I'd be brave and free, prying loose Persian secrets on every street corner. I'd be the first (ex–)CIA man in Tabriz in fifteen years. I'd not once jerk my head across my shoulders, searching for police, Revolutionary Guards, Basijis, or ordinary soldiers. Envisioning this idyllic visit made me laugh to myself as we arrived in Tabriz. I was more scared than at the border, and probably soon to be disappointed. On the way into town, we'd seen squat, mud-brick villages guarded by goats. The peasants surely had overrun Tabriz, as they'd taken most Third World towns. I'd come all this way to see one-story brick huts sandwiched between four-story concrete blocks.

I hoped Hosein had been too harsh on his hometown. Decay is always relative, and in Turkey and Egypt I'd developed demanding standards for centuries-old decrepitude and modern crumbling concrete. The exurban peasant ghettos of Istanbul, almost always without running water, paved streets, or adequately piped sewage, were appalling. In winter, the coal-polluted rain streaked concrete and children's faces a grayish black. Mosques were usually the only buildings with any architectural interest—their painted doors and colored windows were properly cut and attached.

As a student in Cairo, I'd occasionally placed bets in a monthly "housing" pool that tried to pick neighborhood mud-brick buildings ready to collapse. It was a morbid game with short odds. The sand and broken-rock streets of Fustat, the oldest and perhaps poorest section of Cairo, became rivulets of sewage whenever it rained, which fortunately wasn't often. The city's medieval Mamluk cemeteries had become evening hotels for homeless people searching for quiet in Cairo's ceaseless racket. Every fourth person seemed physically deformed, as if by the city itself.

With only one million residents, it was hard for Tabriz to compete. Tehran drew more Azari peasants from the countryside than Tabriz did. Tehran's endless southern slums had become Iran's biggest Azari mass. But Hosein had warned me I might find Tabriz uglier. "In winter, it's dead. When it snows hard, people go indoors. In Tehran, the cold and snow are never enough to silence the streets." But I liked severe winters in the Middle East for just this reason: the snow hid the dirt, and stopped the cars, and made it easier to dream of the past.

Despite its ugliness, Hosein liked his hometown. "The people cheat you less here than in Tehran. It's smaller. Family and friends are closer and can protect you more." Just as important for Hosein, Tabriz's hard-core revolutionaries were now few and far between. "Tabriz *was* as revolutionary as Tehran," Hosein insisted. "We rose before them in protest against the Shah. We crushed our own Grand Ayatollah, Mohammad Kazem Shari'at-madari. Tabrizis feel awful about this now, but we didn't then. And no one gave more sons to the holy war against Saddam than us. But Tabriz is ignored now. Tehran and Qom take the money. Everybody feels cheated. If you don't hate the clerics, you don't have friends."

At the dawn of the revolution, Grand Ayatollah Mohammad Kazem Shari'at-madari had been Tabriz's favorite son. When the city rioted against the Shah in February 1978, one of the first cities in Iran to do so, Shari'at-madari, not Khomeini, was the preferred cleric of the street. In December 1979, part of the city even rose in his name against the hard-core revolutionaries of Tehran.

Like most clerics, Shari'at-madari had joined the revolutionary cause late and remained skeptical of clerics who preferred politics to *fiqh*, the arduous exegesis of the Holy Law that takes a lifetime to learn. Like the vast majority of senior Shi'ite clerics, he feared the corruption of political power. Clerics should defend the honor of the nation and counsel good government, but keep their distance from the *'ulul-'amr*, the men who hold the reins.

Shari'at-madari loathed Khomeini's hubris, his dogmatism, and his hunger for new martyrs for the faith. He realized early Khomeini's intention to wage war against both the Shah and traditional Shi'ism, which is forgiving of man's, especially the ruler's, sins. He knew Khomeini intended to overturn the clerical hierarchy, making young unaccomplished mollahs with revolutionary commitment the masters of church and state. The elderly Grand Ayatollahs, hitherto Shi'ism's guardians, who had looked askance at Khomeini's scholarship and political pretensions, were to be diminished and not replaced.

Khomeini had astutely put his faith in the masses and not in his peers. With the Revolutionary Guards behind him, he shredded the consensual nature of the clerical community and declared himself supreme. In his and his followers' eyes, he had become the vice-regent of the Hidden Imam, whose return as the Mahdi, the Rightly Guided One, would finally vanquish Evil and usher in paradise. The hard core of Khomeini's followers—like Ahmad—even believed Khomeini to be the Mahdi himself. Shari'at-madari, a measured man who saw no glory in violence, never had a chance. His supporters' rebellion in December 1979 was crushed within a week. In 1982, after being named as a conspirator in a failed Air Force coup d'état, he was placed under house arrest. Khomeini's political clergy in Iran's premier clerical seat of learning, Qom, "defrocked" him, banning any reference to him as a Grand Ayatollah. He died in 1986, still under house arrest. He'd been the clergy's last chance to stop the Imam cult evolving around Khomeini. He'd been Iran's last chance to stop the rebirth of the death-wish Persian.

Hosein's words confirmed what I'd always heard: virtually no one in Tabriz had risen in 1982 in Shariʿat-madari's defense. Turkish-speaking Azaris had proved again they were Shiʿites and Persians above all else. Tabriz had decided to follow Tehran. "You have to understand," Hosein implored, "for a few years we all lost our minds."

Azaris and Iranians. One people split by language or two peoples joined by culture? What makes an Iranian? What makes an Iraqi, a Syrian, or a Turk? How do you define identity in the Middle East? These questions are crucial for spies hunting Persians, Arabs, or Turks. Nationalism is a tinderbox issue in the Muslim world because it is so at odds with the past. Except for Iran, and to a lesser extent Egypt and Tunisia, no Middle Eastern state had a "national" identity before the 1918 collapse of the Ottoman Empire. Present Middle Eastern borders have much more to do with European (usually British) inspiration and administration than with precolonial, centuries-old divisions between distinct peoples with irreconcilable, unconquerable loyalties.

In 1900, if you'd asked the average man in Cairo, Damascus, Tripoli, Istanbul, Baghdad, or Khartoum what he was, he would have replied "Muslim" and probably nothing else. If pushed, he might have also mentioned the town or village of his birth, his father and grandfather, and, if he still felt close to the countryside, his tribe. If pushed further, he also might have referred to himself as a subject of his sovereign, which for most of the Middle East had been the Ottomans for more than four hundred years. Though it has become de rigueur in Arab circles to attack the Ottomans as Turkish intruders who oppressed the "Arab nation" for centuries, that sentiment was not shared by most Arabs until the Ottoman general turned Turkish dictator Kemal Atatürk abolished the Ottoman sultanate in 1922 and established the secular Turkish Republic.

For Arab Muslims, as for the Kurds and Turks of Anatolia and the Turkish-speaking European Muslims west of the Bosporus and south of the Danube—the most tenacious holy-warrior "Turks" of the empire—the Ottoman dynasty was the great conqueror and defender of the faith. Sentiments of peoplehood, though they certainly existed, were downplayed in a rather egalitarian society where Islam and martial virtues were the keys to success.

Even Iran, which was never conquered by the Ottomans and whose culture dates back at least twenty-five hundred years, does not have nearly as clear a national identity as the much younger England and France, the parents of the nation-state. Before Reza Shah Pahlavi, the first explicitly Westernizing shah, Iran was commonly known, especially among the clergy, as *mamalek ol-Eslam,* "the lands of Islam."

With the Arab conquest in the seventh century, ancient Persia and Islam began to merge. By the tenth century, the marriage was complete. Persian had replaced Arabic as the literary and court language for the Iranian-Muslim princes of what is now Afghanistan, Tajikistan, Uzbekistan, Turkmenistan, and eastern Iran. Though voluntarily still subjects of Baghdad's Arabic-speaking caliphate, they had become politically and culturally independent. A Persian renaissance had begun—a new Iranian language, rich in Arabic words and written in the Arabic script, had become the vehicle for a universal, ever more cosmopolitan and missionary Islamic faith.

In the tenth century, the great Central Asian Turkish tribal invasion of the Islamic heartlands began. These Turkomans, already converted to Islam by Iranian and Arab missionaries, quickly grafted themselves onto the preexisting Islamic society. Unlike the infidel Mongol invasions three centuries later, this nomadic invasion militarily and spiritually *strengthened* the Islamic Middle East. The Seljuk sultans, the overlords of this tribal irruption, checked the Crusaders in the Levant and fatally wounded the Christian Byzantine Empire in central and eastern Anatolia. The Ottomans, then Seljuk subjects, slowly began to build their holy-warrior fiefdom in Anatolia's Christian–Muslim marches. The Greek language, rooted in this region for over fifteen hundred years, all but vanished overnight.

After the Seljuks, Azarbaijan changed ethnically and linguistically. The dominant Iranian language of the region disappeared as successive waves of Turkish tribesmen settled in ever larger numbers. In the thirteenth century, after destroying the Seljuks and the Abbasid caliphate, the Mongols converted to Islam and made Tabriz their Middle Eastern capital. Tens of thousands of Turkish warriors, cohorts of the Mongol military machine, settled in Azarbaijan. In the fourteenth and fifteenth centuries, Tamerlane, the Skull Stacker, the last great Central Asian conqueror, settled thousands more. But the changes in ethnicity and language did not alter Azarbaijan's historic attachment to the culture of what the ancient Greeks called *Persis* and Iranians *Fars*—the plateau land surrounding Shiraz, the heart of ancient Persia. The Turks quickly became dedicated and successful missionaries of the new Islamic-Iranian civilization.

By the time Shah Ismail established the Safavid dynasty in Tabriz in 1501, the dominance of Persian culture extended from the Balkans to Bengal. With Ismail's decision forcibly to convert his dominions to Shi'ism, geographic borders finally formed around Persian culture based on the ineradicable Sunni–Shi'ite split. The Ottomans in the West, the Uzbeks in the North, and the Afghans in the East checked Safavid expansionism, and contemporary Iranian borders took shape. Persian poetry, architecture, ceramics, miniatures, and carpets still inspired Muslims the world over. However, the love of Persian beauty henceforth had to be watched to insure it didn't lead faithful Sunnis toward conversion. With an older and more refined civilization, Shi'ite Iran became in the Sunni mind the evil whispering Temptress of the Qur'an. Persian poetry became a potentially treasonous intoxicant. Persian pilgrims headed toward Mecca became especially attractive, licit prey for Sunni bedouin. Iranians began to forget they'd once been among the most accomplished Sunni theologians and warriors.

Reza Shah Pahlavi and his son Mohammad tried to undo this Shi'ite–Iranian fusion, placing the ancient Persian glories above those of Shi'ism's martyred pantheon. Iran's numerous ethnic minorities, which today represent more than half of her sixty million people, would become proper Persians. With state encouragement, Farsi, Persian, would become everyone's mother tongue. All Iranians, be they Shi'ite, Sunni, Christians, Zoroastrians, Bahai's, or Jews, would be equally Persian in a new Westernized nation-state.

The Islamic revolution was in part a rejection of this recast nationalist identity. Once again, clerics referred to Iran as *mamalek ol-Eslam* and diligently tried to avoid references to Iran without anchoring them in the faith. Ayatollah Khomeini preferred to damn his foes as the enemies of God and Islam, not the enemies of Iran. In doing so, he returned to the habit of Muslim potentates for fourteen hundred years. If church and state are one, then political legitimacy can come only from Allah. Any enemy of the state is necessarily an enemy of God.

An Islamic revolutionary identity necessarily excludes non-Muslims. By the early 1980s, thousands of members of Iran's religious minorities had fled to Turkey. Most made at least one pilgrimage to a U.S. consulate seeking visas—Christians begging for Christian fraternity, Jews hoping to find fabled Jewish power and intercession, and Baha'is just praying for American mercy. Little did they understand that their special pleas for help damned them in the vice-consuls' eyes. Minorities couldn't overcome the "214B presumption of intending immigration." We'd all seen "the blue sheets," the U.S. Immigration and Naturalization Service one-page bulletins about Iranians who'd violated their tourist visas and remained in the States. Christians and Jews rarely went back to Iran, quickly locking into U.S. charitable and family networks. Baha'is never returned.

With the visa door closed to them, the minorities could try to gain refugee status. But even Baha'is, whom the clerics abused mercilessly, didn't have an easy time. Moving from Istanbul to New York could take years. For Iranian Christians and Jews, the refugee option offered little hope. Second-class citizenship and occasional state-sanctioned murder weren't sufficient reasons for Washington to open the refugee door. For Jews who no longer wanted to endure the vagaries of radical Islamic life and wanted their children out of revolutionary schools, there was always Israel. The Israelis could have a Persian Jewish family transported from Istanbul to Tel Aviv within twenty-four hours; I'd sent Iranian Jews whom I couldn't help to the Israelis.

A Christian with similar concerns was usually stuck. If France didn't give a "tourist" visa on the sly—and the French alone among the Europeans unofficially gave tourist visas to Christians seeking refuge from the mollahs—an Iranian Christian family had little choice but to return to Iran. Since most Iranian Christians are Armenians, a permanent exile in Turkey seemed worse than a return to Iran. Fairly numerous in Tehran and Isfahan, organized, financially successful, and not without clerical contacts, Armenians were usually able to plead or buy off the revolution's anti-Christian hard core.

The religiously persecuted occasionally made their way to me. A few had interesting scientific, medical, and import-export skills— knowledge and talent the mollahs wanted to keep and Washington wanted to learn. The Sunni Kurds always offered information that I needed about the border: the *who, what, where,* and *how much* questions about legal and covert border crossings.

However, non-Shi'ites could never be officials—the CIA's primary targets—in a revolutionary Islamic-law state. When they told me their stories, I offered them solace, sometimes money, but nothing more.

On the other hand, Azaris were everything and everywhere—diplomats, military officers, *Pasdaran,* Central Bank and Oil Ministry officials, *Basijis,* Persian Gulf shipping agents, film producers, novelists, actors, engineers, scientists, and clerics. Ten million strong, Azaris are Iran's historic overachievers. Like the Kurds in Turkey, they cropped up disproportionately in the powerful's family trees. And despite their repeated demonstrations of proper Shi'ite Persianness, a distinction between them and Iranians remained. This distinction was the "vulnerability" I constantly probed. Find a weak link between Azaris and "proper" Persians, and a case officer could slice a man's soul, the regime, and conceivably the country apart.

Twice since 1900 Azari separatist movements have appeared. Since 1991, another Shi'ite Azarbaijan, the ex-Soviet one with its capital at Baku, has been just across the northern border in rapid development as an independent nation-state. Baku and Tabriz are two totally different worlds—one Russian and secular, the other faithful and Persian—but the languages are the same.

Under the Russian tsars, Baku had been the Paris of the Caucasus, with concert halls and outdoor cafés. Upper-class Persian Azarbaijanis regularly visited, tasting pleasures not available at home.

Nowadays, Baku is even poorer than Tabriz. Newly discovered Caspian Sea oil and gas, however, might quickly reverse the situation. Then how strong would the Azari–Iranian bond prove? After all, proper Persians call Turks jackasses and donkeys, and they *always* call Azarbaijanis Turks—with time and an economic seesaw, the jokes might take a toll. As Hosein put it, everybody in his hometown hated clerical Tehran.

In the CIA, I'd often wondered about the covert-action possibilities in the Iranian–Azari divide. I wasn't an unqualified fan of covert action (CA), but now and then it had worked, though even when it worked, you could rarely gauge well what you'd done. CA has more flexibility than diplomacy and fewer casualties than outright war. It covers everything from funding newspapers, magazines, radio stations, international conferences, journalists, academics, and guerrilla operations to orchestrating rescue missions and coups d'état.

U.S. diplomats hadn't won the hearts and minds of Western Europeans tempted by Communism, but legions of left-wing intellectuals wittingly and unwittingly on the Agency payroll did a somewhat better job. U.S. diplomats couldn't make cash deposits to bring Mosaddeq down. They didn't save the Dalai Lama. Spies, less tied to means than to ends, may cross the gray zone between Good and Evil and come home moral survivors: if the other side is bad enough, you can always forgive yourself most sins.

One purpose of U.S. covert action against Iran should be to reinforce Persian awe of American power and omniscience. Nothing in the world scared Tehran's clerics, like the shahs before them, more than an Iranian–Azari divorce. So why not feed their fears? I had no qualms about certain types of covert action against the clerics. They weren't angels. They'd killed and tortured far more people than the Shah. They'd converted Islam into an ideology where teenagers toting German assault rifles became the sentinels of public virtue. They'd sent Persian hypocrisy and corruption into overdrive. They'd kidnapped U.S. diplomats, encouraged the bombing of U.S. Marines in Lebanon, sent assassins after Salman Rushdie, and aided and abetted terrorism against Jews worldwide. They'd also beaten, jailed, and robbed a few of my friends.

Still, I knew any CIA effort wouldn't really get off the ground. If case officers can't read or speak the "target language" and don't know Iranian history, how can they seriously engage in anticlerical CA? Without Persian-literate officers, you have to rely on Iranians for the truth. Brilliant older officers from another epoch might be drafted into service to fill the void. However, such wise men can do only so much in offices where Persian books and newspapers are stacked unopened along the walls. Inevitably, they retire to New England seashore cottages, and spy-bureaucrats deepen the void. These men target congressmen and their staffers instead of Persians.

The dirty little CIA secret is that it's easier and safer to do nothing and pretend the utmost has been done. With Langley's barbed-wire fences, cipher locks, and endless mantras about protecting national security, senior CIA officers can usually frustrate congressional watchdog committees. Congressmen are far easier to recruit than Persians. They work for the same country and rarely have the time, patience, and wherewithal to penetrate Langley's defenses, mediocrity, and lies. Even after the arrest of the KGB mole Aldrich Ames exposed the rot inside Langley, most congressmen still believe it's easier and more patriotic to legislate millions for the Directorate of Operations and hope that something good is being done, somewhere.

Despite the operational pointlessness, I continuously scripted possible covert-action mischief in my mind. Iranian Azarbaijan was rich in possibilities. Accessible through Turkey and ex-Soviet Azarbaijan, eyed already by nationalists in Baku, more westward-looking than most of Iran, and economically going nowhere, Iran's richest agricultural province was an ideal CA theater. Incompetence aside, all the Agency had to overcome was a cardinal rule of U.S. diplomacy in the Middle East—the territorial integrity of modern states.

In 1991, U.S. fidelity to this land-over-people creed caused Washington to blow a rare chance to topple Saddam Hussein and psychologically unhinge the mollahs. Immediately after Operation Desert Storm, Iraq's Shiʿa revolted. Although more than half Iraq's population and draftee army, the Shiʿa were in desperate need of U.S. assistance to counter the Republican Guard, Saddam Hussein's Sunni shock troops, who'd escaped the Allied victory virtually unscathed. Washington, however, viewed Iraqi Shiʿites as potential Iranian allies and, instead of supplying them with arms and enforcing the flight ban on Baghdad's helicopter gunships and planes, turned a blind eye to Saddam's anti-Shi'ite counterattack. His helicopters and tanks slaughtered the Shi'a, reducing much of Najaf, Iraq's oldest seat of Shi'ite learning, to rubble.

Holding firm to the belief that Iraq's territorial integrity and Arab Sunni dominance were necessary to preserve the region's equilibrium, U.S. intelligence couldn't see the Shi'ite versus Shi'ite possibilities. Iran's clergy viewed their Arab co-religionists as traitors, not allies. Iraq's Shi'a had unforgivably failed to rise against Saddam during the 1980–88 Iran–Iraq War. So when Saddam attacked Najaf, Tehran remained silent. Except for the odd shipment of supplies from freelance Iranian smugglers, no Iranian weaponry or soldiers crossed the frontier.

This struck me as a huge missed opportunity. An independent or autonomous Shi'ite state in southern Iraq would have reenergized Iraq's Shi'ites, long docile under ferocious Sunni rule. The age-old clerical rivalry between Najaf and Qom would have been reborn. Hostile to the clerical hubris of Khomeini's Iran, Najaf's Arabic-speaking mollahs would loudly have debated the fundamentals of Khomeini's theocratic rule. Dissident senior Iranian clerics disgusted with Tehran could have repaired to Najaf, as the Ayatollah once did under the Shah. A network of anti-regime clerics could have formed. At minimal cost to the United States, Washington could have encouraged a Shi'ite civil war.

In the process, Saddam Hussein might have fallen. Though well armed, the Republican Guards couldn't have beaten simultaneous insurrections north and south. The Kurds and Shi'ites would possibly have finished the job America left undone.

Covert activity in Azerbaijan couldn't possibly bear so rich a harvest. But a well-constructed program, even if it failed, could still unnerve the mollahs. Here CA needs only to scare—to let the mollahs know the Great Satan is toying with the idea of tearing Iran apart. Even hard-core Iranians know they'll lose if the United States really takes aim. Worldwide Islamic revolution, terrorism, or assassination wouldn't look so appealing if the price were Azerbaijan.

Would we be playing with fire, tempting a geographic implosion of the Muslim world? Perhaps. But nation-states don't take shape unless there is a popular will for them. A lavishly funded CIA covert-action program to tear Brittany from France wouldn't work. Bretons may hate Paris, but they are French. The same may be true for Azaris and the Islamic Republic. Still, a little CIA mischief would help the two make up their minds—while convincingly reminding the mollahs of U.S. omniscience and power.

Provocative CA questions in Langley didn't seem so pressing in Tabriz. I wanted to talk to Azaris and Persians to test their marriage vows; I also wanted to hide. As I felt the truck slowing for another checkpoint, my nerves and the muscles in my neck stiffened. Once more, I realized what I'd done. At least the Revolutionary Guards wouldn't shoot me: A dead American wouldn't be worth much. And a dead American spy would be a pointless waste.

They would certainly discover the truth. I'd have to tell them I'd worked for State—I couldn't erase completely a decade of government service and have it hold up in a physical cross-examination. And a State Department confession would be more than enough to damn me. Once I was damned, they'd take their time. They'd hang me by my arms behind and above my head—the Ottoman way popular in Persia that very slowly tears your arms from their sockets. They'd probably leave my face and hands alone. The odds were good that I'd get on prime-time TV, and Iranians always like to show they treat foreigners better than their own.

The words of Robert Strausz-Hupé, a former U.S. ambassador to Turkey, kept returning: in societies "where men kiss each other they also beat each other." And Middle Eastern men regularly embrace. If I were lucky, they wouldn't use electric shocks. I'd debriefed several Iranians who'd been tortured by the mollahs. Not one had encountered cattle prods or genital toasters. SAVAK, the Shah's secret police, had used such things; perhaps enough clerics had been fried to engender a little compassion. Perhaps electric torture seemed unmanly—the type of thing Iraqis did to Iranian prisoners of war. Perhaps it was too modern to be cricket with God. To me in the truck, this seemed like progress.

However, they'd hit Hosein everywhere with real force. In the end, they'd kill him. If he was lucky, they'd shoot him. If he was unlucky, they'd vise-grip his testicles into tomato paste and let him bleed to death. The clerics had dealt similarly with other "traitors."

I'd had these nightmares before. I hadn't resigned from the Agency when I first realized its decrepitude. For years I'd excused the Agency's incompetence around me by appealing to patriotism and higher ends. I'd wrestled with the possible consequences of my efforts to convince Iranians to work for Uncle Sam. "If good men always leave, the bastards always win," a former professor, once in intelligence, had chided me. Also, others' incompetence didn't prevent me from doing my best.

My professor had been right. Good men were leaving the Agency in ever greater numbers. And good men entering were rare. Long before the Cold War ended and Aldrich Ames went to prison, the clandestine service was falling apart. The unforgiving law of bureaucratic rot—first-class people may choose first class, but second chooses third, third chooses fourth—had come brutally into play in the CIA's closed society. First-class people, like Agency successes, were now few and far between.

The Directorate of Operations Iran desk officer sent in 1985 to debrief Manucher Ghorbanifar, the slick and savvy Iran–Contra go-between, couldn't recognize the names of senior Iranian officials involved in the missiles-for-hostages game. Without Persian or a background in the Middle East, he had to ask Ghorbanifar to spell the officials' names over and over again. The same officer once remarked with pride that he hadn't finished reading a book in four years. "You should put your faith in the system," he advised me one evening. "The organization makes mistakes, but in the end the best people always rise." Within a few years, despite major mistakes, he'd become the acting deputy director of Operations, America's most powerful master spy.

When I stopped playing by Agency rules, my nightmares ended. I'd never tell another Iranian that if he took care of himself, we'd look after him. I'd never again be an intermediary for men I didn't know and trust. There would be no more promises and gifts.

Yet, here I was again putting an Iranian into danger. There was no way Hosein could survive the discovery of an American stashed in his truck. If the authorities even caught us on the street together, he'd still have an onerous interrogation. Our prepared stories might not hold. So was I any different than before? I was still trying to ride to the center of the Iranian mind on an adrenaline rush. And if something went wrong, we'd both go down, but only Hosein would die.

Still, it seemed more moral. Neither of us now cared much for grand causes. I couldn't remember a single Special National Intelligence Estimate on Iran I'd read, and I'd read them all closely. Eight-and-a-half-by-eleven-inch, red-white-and-blue, graphics-rich reports whose sole insights came from satellite imagery and intercepts. To an Iranian, dying for a cleric-free Iran made perfect sense; to me, an Iranian dying for "classified" information usually expressed more fully and accurately in an academic journal, the *New York Times*, or *Petroleum Weekly*, had not. A truck ride to Khomeini's tomb seemed a far higher calling.

We were crawling now. Cars were honking around us. Whatever security check there was obviously didn't elicit much fear. I couldn't imagine Iraqis honking at security checkpoints or Frenchmen or Germans. I couldn't imagine Iranians honking in 1981 during the *Mojahedin-e Khalq*–Revolutionary Guard shooting free-for-all.

With a little luck, I'd be out of the box within an hour and my legs would still work. Tonight, I'd have Hosein walk me to the Citadel. During the revolution, the town's radical mollahs had blown part of it up to make more space for public prayers. Later the mollahs apologized. The Mongols had become Muslims, after all.

We'd stopped. No voices. Only Iranians riding their horns in disgust. Cars, not trucks. One line of traffic, not two. Before I could put my ear on the wood, we started moving again. Stalled traffic or a wave-by? Nothing from Hosein.

I'd hit roadblocks before Iran. During training at the Farm, you'd have at least one. The instructor-turned-cop who'd stopped and drilled me was an alcoholic who couldn't remember his lines. In the real world, I'd been caught in routine security checks, but never with an agent.

Unexpected roadblocks had occasionally caught Agency officers with their "assets." It didn't ruin their careers. In theory, you'd always try to have a cover story. But cover stories can work only if two men plausibly can be together—with some agents I'd chosen black leather and feigned a homosexual affair.

Hosein was unquestionably better at this than I, though I was a decent liar. But lying to Americans, even case officers, is easy: they assume you're telling the truth. I'd lied successfully to Persians, but only when I'd controlled the terrain. Because I was Washington's representative, they assumed I was too powerful to fib. I'd never lied if the penalty was mercilessly severe. An undiplomatic state like the former Soviet Union or Saddam Hussein's Iraq had occasionally played rough with an American case officer caught with his hands in the cookie jar. Yet in most countries it was not even a night in jail. With diplomatic immunity in the back of your mind, lying could never become more than an avocation.

Hosein, however, lied constantly to armed men. And unlike most Iranians, he always sounded as if he were telling the truth. Persians don't always lie, but their manner—the effusive explanations, entreaties, and obvious mismatch between abilities and words—makes you think they do. Hosein's delivery was disarmingly quick and straight. More American in style, he was parsimonious with his dishonesty. Perhaps he even believed in the truth.

Again the three taps. "American, get out!"

The engine sounds had been enough to tell me where we were. Company semis and smaller freelance trucks personalized by rainbow colors and freehand *nastaliq* were parked every which way. I'd been in the box less than an hour, the time Hosein had estimated for reaching his truck park. We'd slowed once—the checkpoint—but never stopped. Only when Tabrizis rioted did the *Pasdars* turn the checkpoints into killer searches. Tabrizis, fortunately, hadn't rioted lately.

"We're in Tabriz?" A stupid question I nevertheless couldn't stop. From a coat pocket, I pulled a small folding mirror, acquired in my first disguise class. I'd shunned disguises ever since—quick, do-it-yourself wigs, mustaches, and facial coloring are almost always more trouble than they're worth—but I'd kept the mirror. It had been my constant companion when I was a walk-in officer in Turkey, where Russians, Ukrainians, Bulgarians, Romanians, Poles, Czechs, Libyans, Syrians, Iraqis, Uighur Turks from Communist China, and Iranians descended on me without consideration for office hours. Most were of no value whatsoever. Rarely did I find one matching the Agency's or my criteria. Most I never reported. The Marine Guards, the State Department security officer, and consular officials did their best to keep them from overwhelming me. But I'd have to check them all, directly or indirectly. Simple questions revealing the essentials while maintaining cover quickly separated the dross from the gold. Separating fool's gold from the real thing, however, could take hours.

A look in my hand mirror before long debriefings would ensure I'd not left bits of kebab in my teeth. It also reminded me of the silly training at the Farm.

"We're in Tabriz. Not too far from where I live. Tonight you'll sleep on a bed. You're tired of my truck, I think?" Hosein asked, backing it into place.

"I love your truck," I answered.

Hosein's smile was cut by a hard turning of the wheel. I fell awkwardly over the passenger seat to get a better look. There were around thirty men in the lot, gathered in groups of threes and fours. Over half were men with mustaches and no beards.

"Are they mostly Iranians, or Turks?" In Hosein's side-view mirror I could see a semi's Turkish license plate.

"You think every man who doesn't have a beard is a Turk?" Hosein jerked up the parking brake.

"No, but they seem more Turkish. Their frowns are deeper in their skin. Perhaps it's just the Azari look."

"They're Turks," Hosein shot back. "Most of the Turkish drivers stop in Tabriz before going to Tehran. They have more work than we do. More trade coming than going. But more and more Iranians don't wear beards, to show their hatred for the clerics. There's nothing in Islamic law that makes you wear a beard, you know."

Islamic law encourages, though does not command, men to grow beards. The Prophet Muhammad wore a beard; a good Muslim *should* follow the Prophet's practice. The *Shar'iat*, with its shaded areas between right and wrong, allows Muslim men, and to a lesser degree women, considerable moral maneuvering room. Something may be "encouraged but not compelled" or "scorned but permitted."

"Iranian truck drivers don't want to be seen as Iranian or confused with Turkish fundamentalists?" I asked.

Hosein was smiling again. He liked it when I needled him. "It's not good to be an Iranian in Turkey. They don't take you seriously when you have a beard."

"You have a beard."

"They know I'm a 'Turk.' They leave me alone." Hosein mixed pride with pity whenever he said "Turk." He reached across my knees to the glove compartment and pulled out a hammer. "Iranian officials cause me more problems. I bribe Turks occasionally, Iranians all the time. When it comes to money, *akhunds* don't care about beards."

"You'd look like a Turk if you shaved," I said, shutting the compartment Hosein had left open on my knee.

"You're not my friend," Hosein snorted. "Besides, I don't like to shave when I'm on the road."

In Turkey, almost all the Iranian visa applicants had shaved. Little cuts and neck rashes suggested they did so only to visit the consulate. A clean appearance, they were sure, would help their chances. Of course, it did just the opposite. If you were an Iranian applicant, your chances were better if you didn't try to please. You wanted to look prosperous but traditional, as though you couldn't survive culturally outside Iran. Only Stateside family pressure had forced you to apply for a tourist visa. Under no circumstances would you stay in the United States a long time.

Hosein killed the engine and got out of the truck. I caught myself again in the side-view mirror. Not Iranian, not Turk, not American; no longer exhausted, but still scared. I jumped down onto the running board and took a long look around. The truck next to ours was empty. Just past it, the lot became a road, and behind the road, short, square concrete and beige brick apartment buildings blocked my view. In front, trucks, Turks, and Iranians. Behind them, more concrete buildings and open flat ground running into a village of one-story flat-roofed houses. Behind them, snow-streaked yellow-tinged brown foothills and burnished mountains.

I hit the ground and dropped. Snow barely stuck to the dirt and gravel. I looked under the truck: on one side, the feet of several men two trucks down, on the other, Hosein's boots and pants legs, the wheels of two other trucks, and then open ground.

I walked to the rear. Dented and dirty old cars were parked on the road. A dusting of snow covered their roofs and windows. Just across the road were three middle-aged women wearing raincoats and dark, heavy head scarves. They were carrying plastic garbage bags. I stared at them. They stared back.

In Turkey, I'd learned that even peasant Iranian women could look intensely at a man. Of course, Iranian women seeking visas to the United States would want to grab my attention. But, visas aside, Iranian women weren't timid with their eyes.

"Help me with the door," Hosein requested from behind. I grabbed the opened door, he jumped in, and I looked back. They'd passed me. Amply hipped, they wore their raincoats tight around their rears.

Since Hosein was still buried in the truck and didn't want help, I walked. Hosein had warned me there were always *Basij* and Revolutionary Guards in the neighborhood. They'd grown up here. And ever since the revolution began to fail, and neighbors started switching sides, they worked here, monitoring and occasionally squelching the poor.

As I walked, I kept turning. If I'd been on a surveillance-detection run, I would have failed miserably. I kept rubbernecking, half-turning to the side, looking between the trucks, occasionally twisting 180 degrees to see the empty street behind. I was determined to walk the periphery of the truck park without Hosein. My clothes fit in; only my face and gait could give me away. There was no crowd, no constant press of Third World flesh and noise. If someone approached, I'd see him. If someone spoke to me, eventually I'd understand. Persians were kind to strangers, I told myself.

And Hosein had promised me Azaris wouldn't stick. They or I could start a conversation and I could walk away whenever I wanted.

Proper Persians might hang interminably, but Azaris grant more private space. A residue, perhaps, of once being the Turkish ruling race.

The women disappeared behind a building. A few leafless trees along the streets caught my eye, an attempt to break the array of concrete and frozen ground. Sadly, the trees seemed short-lived: eventually, someone would remember to come and cut them down.

Again, I searched for American parallels: the cityscape was too barren, the apartment-building concrete too cracked and cold. American urban squalor is dirty, dense, busy, and broken—cutting-edge modern. Tabriz's poverty is the back side of modernity. These buildings were never pretty and the streets never well paved. There had never been any charm; the quaintness of century-old peasants, artisans, and landed aristocrats had given way long ago. Mollahs, no less than Pahlavi shahs, had to be modern. Too many people, too little time, too many earthquakes, and too much oil for an aesthetic sense to survive. Also, Tabriz had been occupied by the Soviets during World War II—aesthetically always a bad influence.

The neighborhood wasn't despicably poor. There were packed-earth sidewalks, planned streets, and cars. The buildings had TV antennas and glassed windows, and the streets a few lights. Despite the constant traffic, you could breathe the air and there was little garbage on the ground. Truck, automobile, and electronics-parts stores, two teahouses, and a one-room grocery store, with cans and big white plastic bottles lining the walls, were nearby. A few businesses used lighted plastic advertising signs, evidence that commerce was worth higher electric bills. With the mountains looming, I imagined Tabriz a declining mining town.

Two men, one of them wearing a bright red bandanna folded into a low-rising turban, pushed a cart full of knotted gunnysacks. His headgear, the advertising signs, and the wildly painted trucks bore the only man-made colors around. I wanted to keep walking until I found swaths of color—some trace of medieval splendor that had survived Tabriz's innumerable earthquakes, invasions, modernization, and revolutionary mollahs. I wanted to find the Citadel and pick up a ceramic fragment of Ilkhanid rule, the rule of the Persianized Mongols who rivaled the Safavids in their love of beauty. I wanted to see the Quri Chay River traversing Tabriz. In the city, did it run blue, green, yellow, or brown? And I wanted to enter one of the teahouses and see what would happen.

Suddenly I turned. Hosein was behind me with a man. He was short, balding, with more gray stubble on his face than hair on his head. He wore green army pants and a dark-gray cardigan down to his knees.

"My friend Fazel wants to meet you."

The old man was smiling, revealing yellow-stained teeth and a couple of gaps. "Welcome! Welcome! Welcome!" he said in Persian. "I'm very sorry you were mistreated. Please have tea with me. I've not had tea with an American in years."

I wanted to kill Hosein. This wasn't the roadside. Tea with one could be tea with six. Here we had neither anonymity nor privacy. I walked toward them, praying again Hosein knew what he was doing.

"Fazel sometimes looks over the trucks here. I've been drinking his tea since childhood. It's the worst tea in Iran." Hosein had the hammer tucked under his arm.

"Please come. It's cold and the tea is ready. We can drink and Hosein can stay in his truck." The old man beckoned me slightly with his hands.

"Your shack is warmer than my truck, and your tea is, as you know, better than mine. I ask pardon," Hosein said to his friend.

The old man snorted.

Hosein should have told me about Fazel, as he should have told me about Hamid. But the joke was on me—that's what it's like to be an "agent." Your case officer tells you only what he wants. And if you need him more than he needs you, that's too bad. In the espionage manual, that's the ideal CO-agent relationship.

"Your tea must be better than his," I said as I walked past Hosein.

"What Persian! By God's blessing, an American who speaks Persian like a nightingale!" the old man answered, flattering me fulsomely like all Persians do. He was Azari. I heard the Turkish shortening of long Persian vowels.

We headed back through the truck lot toward a small concrete building with a window and a door. The old man and Hosein kept talking.

Fazel's hut was on the back side of the building, tin-roofed and with a dirt floor. Two metal chairs, a few plastic crates, and a knee-high gas bottle with a small circular grill rammed on its nose. On the grill, a silver-metal teapot spewed water and steam.

Fazel immediately gave me his cushioned chair and handed another, cushionless, to Hosein. He sat down on a plastic crate. Quickly preparing the tea, he served me, ignoring Hosein, who was trying to force him to sit on a chair. Immediately I felt guilty for not doing the same.

"The tea is delicious," I said, eyeing Khomeini's photo on the wall. In the Middle East, rulers' pictures are everywhere. Sometimes it's an expression of admiration bordering on love; more often, it's like an evil-eye amulet hung above a door or a baby's crib. More awe and self-interest than affection. But the Imam was different from other Muslim rulers. He had transcended earthly norms, becoming an expression, however perverse, of Persian glory. I knew for a fact that Iranians could loathe the clergy, love Khomeini, and spy for the CIA.

The picture was countered on the opposite wall by a glass-framed Persian miniature depicting a bow-and-arrow nobleman killing a lion. In Istanbul, thankful Iranians had given me dozens of these mass-produced fluorescent-color miniatures. I'd kept a couple, put a few on the walk-in room walls, given a few to Turks, and slid the others under my bed.

"No, no, it's not very good." Fazel probably thought the tea superb, but Persians can't take compliments, at least not the first time around.

"No, no, it's very good," I insisted as Hosein grinned. Fazel's tea had a distinctly sharp, metallic taste, perhaps coming from his tinny teapot. Tea from a samovar would have been better.

"No, no, it's not good. If you come to my home, I'll make better."

"That's very kind," I answered, looking at Hosein for a sign.

"Do you want to come tomorrow?"

Still nothing from Hosein indicating yes or no. I'd never been a master of polite Persian chitchat. I knew many of the obligatory polite phrases. "May your shadow not be shortened" was my favorite, a polite alternative to "Goodbye, I have to go."

In Turkey, I'd regularly violated rules of etiquette, though I was always quickly forgiven. My old Persian instructor Shahpur had suggested I say yes to everything and then do as I pleased. A dodge unfortunately not open to an American spy. Against unending entreaties, I usually fell back on *inshallah*, "If God wills," a polite way of saying yes and meaning no.

"We have to leave for Tehran tomorrow. I have work, and he must catch a plane," Hosein mercifully interjected.

"Please, I beg you, you can come to my house tonight," requested Fazel again. Three requests are the usual minimum in Persian.

"We can't, uncle. We have a dinner with a friend."

Amu. I didn't know whether the Persian for "uncle" could only be used with a blood relative.

"Thank you for the invitation," I added quickly. "Next time in Tabriz, *inshallah*."

"I won't last another twenty years," said Fazel, offering me more tea.

"It could be a year," I answered, handing him my empty glass.

"It could be anytime you wanted," he continued, pouring me my tea. "You know America can bring the mollahs down."

I couldn't tell whether his statement was an appeal, a reproach, or a setup. Hosein could respect America, Fazel could loathe it, and I might not detect the slightest animosity between them or toward me.

"Should America topple the clerics?" I asked, hoping he'd say yes, I'd agree, and we'd head toward Hosein's home or the Citadel.

"Don't America and the clergy work hand in hand?" Again Hosein's question caught me off guard. Did he really believe all the preposterous U.S.–clerical conspiracies? Or did he believe them only on Sundays, Tuesdays, and Thursdays? Whatever: his understanding was obviously fluid enough to protectively encompass me.

"Do you really think Khameneh'i and President Clinton are friends?" I asked.

"Do you really think the mollahs could beat America?" he countered. A man passed in front of the hut, looked in, said hello, and slowly walked away. Talk about politics among Iranians and you draw a crowd.

"Didn't America put the Shah in power, and Khomeini overthrew the Shah," I replied.

"Khomeini was better against the Russians," Fazel interjected. "I remember listening to American radio during the revolution. They always talked about Khomeini and Islam scaring the Russians."

More likely it was the BBC. Iranians listened to the Persian service of Voice of America after the revolution, not before. The VOA didn't restore its Persian service, eliminated in October 1960, until after Khomeini had come to power. The BBC had been king, and Radio Israel was next in line. But differentiating between VOA, the BBC, and Radio Israel was niggardly. They were all part of the cabal.

And Fazel was right: the BBC had been sympathetic to the revolution. Good liberals couldn't like the Shah. The BBC in particular gave generous coverage to the opposition. Khomeini's voice via British airwaves must have seemed to Persians like the voice of God.

"Do you want America to overthrow the mollahs? Shouldn't Iranians remove their own rulers?" I asked, hoping Hosein would let him finish.

"God knows what to do with the mollahs," said Fazel. "The Iranian people are too tired to fight them. But America could easily get rid of them."

I agreed and let the subject die. I was pretty sure Fazel had supported Khomeini. He'd not given his soul as Hosein had done: he was too old in 1978–79. But when the revolutionary bandwagon started to roll, when Persians started hearing Khomeini on the BBC and realizing the *Shahanshah*, the King of Kings, had lost control, Fazel had joined in.

Now he probably didn't like living with failure. As a Persian, of course, he didn't have to. America Almighty could take the blame. Eventually, *inshallah*, the CIA would intervene and make amends for 1953. Persian life is a constant irony, another thing Iranians and Americans don't have in common.

Hosein and I left Fazel in the hut after one more tea. We talked a little about Hosein's father, Fazel's closest friend. Fazel had gotten

Hosein into trucking. I had a suspicion he'd helped him start hauling Iranians over the border. Iranians talk constantly on the phone:
I also suspected Fazel had got word of my coming. Fortunately, Iran
has direct dialing abroad and the Ministry of Intelligence probably
has neither the inclination nor the computers to monitor peasants'
calls between Turkey and Iran. An agent can't and shouldn't know
all the details of his case, I reminded myself. He must put his trust
in his C/O. He mustn't look back or second-guess.

Hosein's home in the city was a long walk from Fazel's shack. It
wasn't pretty. Except for the occasional factory, smoldering trash
dump, and used-car junk heap, squat brick houses and two- and
three-story apartment buildings covered most of the land. The older,
one- and two-story houses were built of smoothed, dirty ocher bricks
and had walled enclosures usually to one side. The newer structures,
mostly brick, not concrete, didn't have enclosures; a few of them
had stretched black plastic instead of glass for windows. Almost all
of them had TV antennas. Given the concrete highway poles with
fat and skinny wires, it appeared Tabriz's exurbs were electrified and
hooked up for telephones.

Dirt roads with deep frozen ruts snaked through this endless peasant agglomeration, which paralleled the two-lane highway we were
following into town. When it rained, these roads probably ate cars,
and even trucks. Despite the cold, several packs of little boys played
behind the buildings or ran across the highway in front of oncoming
trucks. Dust and fumes from the heavy traffic kept getting into my
eyes and mouth. I was jealous of a chador-clad woman walking by.
With the chador's black fabric over her nose and mouth, she
screened out the larger road particles without raising a hand. She
looked a little odd, however, wearing a heavy wool coat over her
chador. With a thick scarf also wrapped around her head, she looked
like a winter-proof mummy. A man with a tethered line of goats
passed us on the opposite side: my first Persian caravan. Behind him,
a beardless young man wearing a dark ski cap topped with a sky-
blue ball pushed a dilapidated wheelbarrow full of used automobile
batteries.

When Tabriz's brutal summers sizzled and baked everyone and
everything, this area often smelled awful, Hosein warned. The un-

derground sewage system and septic tanks needed to be expanded to handle the peasants continuously arriving from the countryside. In the winter, no one was going to pickax a new toilet into the ground.

As we got closer to town, concrete and cinderblock gradually superseded brick and packed earth, and cars outnumbered trucks. We were in Hosein's side of town, a low-end merchant district where one-room shops occupied the ground floors of low-rise apartment buildings. I couldn't see any neighborhood commercial themes, as you often can in the Middle East, where one or two types of trade dominate a neighborhood, reflecting centuries-old family, ethnic, or religious specialization. Hosein said I could find little communities of merchants toward the center of town, and of course in the Bazaar, where the residue of medieval commercial guilds and family specialization tended to put carpets, copper ware, and jewelry in different places. Hosein's neighborhood was too modern for this. An electronics-parts store with Sony, JVC, and Panasonic English signs was located next to a cobbler with a sidewalk display of dusty, crinkled leather shoes, and a butcher with skin-stripped mutton hanging from blood-speckled white walls.

As soon as we'd left the highway and started walking through Hosein's neighborhood, I noticed people looking at me. I was sure they knew I was a foreigner. I was too tall to hide. So I just kept moving, returning the stares of some, dropping my eyes with others. When Hosein unexpectedly stopped at a side-street flea market to buy socks, I almost yelled at him. I couldn't believe he was so laid-back with my security. I couldn't believe he'd immediately started to converse with a sock-and-underwear vendor about the hated mollahs. Then another man joined in cursing the clergy. I stood aside, not wanting to be dragged in. The sock vendor eyed me but didn't say a word. As they were speaking Azari, I couldn't catch much, but what I caught wasn't kind. I kept glancing over my shoulders, trying to see whether anyone was looking at them or me. Several men and women were moving between the covered stands. A few glanced at me but turned away when I glanced back. Two chador-clad young women close by stared at me, turning their eyes away only as they passed. Other vendors looked up at me several times. But no one was approaching. No street urchins wanting bonbons, or older men with "Hey, Meester, change money cheeep." Still, I was scared, my senses so taut they were almost useless. I couldn't believe Hosein had stopped without asking my opinion, or at least giving me warning.

While Hosein and the other men animatedly lambasted the clergy, and probably everyone and everything else, I imagined *Basijis* or Revolutionary Guards coming to drag us all off. Two more men had joined the conversation. Soon we would have an anticleric crowd. I feared someone would finally ask the foreign-looking, bearded, tall fellow in the army coat what he thought, and then I'd have to say something in Persian. In the open, with dozens of ears about, I'd surely become the center of attention. I took a few more steps away from the stand, hoping to catch Hosein's eye. Looking forward and moving backward, I bumped into a chador-clad old woman. I blurted *"Bebakhshid!"* ("Excuse me!") and stepped out of her way. She glanced at me, said nothing, and walked off.

The collision caught Hosein's attention. The five-man conversation, which Hosein halted briefly to haggle over sock prices, was still raging. I jerked my head and Hosein walked over, pivoting to continue bickering about a pair of socks in his hands. Barely checking my anger, I asked Hosein whether it was wise to publicly trash the mollahs with me in tow. "Everybody hates them," he said. "You can't get arrested for cursing the mollahs in the streets. Everybody would be in jail."

I believed him, but I still didn't like him cleric-bashing with me around. I didn't like standing still in a crowd. Next time, I might bump into an off-duty Guardsman bitching about the clergy. Hosein saw the fear and anger in my face and said he'd be more careful next time. As soon as we started walking, I regretted my words to him. I'd overreacted: he wouldn't look me in the eyes. He had more on the line than I did, I reminded myself. My nerves were so fried I couldn't control myself.

A four-wheel-drive Land Cruiser with armed security forces turned a corner a few blocks from Hosein's apartment. I didn't see it, but Hosein did and pointed it out. He smilingly assured me we'd see others, possibly when we went downtown to the Citadel and the Bazaar.

I'd stopped thinking about the fourteenth century and Mongol rule. You don't think about history and beauty when you're scared; you think in small increments, a hundred feet away. And you keep looking behind you.

6 HAZRA AND THE BAZAAR

She opened the door before Hosein could unlock it. Partly covered by a blue scarf, her wavy black hair fell over her forehead, temples, and in front of her ears. Her calf-length, long-sleeved nightshirt didn't hide her form. Her face was her brother's: long, high-cheekboned, with thick brows straddling brown eyes and an aquiline nose. Given her good looks, I was surprised she was still unmarried in her late twenties.

Hazra was smiling at both of us. I was sure she'd seen me through the peephole and chosen not to put on more clothing. The suspicions Hamid had started and Fazel increased, Hazra confirmed. She knew I was a "family friend" because her older brother had telephoned. My reflexes started twitching again even though the odds were all in my favor. I kept reminding myself of all the operational errors I'd made.

Treasonous case officers and general C/O incompetence aside, nothing has undone so many agents as telephones. I didn't warn Hosein about telephoning. I didn't want to offend him before we even reached Bazargan. He knew the rules about the border better than I, and if calling was dangerous, he surely knew it. Also, Hosein didn't have an intelligence profile, the type that provokes the Ministries of Intelligence or Interior to tap a line. He'd never been politically involved. He hated the mollahs, but, as I was learning, so did everybody in Iran. He regularly crossed the border, but so did thousands of other Iranians for work and pleasure.

Persians don't have a police-state temperament or American technology, I reminded myself. They don't bug everybody under the sun. Technically unable to carry out effective random microwave intercepts against a direct-dialing system, the security services would have physically to tap Hosein's line. And hard taps mean you're already suspect. If Iranian Intelligence had known about Hosein's nefarious deeds, he'd be dead or in prison. No matter how I twisted it, the worst-case scenarios didn't make sense. Being at the wrong place at the wrong time, not technology and loose lips, would be my undoing.

I'd just read too many intercepts in the Agency, listened to too many National Security Agency officials brag about international eavesdropping. Hosein wasn't stupid. Whatever he said, it couldn't have been much. And I couldn't blame him. Without parents and other siblings, the two of them, after all, had to keep each other informed.

I smiled back at Hazra, said "Good morning," and tried not to stare. After two days in a box, meals and tea with unshaven men, and the expectation of seeing females only in coats, scarves, and chadors, I couldn't stop looking at her hair.

After hugging Hosein, she asked whether I'd like tea or coffee, a rarely offered drink in Iran except among Armenians, and disappeared under an arched doorway. I could smell unrefrigerated food. The apartment was larger than I'd expected. The living room was American-sized, with at least one large adjoining room. The furnishings were modest: a linoleum-and-metal dining table, four wooden chairs, and three partly rolled futons. Cheap carpets and kilims chaotically covered the floor. Two colorful miniatures and a black-and-white photo hung on unpainted plastered walls. A television with immense rabbit ears sat on a chair in a corner; under the chair was a wooden backgammon box. Near a window, a Qur'an lay open on a stand.

The two had always been together, Hosein told me. Only once had they parted, when Hazra had gone to university in Tehran. She'd hated her studies and the uncle who'd given her a home. After three years, she returned to Tabriz and never finished her degree.

I didn't know if Hazra had numerous aunts and uncles offering advice about when and whom she should marry. Without a mother or a father, Hosein, the aunts, and the uncles would be the ones to worry about a single woman in the family. But Iran isn't Pakistan: generally, women aren't forced into marriage. They can be picky and take their time. When they do take their time, of course, they become like their Western sisters, constantly worried they won't find a man with a good job before they're too old. The women I'd met outside of Iran who spoke to me about such matters described even headstrong Persian women as wanting their family's help in finding a mate. A loveless marriage was awful; a life without children worse. In Iran, childless women are nothing.

So far as her brother knew, Hazra had loved a man only once, a cousin three or four times removed. He'd died in one of the 1987 offensives, Iran's bloody last pushes against the Iraqi lines. Besides Hosein, he'd been the only single man in the family she liked.

Though men and women can mix at university—higher education in clerical Iran is divided within classrooms but not by school—opportunities for romantic mingling are rare. Agents of the morals police are everywhere. Conversations are rarely private enough to allow students maneuvering room. You can't reinforce your words and glances by holding hands. Unless you come from the upper classes, who have the time, money, and walled houses to entertain extended family and friends, courtship is a rudimentary affair. Dating simply doesn't happen.

Hazra reminded me of the good-looking single Iranian women I'd often seen in Turkey. I'd been surprised by the number who'd come alone to try their luck at the visa windows. Most were somewhat secularized and middle class, but many were poor and wore raincoats and chadors. At home, they'd not been chattels. Shi'ism has a historical feminine birthright: Fatimah, the Prophet Muhammad's daughter and Ali's wife, sanctified Ali's line. Ever since, Shi'ism has always given a little more to women than Sunni Islam. Nevertheless,

I was meeting hundreds of ordinary women running from their homes.

They were dreaming. The Western ideas of happiness and progress, which have no real Islamic parallels, had taken root. Despite all the propaganda depicting the United States as Sodom and Gomorrah, these women believed they'd get a better deal there. Many had marched in the streets screaming "Death to America!" just a few years before, believing that only Islam protected female virtue and the poor. As happened to their brothers, Good and Evil later flipped in their minds.

The revolution's unfulfilled promises were now sending them abroad. They worried about finding good Muslim men in the United States. They worried that non-Muslim men wouldn't find them appealing. They worried about jobs. Most of all, they worried about the visa window. They practiced their stories constantly and asked advice from applicants who'd gone and failed. They prayed they'd get into the queue of *siyahpust-e kucheek*, "the little black man," the U.S. consular officer whose kindness was known throughout Istanbul's Little Tehran. They dreaded *Agha-ye Gardankoloft*, "Mr. Thickneck," the six-foot-six ex-Marine who loved informing Iranians they'd never see the States except in the movies.

Each year I'd visited a few of these women's hotel rooms to see where and how they lived. They let me enter, since I was *the Angel*. Most stayed near the consulate, in Beyoğlu and Taksim flophouses often used by neighborhood bar whores. If they didn't get snared by a Turkish consulate security guard or a policeman who promised visas for sex, they made it to the consular windows with their dignity intact. With two I interceded, stretched the rules, and got them visas. They were no different from all the others, but I'd grown weak listening to their stories.

I couldn't make up my mind what the Islamic revolution had done to women. Those openly challenging the dress codes and sexual segregation were harassed and jailed. Romance, lipstick, and nail polish were driven indoors. Evin prison had a special section for women who misbehaved "morally." Wives wanting to travel abroad without their husband's permission often found themselves interrogated at Tehran's airport or border crossings. Divorce had again become a male prerogative, though wives usually could win their freedom informally. However, under Islamic law, children always belong to their fathers. Female child marriage, a practice sanctified by the Prophet Muhammad in the Qur'an, was once again legal, yet I doubted many Iranians outside of the clergy approved of it.

The revolution hadn't eliminated the traditional decency that Persian men have often shown their women, or the Western principle of sexual equality the Pahlavi shahs first imported into Iran. Khomeini railed against Mohammad Reza Shah in 1963 for giving women the right to vote in local elections, but in 1979, after taking power, he didn't challenge women's voting rights. The mollahs didn't drive women from the universities, nor, as in Saudi Arabia, from their cars. Iran still had women's volleyball, Ping-Pong, crew, and track-and-field teams. There were female doctors, actresses, artists, writers, parliamentarians, diplomats, and central bank officials. Of course, they all wore chadors.

The Iranian revolution covered women's heads but put assault rifles on their shoulders. This tension hadn't existed before. SAVAK, the Shah's secret police, occasionally tortured women; the revolutionaries shot hundreds of female "counterrevolutionary terrorists" by firing squad. Before Khomeini, armed women had never marched through the streets yelling "Death to America!"

In 1977, a middle-class Tehrani woman could wear a miniskirt, but she respected most conventions. With her husband living well off Iran's oil wealth, she didn't work. Her children were her first love and her primary responsibility. In general, modern Iranian women had been like the female elites of most Westernized Middle Eastern states: pretty, made-up, and dedicated to socializing and family life.

The revolution took away female beauty and replaced it with female virtue. Every man's concern with *namus* became a matter of national defense. Persian women weren't blind to this frenzied attention. It concentrated their minds. You can't give women automatic weapons and tell them to shut up. The leftism of the Iranian revolution, the militant belief in the masses and popular struggle, is incompatible with *namus* and the second-class status envisioned for women by Islamic law; sexual restraint and a well-ordered family fray when women are taught the glories of martyrdom.

I'd had the impression that Iranian women generally didn't make good martyrs—women rarely worship death and violence as fervently as men do. However, the psychology of martyrdom, so vivid in the early revolutionary years, and the ideology of popular struggle had their effect. A new woman had been born, and she was neither what the Shah nor what Khomeini had planned. Perhaps even more than her brothers, she was the anvil on which Islam's future would be hammered out.

Hazra came back with coffee and immediately suggested food. Before I could answer, Hosein informed us we wouldn't be staying for lunch. He had to see a money changer at the Bazaar and we'd eat on the way. In Azari, Hazra said something harsh. I caught the drift: she'd already prepared a meal.

With Hosein always on the road, Hazra managed the family's money. She, like most Iranian women, controlled the home. She usually changed Hosein's dollars and Turkish lira into Iranian riyals. Hosein never kept much Persian money—given the 100 percent inflation rate, no sensible Iranian did. So changing money took a lot of Hazra's time. Regardless of the food, she didn't want to go to the Bazaar. I didn't either. This was the first time in two days I'd been warm and uncramped. In the streets, we'd seen two security vehicles and armed young men in disheveled blue uniforms. Hosein's remark that security wasn't heavy did little to diminish my concern. The Bazaar would be there tomorrow. I wanted to sit on a futon and have Hazra bring me food. I wanted Hosein to slow down and check out our excursions in advance.

Hazra was protesting in Azari again, but this time I couldn't catch the theme. In Turkey, when I'd asked Hosein if he was married, he talked about his sister. I thought seriously then about canceling the journey. I hadn't wanted someone with a wife and kids, or a sister attached at the navel. I didn't want women gossiping.

When you're a case officer you don't hesitate to recruit a man because he's married. If an agent signs on, then he's responsible for his family. You could, of course, tell an agent not to tell his wife about his extracurricular activities. The fewer people who know, the better. I'd never intruded between a husband and wife, however, as I never thought the likely gain was greater than the loss. Wives are touchy subjects, especially in the Middle East. Also, a wife can aid her agent-husband, allowing him to be in two places at the same time. With an accomplice-wife, however, the general rule of espionage—wives and children of caught spies are left alone—is cast aside.

The finest agent I ever had walked away because he realized he'd jeopardized his family. At first, of course, I'd convinced him he hadn't. But when I "passed" him to another C/O, reality arrived. Turnovers often break the espionage bubble, where both agent and officer believe they're greater than they are. He refused the handoff and went back to Iran. A few months later, I received a mailed apology attached to a photo of his daughter, with whom I'd played while explaining to her father how I'd improve their lives. After the failed turnover, I waited. I knew where he would be during the next few months. I assessed him as an untapped adrenaline addict who needed another push. This time there wouldn't be a turnover to an unknown case officer. This time I'd keep control.

Fortunately, I miscalculated his comings and goings. He took a little longer than I'd planned. By the time he exited Iran, right and wrong had flipped in my mind, and I no longer could send an agent into harm's way. Patriotism could no longer excuse Langley's rampant incompetence. I could live without the intense pleasure of a recruitment adrenaline rush. When a friend called and told me he'd been spotted, I took my time. When I told my boss in Istanbul I was ready to catch a flight, he was gone. A few months later, I received another note in the mail. Somehow my Iranian guessed what had happened. He thanked me for not coming: the second time around, I might have convinced him to put his family into danger.

Hosein and Hazra went back into Persian. I couldn't tell who'd won until Hosein told me again we were eating out. He would first, however, go without me to the Bazaar. I knew I should make a fuss about his going and our staying. But he was wrong. A Persian host should never make a guest wait for a meal. A good guardian shouldn't put his charge into danger.

As soon as he was gone, Hazra asked me if I was hungry. Within minutes, food was on the table. Hosein might be angry, but neither one of us cared. I quickly started on the cucumbers, onions, and yogurt.

"Did you learn Persian in Iran? I've never met an American, let alone one who speaks my language."

Hazra's physical informality distracted me. Slouching forward in her chair, an elbow on a raised knee, collapsing white gym socks beneath a bit of leg, hands folded just above her chest, the loose nightshirt pulled tight from shoulders to hips, she appeared American—except for the scarf on her head.

According to Arabian custom, an unmarried man and woman alone in the same room inevitably leads to sex. Thus, a man may kill any male nonrelative caught alone with his family's unmarried women—the Holy Law's prohibition of such killings guiltlessly ignored. The *Shar'iat* requirement of four witnesses to unlawful sexual intercourse is too much to ask for when your sister is in question.

I didn't think the same attitude now prevailed in Persia, even among the poor. Still, I wondered what a friend or relative would think if they unexpectedly knocked on the door. Iranians aren't Saudis. *Namus* didn't mean that men and women indoors couldn't innocently flirt. However, I didn't know whether such leniency applied to a black-clad foreigner.

"This is the first time I've been in Iran," I answered. "I wanted to come in 1979, but the hostages had been taken."

I hadn't heard Hosein call me an American. In Persian or Azari, I wouldn't have missed it. I was waiting for it in the introduction. She'd known I was an American family friend before I arrived. Talking to Hazra, I realized there could be a network from Tabriz to Tehran aware of an American en route. Was I an American denied exit at the Turkish-Iranian border town of Bazargan, or an American hauled over the frontier in a box? In Iran, two weeks is a long time to keep a secret.

I should have asked Hosein about Hazra at the beginning, absolutely no later than the roadside dinner with Hamid. I recalled I'd often got messages from agents' families, even friends, out of the blue. I should have expected no less from Hosein. Hazra's calmness belied the problem's gravity. If she knew what Hosein had done, then she, too, was at risk.

Or was she? If she'd frequently been involved in Hosein's cross-border trade, then the two of them must have worked out a story. *I was a tourist on the way back to Tehran.* For Hazra's own good, Hosein shouldn't have told her more. But if he'd told her that, then there was no reason why she shouldn't tell others. I kept knocking back and forth the possibilities while staring at Hazra, so generous and calm.

"Did you study Persian at university?" she asked, after running to the kitchen for a bottle of Iranian Coca-Cola, which tasted sweeter than the American version.

"Yes. A couple of Persian girlfriends also helped."

Too quick, but I wasn't going to spend a week in Tabriz. We'd soon be on the road to Ardabil, unless it snowed. On our return, we planned only a pit stop. I didn't know how much time I'd have with her. If she'd talk about men and women with a stranger, she'd talk about anything. Hosein had done the hard part by letting me in.

I was no longer *the Angel*, but being American was always at least half of *the Angel*'s charm. At least, she might tell me more about why her brother took me across the border and how many in the family knew I'd not started in Tehran.

Persians build high walls around their homes because they talk too much. Unfortunately, I got a big smile and nothing more.

"Why did you study Persian?"

How many times had I been asked this question? I always gave the same response: "Persian is a beautiful language." True, of course. Push the scan button on a shortwave and find the sweetest voices; Persian usually wins. But I'd not fallen in love with Iran because of its language and literature. I fell victim to its history, its hellish twists and turns.

"Don't Americans hate Iran?"

"Some do. Some don't. In any case, Persian *is* a beautiful language," I said, trying to avoid a discussion of whether America hates Iran.

Before I'd finished answering, Hazra was back in the kitchen.

"Did you study the mollahs when you were in school?" she asked from around the corner.

"Of course. You can't study Iran without studying the *akhunds*."

I heard a chuckle. A minute later, still grinning, she came out with a plate of *kofteh*. With the first bite, I tasted saffron. I hadn't tasted it in years. It costs less in the Middle East than in the West; still, it costs a fortune. She must have known a "friend" was coming to dinner.

"So you can tell me why America supports the mollahs."

Her intonation told me it wasn't a question. Although I could understand how Hosein, Hazra, and probably millions of Iranians spliced together the conspiracy of U.S.–clerical ties—gluing those parts together was Politics 101 in the Iranian mind—I was nonetheless jarred whenever I heard it. A blind man could see the hatred between Washington and Tehran. Secretary of State Warren Christopher, in public a cold fish, glowed when he attacked the clerics. And Ali Khameneh'i, Khomeini's humorless successor, grinningly derided Christopher as *Agha-ye Karih ol-manzar*, "Mr. Ugly Face."

Most Iranians I knew saw the animosity. However, Persians rarely believe what they see. The truth is always *posht-e-pardeh*, hidden behind the curtains. And a happy Persian has always thought of someone else to blame his problems on. Also, sometimes, surprisingly, they aren't self-deceived. They *had* seen friends and foes change sides. Not many Iranians were surprised when President Reagan and CIA director William Casey sent a planeload of missiles to clerical Iran. Iran–Contra was, of course, an exception, not the rule, but explaining that to a Persian could take years.

"I think America hates the mollahs," I countered.

"In Iran, everyone hates them," she shot back. "Even some of the mollahs hate themselves."

Both of us laughed.

"Do Iranian women hate the mollahs more than men do?" I asked, hoping this time she'd drop her guard.

"Everyone hates them."

"But do you think women hate them more?" I asked again. Ask

the same question five different times with a Persian, with luck you get five different answers.

"I don't know. We all hate them."

"Why do *you* hate them?" The question was too sharp. However, Hazra had used saffron in her *kofteh*. I was her brother's guest. I had to be indulged. More importantly, she was as curious about me as I was about her.

"They've destroyed Iran."

"How? I've never visited Iran before."

"They ruined the revolution."

The words rang in my mind. In Istanbul, a consular officer had once asked an Iranian peasant what he thought of Khomeini's Republic. His identical words provoked an approving chant in the sea of applicants behind him. I'd sincerely hoped one of the Iranian consulate's spies was in the audience that day. Reluctantly, I had to ask the applicants to quiet down.

"But what exactly did they ruin?" I asked, hoping Hazra would give me a target.

"Everything."

"For example?"

"Everything," she said, raising her voice.

"Have they ruined Islam?"

"I don't think people believe like they used to. Every time a mollah says 'Islam,' I'm disgusted. Most people are. The most beautiful word is ugly in their mouths."

"Why? Because of the economy, defeat in war, the mollahs' corruption?" I asked, hoping she'd run with something.

"Yes, everything. Most people I know have two or three jobs. Many work until midnight. We fought for Islam, the oppressed, and . . ." Hazra nipped the sentence and averted her eyes.

"I'm not offended," I said. "You're doing me a kindness by being honest."

". . . against America and the Communists. We didn't fight for this," she went on, her eyes firmly on the table. "Many people believed that through the Imam and the Holy Qur'an we could hasten the coming of the Mahdi. Just looking at the Imam made us feel strong. Even my brother, who hated Khomeini, mourned his death."

"So it was the Imam's death—not the war, not the economy, not the corruption of the mollahs—that stopped the revolution and weakened Islam?"

She, not her brother, had been the family's revolutionary. Hosein, like most Iranians, had gone with the flow. She was different, an earlier convert and later repenter. She still had a revolutionary's vocabulary—and eyes.

"Yes," she answered.

"You believed in the Imam?"

"Yes. He and Islam were the same. I loved the public prayers where we were all brothers and sisters. The Shah divided Iranians. The Imam made us all a family."

"Yet you don't believe in the revolution now?"

"No."

"How do you feel about Khomeini?" I asked, wondering whether the question was even fair. Once Khomeini got into the blood, could he ever be expunged? Could a once-devout Catholic ever have his imagination, dreams, and sense of sin liberated from the confessional?

"I don't think about him anymore."

"When did you stop?"

Even with my most urgent walk-ins, I'd never grilled someone so quickly and crudely, never sliced into God before dessert. I was feeling like a case officer again. Allot three minutes for pleasantries and questions about the kids, then get straight to the debriefing notes and treason.

"I was at university," she answered, collecting dishes from the table.

"Was that before or after your cousin died in the war?"

Hazra's eyes opened wide and then receded. Perhaps I was betraying Hosein's trust. If Hosein had told me about her and the cousin, then we'd obviously got close. With strangers, Persians rarely gossip about their families. Now she would know that her brother and I had exchanged more than money.

"I'd stopped believing before."

"Because your brother stopped?"

"No," she answered, gutturalizing the Persian word for "no" a little louder than before.

"So why? Did you drop out of university because you no longer believed?"

The collapse of faith in women is always more intriguing than in men. Men slam into faith, and it in turn propels them. Even with assault-rifle training, Iranian women hadn't run across minefields into flaming oil pits. By the time their beloved men were buried, they'd missed the stench and slaughter. At mosques, women always pray or play with their children along the walls. A female Islamic radical always gains, expresses, and loses her faith at a distance from men. Again, I was trying to push backward my professor's theoretical question about females in heaven: how do Muslim women believe in God?

"No. I dropped out because I needed a job. Hosein had found one in Tabriz. I couldn't have found work with a literature degree."

"You weren't alone at university in your loss of faith?"

"I think most students didn't believe. Certainly, all my friends no longer thought of themselves as revolutionaries. After the Imam's death, I don't think we even knew what the revolution was. We definitely knew we were going to graduate and stay unemployed."

"Weren't there any radical students who continued to believe?"

"You didn't express your opinions openly to students you didn't trust. I had radical friends. Some were ex-*Basijis*. If you'd asked them, they would have said the Iranian revolution was going to liberate the Muslim world. Privately, all they wanted was money."

"The Imam wasn't corrupt, was he?" I asked, hoping to snap her Persian habit of viewing men as either good or evil, corrupt or pure.

"No. I don't think he ever touched money. I don't think he knew any pleasures. But most mollahs touch it. They, the Revolutionary Guards, the *Basij*, even the army are on the take. The mollahs always change riyals into dollars."

"Before Khomeini died, Iranians didn't worship money as much?" I asked, sensing the question wouldn't sting. Once friendly, Iranians—like Arabs but unlike Turks—love to rip themselves apart for the benefit of strangers.

"Iranians have always been corrupt. However, Khomeini reminded us there was more to life than money. Rafsanjani and Kha-meneh'i have taught us Khomeini was wrong."

The reverence fallen revolutionaries still gave to the Imam was perversely compelling. He'd tried to gut Persian culture of its ten-derness and joy and to bore Iranians out of their minds, yet good people still held him dear. Or at least they didn't curse his soul. Fan the spiritual wound left by Khomeini's death, and you could still get the ash to glow. Often, it was the only efficient way for a C/O to gauge an Iranian's proportions of friend versus foe.

"Where were you when Khomeini died?" I asked.

"In Tabriz, though I'd been in Tehran a week before, when we'd suspected he was finally dying."

"And Tabriz and Tehran were nervous?"

"No, not really. We knew the rumors about his approaching death were true, but I guess we didn't really believe them. Both cities were quiet. They stayed quiet until the funeral."

"Did you go to the funeral?"

"Hosein insisted on going. We spent nearly a month with my uncle in Tehran. Hosein thought something violent might happen. When nothing did, we came home."

I could easily understand why Hosein had gone to the burial. Even as a hater, he couldn't resist the Imam's pull. With Hazra with him, he wouldn't have got close. The seething mass of mourn-ers at its core was all male. And Hosein wouldn't have left Hazra alone in the crowd. I wondered if he'd got near to the Imam's corpse whether he would have kissed it or spit on it.

Whenever I remembered Khomeini's funeral, my memories went back to Istanbul. A Persian friend and I had got together to watch the obsequies, the most powerful, chaotic spectacle of modern times. Before turning on the TV, we toasted the Ayatollah into the ground, then we stared speechless, watching hundreds of thousands, perhaps millions, of Iranians moving in waves toward the grave. Those closest stampeded to touch the Imam's elevated body, nearly stripping off his shroud and overturning him. Millions of death-wish Iranians were in south Tehran's streets. Tearfully, my friend con-cluded the Ayatollah had irrevocably destroyed the Iranian mind.

But my friend had been too quick to judge. He'd lived in the

States too long. In Iran, first impressions are often misleading. Khomeini's most militant followers were writhing in mortal pain. The frenzied clawing of his corpse would bring no benediction. His charisma wouldn't pass to his son or to Khameneh'i, his successor. The immense mausoleum that had been built over Khomeini's grave, I'd been regularly told, was rarely more than a quarter full, even though it was a carpeted, roofed refuge from the sun, sand, and cold, which once a week offered free food. The riyal notes strewn near the tomb were sure signs of the Imam's fall from revolutionary grace. Religious Turks did the same thing for victorious Ottoman sultans they didn't even know by name—standard peasant tokens given to your average man-cum-saint.

The average Iranian wasn't even twenty when Khomeini died. His sense of history and patience was poor. Like his father, he needed a living, errorless man to ignite his soul.

Shi'ites, unlike Sunnis, believe ardently in perfection. An orthodox Sunni cleric looks askance at the faithful who liken the Prophet Muhammad to God. The Prophet, the best of all men, had his faults. Even revolutionary Sunni clerics were uncomfortable with Khomeini's impeccable pretensions.

Perhaps influenced by Christian doctrine or the East's penchant for merging the mundane and the divine, Shi'ites are tormented by their faults. They adore their Imams who have none. More than anything else, devout Shi'ites want to be pure. I'd never encountered a Sunni Muslim scared of a foreigner's touch. I'd met Iranian peasants, even diplomats and spies, who never extended their hands. According to the rules, a devout Shi'ite should wash himself after touching a non-Shi'ite, and if the outsider is non-Muslim, a Shi'ite should cleanse his hands especially well. Preferably, he shouldn't touch an infidel at all.

The drama every Iranian knows by heart is the *ta'ziya*, the passion play about the death of the caliph Ali's son, Hosein, the third Imam. He died on the sand plains of southern Iraq at Karbala in 680, a martyr for his family faith. He'd been abandoned, so the Shi'ite story goes, by most of his followers, who were unwilling to face death for spiritual rewards. Perfect men, like Hosein and his companions, held firm and went to heaven. Once a year, Iranians see themselves standing by "the prince of all martyrs." The rest of the year, they see themselves for what they are. For a Persian, atonement is a painful, inflammatory exercise.

When Khomeini died in 1989, Langley's analysts and case officers wondered whether Iranians might be ready to atone for their revolutionary excesses and moderate their international behavior. Not long after Khomeini's death, the Iran desk chief asked me whether I'd be interested in serving in a reopened Tehran station. Like Hosein, Langley was praying that, with the Devil dead, the revolution might disintegrate. In 1989, the CIA didn't consider Rafsanjani a "moderate" anymore—Iran–Contra had ended that—but with the Ayatollah buried, his government just might redefine itself. Rafsanjani kept saying he wanted the Shah's billions that Washington had kept when the embassy went down. Of course, the billions were never as many as the clerics claimed, and much of the frozen funds had already become compensation to U.S. companies burned in revolutionary Iran. Nevertheless, the mollahs truly believed Washington still had their billions, and clerical Iran was desperately short of cash. Rafsanjani and Khameneh'i just might compromise, so the theory went. Wise men in the Directorate of Operations thought it unlikely. Nevertheless, contemplating case officers roving again in Tehran was a thoroughly enjoyable exercise. The thought of walking among Tehran's wounded delighted me.

Yet I wondered whether the clandestine service could possibly send me to Tehran. The desk chief liked me, and (according to corridor gossip) I was still a Near East Division golden boy, but doubts were beginning to appear. I'd become progressively less of a team player. I'd accepted an onward assignment beyond Istanbul based on my wife's professional ambitions as well as my own. I no longer churned out quite so many cables. Rising in the Agency is a bit like rising in an army's officer corps: by the time you take command, your peers know you down to your underwear. The chances of opening an embassy and station in Iran within a year were thin. Five years would be a miracle, fifteen years a more plausible bet. The ruling clergy couldn't change its spots overnight.

"So one day you woke up and no longer believed in the revolution?" I asked, hoping Hazra would lift her eyes.

"I can't tell you when," she said impatiently. "I lost hope gradually. Khomeini always told us that material things didn't matter. We believed him. We didn't have much in our lives. Others were rich. They still are.

"Sometimes, I still go to the mosque for prayers. Hosein won't come with me. Except for the mollahs giving speeches, no one says brother and sister anymore."

"But you still believe in Islam?"

"I'm a Muslim. The mollahs betrayed God. I didn't."

"Do you believe the Holy Law is just?"

"Yes, though I don't know it well."

"But you no longer believe in Khomeini and the revolution. What's the difference?"

We looked at each other quietly, both of us listening to apartment and traffic noises. Women and children were stomping loudly down a stairwell. If the noise carried so clearly this way, it went the other way almost as well. Recoiling from the sound, I glanced toward the window and Hazra's Qur'an.

My first Arabic professor had introduced me to the Muslim Holy Book. He'd learned to chant it in Cairo. Fascinated by every word, always faithful to its cadence, he could easily convey a student from an ivied campus to crowded streets bowing to a muezzin's call. The Qur'an might not be the most beautiful Arabic ever written, but fourteen hundred years of constant recitation had certainly made it the most impassioned. Even perfectly secularized Muslims have a hard time gainsaying the Book. No comparable loyalty exists among fallen Christians and Jews for the recorded Word of God. Make a try at the Qur'an, memorize a few suras, know the differences between the Meccan and Medinan sections, and you can go far with Muslims, no matter how they have fallen. I searched my memory for a line to show Hazra my sympathies and concern.

Her voice brought me back from the window. "I didn't know much about our faith when I was young. Our family was conservative, but not religious. My mother and I went only a few times to a mosque before she died. She always thought mosques were for men, not women. And my father would never take me. He and Hosein rarely went.

"I discovered my faith through Khomeini. I'd known I was a Muslim, of course, but I hadn't felt my faith. The Imam changed that. Then I went to university and met people who'd studied Islam for years. Most of them no longer revered Khomeini, but they weren't traitors or counterrevolutionaries. They cared deeply about Iran and Islam. They told me Khomeini was a revolutionary and a religious scholar. He shouldn't have allowed us to call him the Imam."

Hazra was living proof the clerics hadn't successfully Islamicized Iran's universities. They'd fired thousands of teachers and overhauled the curricula. Both professors and students had to have a razor-sharp idea of the sacred and the profane. Yet Tehran University remained quintessentially Western: it could still unsettle the mind.

With thumb and forefinger, Hazra was rubbing a couple of strands of hair just below her ear. Nerves, or a pleasurable indoor habit? No doubt, she was a better Muslim than her brother. She still went occasionally to mosques, through good Shi'ites need not go to a mosque to pray. Yet her Islam hadn't obliged her to put on more clothing when I came to the door. She averted her eyes when we spoke, but she didn't try to hide the outline of her breasts through her nightshirt.

"Do you remember not wearing the chador?" I asked, finishing off another piece of baqlava.

"Of course," Hazra replied, smiling.

"Do you ever think about wearing dresses again in public?"

"Yes."

"Often?"

"No."

"Why not?"

"I'd feel awkward and ashamed. I couldn't protect my dignity."

"So you don't mind wearing the chador or a coat when you go out?"

"No. Men don't bother me when I'm covered. I can go wherever I want."

"So, in your dreams, you wear a chador?"

For the first time, Hazra laughed aloud.

"Sometimes."

"What do you dream of?" I nearly shouted, trying to overcome a surge in the traffic noise.

"I dream about Hosein staying home more and about me having a better job," she answered once the trucks had passed.

She was aiming low; I wanted her high.

"Do you dream about marriage?"

You have to try several times with Iranians, each time at a slightly different angle. You have to chip patiently through the thick walls that separate women from men, then wait. I was more a sledgehammer than a chisel, but I was her brother's friend, a Persian-speaking American in Tabriz. I wasn't part of her world. Within the week, I'd be gone.

"Yes," she said, barely enunciating the word.

"Did you dream of marriage when you were eighteen and believed in the Imam?"

"Iranian women always dream of marriage."

"Did you dream of marrying your cousin?" I asked timidly, fearful I'd shut her down.

"No. I didn't know him well then," she said cleanly.

"Did you want to find a man, get married, and fight together for the Imam and Islam?"

Blessedly, Hazra grinned and raised her eyes. "Yes, more or less. I would do my part. My husband would do his."

"And your part would be what? What did young women like you dream of when the revolution was young?"

"I dreamed of fighting. Fighting for the Imam, Islam, and against"—she hesitated—"imperialist America. I dreamed of having children who would fight. I wanted to volunteer to help behind the lines, but Hosein forbade it. He wouldn't permit me to have anything to do with the war."

"Was your cousin the only one in your family to die?"

"No, there were others. Distant relatives. I didn't know them well," Hazra answered, her voice tightening slightly.

"Was your family proud to have martyrs?"

"Yes, very proud."

"Did you ever want to be a martyr?" I asked, simultaneously asking for more pistachio-laden baqlava. Standing and serving, Hazra couldn't look away.

"Yes."

I didn't want her crying. I didn't have a case officer's privileges anymore. Also, Hosein might be home soon.

"When?"

"After funerals. We were always in mourning for somebody. We'd done so little, compared to those who'd given their lives."

"Did you ever talk with Hosein about the revolution?"

"Not often. Hosein screamed whenever I started talking about Khomeini, and I didn't want him mad. He was home so seldom because of the war and his work."

"You were never ashamed of him?"

"Yes. But he's always thought of me before himself. When he was at the front, he'd somehow send gifts. He's always allowed my friends to visit even though he generally hasn't liked them. He's never hit me."

Before I could ask more, she was back in the kitchen. I smelled more sugar cooking. By the time Hosein returned, I wouldn't be able to move. He'd find me asleep on a futon, stuffed with baqlava, halvah, and honey cakes. Hazra would tell him of all the questions, and he would tell her of many more. If I could stay awake with my eyes shut, and they would be kind enough to speak in Persian, I might learn their secrets.

With my boots off and my feet warm, I wouldn't stay awake. A corked carafe of whiskey was on the table, an illicit leftover from one of Hosein's earlier trips to Turkey. It was early afternoon, but I'd made an exception. Once horizontal, I'd be gone. And once I was asleep, Hosein would leave me alone. By the time I woke, it would be dark and the Bazaar, *inshallah*, would be closed. There wouldn't be any long cold walks, no blue-uniformed young men with automatic weaponry, and no 360-degree sensations of Tabrizis seeing through my beard, dirt, and army overcoat. I wouldn't have to ask a single question about Hazra and the family network. My second night in Iran would pass far better than I'd feared, and far more comfortably than the first.

. . .

I vaguely remembered a Hazra somewhere in the classified cables of *The Nest of Spies*. A personal letter of the last U.S. chargé in Tehran mentions a teenage Iranian girl who'd been curious about a U.S. embassy limousine. The girl had insisted on knowing the car's owner. When told, she warned, "We're going to chase them out!" A few days later, the embassy was seized.

Change Tabriz for Tehran and Hazra had been that girl: poor, ardent, and probably even a little savage. Yet, fifteen years after the U.S. imperialists had been thrashed, she was welcoming an American into her home with whiskey. Fifteen years isn't long for the world to go topsy-turvy. In November 1979, I would have thought visiting Iran in a box a nightmare, not a dream. And the CIA seemed then the pinnacle of public service.

History is, among other things, an unending chain of accidents. If I'd not had provocative professors of Islamic history, my early curiosity might have faded. I could have ended up a lawyer. If Hazra had lost Hosein in war, she would have lost her soul. With a martyred brother, she would have given herself wholly to the cause. Permanently crippled, she would have ended like Ahmad—no home, no future, a collapsed faith providing her only sustenance and solace. She could have ended up a streetwalker in Turkey.

If Ruhollah al-Musavi al-Khomeini hadn't lost his father when he was five months old and his mother at sixteen, perhaps he wouldn't have become the Imam. His uncompromising will and his cold eyes could have softened in a normal home. The Shah would have survived modern Iran's growing pains, and the CIA intelligence estimates of 1976–77 predicting Pahlavi rule and Persian Gulf stability into the twenty-first century would have been considered humdrum prescience. The organization would happily have declassified the top secret documents through leaks to the *Washington Post* and the *New York Times*.

Before falling asleep, I heard Hosein come in. I was too tired to try to understand. In any case, they were speaking Azari. I turned away from their voices to the clank, grind, and belch of Third World noise. I started wondering again what the hell I was doing. I wasn't a total wreck, as I'd been at the border. The whiskey had calmed my nerves. Hazra's food had stopped the shivers from the night before.

I hadn't, however, walked out the fear. I'd seen thousands of Azaris in my years in Turkey. Most had come from Tabriz. All I needed was one to pop out from a doorway or a street-side circle of unemployed men and say, "Sir! Sir! What are you doing in Tabriz? Is the American consulate opening again, sir?" Within a few minutes, I'd have a hundred applicants and I'd spend the next twenty years in prison.

If something like this happened, Hosein was to keep walking. If he got involved, I'd have nowhere to hide. Somehow, I'd return to the truck. With fear working against my sense of direction, I'd be damned lucky to find it.

Soul-searching is a case officer's worst enemy. C/Os are action oriented. They recruit, not analyze. Someone else will determine whether it's all worthwhile, preferably long after the C/O has been promoted and departed post.

At HQS, agents' orange-bindered operational files are stacked in gray metal filing cabinets, usually next to the books along the walls. Reading files is a boring exercise. Spyspeak is standardized bad English. Character assessment of agents is kept to a minimum. A field C/O doesn't want some desk officer second-guessing him on how to run a case. He doesn't want some C/O-turned-alcoholic-turned-counterintelligence officer-cum-shrink locking onto a foible. Only one out of twenty or thirty files is flesh and blood.

Before Tabriz, I didn't really care about Hazra. She was too abstract, and my own fear was too consuming. It was Hosein's decision, not mine, I told myself again. He was responsible for his family and friends. But the old dodges didn't work as well; arguments with Hosein didn't apply. Hazra didn't gain anything by my presence. She hadn't volunteered and, worse, she was a woman. In the Agency, I'd never recruited one. Generally, women don't live and die for abstractions. Lying on the futon, I imagined Hazra tortured; it seemed obscene.

I stopped listening to the traffic noise and my conscience as the alcohol spun my head. I stopped listening to Hosein and Hazra's incomprehensible high-speed chatter and felt the pleasure of having warm, free toes.

I slept soundly into the night. When I awoke, Hazra was cooking again. It was an ideal Persian dinner: they talked about their childhoods while I ate and listened without asking a question about martyrdom. Stuffed, we all went to bed. Again I had a few flashbacks to Langley and Iranian agents I'd known. As soon as I'd crossed the Iranian-Turkish border, I kept a promise I'd made years before. *Never ask someone to do something you wouldn't do yourself.* When the agents' faces finally vanished, I didn't see or hear a thing until the morning traffic woke me. As in the old days, my worries and guilt left my sleep alone.

While visiting Headquarters from the field, I was once unexpectedly called to the Near East Division's Front Office. It was Christmastime. I'd already seen the new division chief that day, ushered in and out for a little season's greetings. On this visit, I was alone.

Late in the afternoon, Langley's shiny rolled-linoleum hallways were nearly empty. The Directorate of Operations' Christmas party had already come and gone. After only two days in Washington, I hadn't adjusted. Headquarters' randomly painted blue, yellow, green, and chartreuse cipher-locked steel doors jarred me. The heavy air inside the building's hermetically sealed windows and innumerable little office cubicles made me feel caged. Thinking still in acronyms and pseudonyms, I'd forgotten everybody's real name. More than usual, I felt that I wasn't at home.

Except for the chief's secretary and a personnel minion down the hall, the Front Office was empty. Outside the chief's door, a large Sony television had Rafsanjani on the screen. I'd never seen a television, let alone a cleric, in the Front Office before. The *gorbeh* was speaking in Persian with neither subtitled nor simultaneous translation. The chief had been the deputy chief of station (DCOS) in Tehran before the fall. Perhaps the video was an eccentricity from bygone days. Still, it was odd. The chief didn't know the language. With his desk far from the door, he couldn't even hear the sweet singsong of the cleric's voice.

Then it dawned on me. The Front Office must have had VIP guests, and the chief had put on a special Christmas show—a high-tech version of Persian newspapers and books stacked along the walls. Unfortunately, the chief's secretary would neither confirm nor deny my suspicions.

"I'd like you to read something I've written," the chief politely requested after beckoning me into his office.

Unhesitatingly, I agreed. He handed me his fifteen-page review of a recently published book critical of the U.S. government's reporting on prerevolutionary Iran. He was angry. He'd heard the academic who'd written the book was pro-clergy. Did I know the man?

"By reputation only," I explained. He was a "Peace Corps professor" who thought the United States was on the wrong side of Iranian history. Perhaps he'd grown too close to Persians, too close for a scholar. Still, not long before the revolution, the gentleman had warned the U.S. embassy that something was going seriously wrong. He might be a blinkered leftist, but you had to give credit where credit was due.

"Have you read *this* book?" the chief asked, revealing his critique in one word.

"It's flawed. Better on Washington, D.C., than on Tehran."

"It's a very inaccurate book," he snapped. "We didn't do a bad job." The chief's halting British accent added authority to his speech. He'd grown up in India, I'd heard.

"We did good work in Iran?" I did my best to suppress an eyebrow twitch.

"We did excellent work."

"Then why do the 1976 and 1977 Special National Intelligence Estimates have the Pahlavi dynasty lasting into the twenty-first century?" I asked sincerely.

"The analysts made a mistake, we didn't."

"So the DO [Directorate of Operations] foresaw the revolution and the DI [Directorate of Intelligence] didn't put it into finished intelligence?" I continued, aware that I was heading for trouble.

"We gave them the best information we could. We didn't fail in our mission," he declared.

His eyes were boring into me. His hands were flat on the desk. He didn't want further questions.

"I was told by a C/O who was then in Tehran that we didn't really do any Iranian reporting," I went on. "He said we spent most of our time chasing Soviets, that we didn't even have a Persian-speaking officer in the station."

"We did good work on internal events, as good as anybody. This officer doesn't know what he's talking about. Who told you this?"

I didn't answer or ask another question. Agency field assignments are very informally made. Division chiefs, not assignment panels, really make the rules. Awkwardly, we shifted our conversation to Turkey. I read his draft, but didn't call back. "This book is about . . ." is how it began. I planned to leave it with the Iran desk chief with a meaningless complimentary note attached. However, the division chief tracked me down by telephone. He'd not known I'd left the manuscript with the desk chief. Tensely, he asked me what I thought.

"Interesting," I told him. "Contained information I hadn't known before." Trying to be complimentary, I added that the academic "certainly wouldn't be pleased with what you've written."

"He'll never know what I've written. It's classified," the chief snapped back.

"Of course. I didn't mean . . ." I said haltingly, trying to recover. "I just meant you trashed his position well."

The chief hadn't, of course. After reading his review, I'd liked the academic's book more.

"He'd better not read my article," he repeated menacingly, oblivious to all I'd said.

"I believe the fellow has State Department friends," I answered after a tense pause. "It wouldn't be the first time an essay from the CIA's *Studies in Intelligence* got circulated outside. Who knows, you might provoke him to write another book."

We listened to each other breathe, neither uttering a word.

"Thank you for taking a look at my article," the chief replied finally. "Please return it as soon as possible."

He hung up. I never spoke to the chief again. I later heard the essay had won the intelligence journal's highest award.

As a general rule, senior DO officers are incredibly insecure about their knowledge. Case officers jump from country to country and rarely gain much substantive expertise. Learning how to spot surveillance and arrange a clandestine meeting doesn't really require much skill. Even under difficult circumstances, it's a common-sense exercise. With HQS analysts and diplomats supplying you with country-specific questions, you can debrief most assets and know next to nil. After a tour or two, case officers are generally mute or in the corner at serious diplomatic parties. It's too easy to get burned by diplomats and journalists who know more. It's safer to hide behind the cipher locks and colored doors and pretend that knowledge arrives effortlessly through "recruitments" and clandestine meetings. Unintentionally, I'd hit one of the chief's most sensitive nerves. I'd suggested he knew little and complimented the enemy. I'd turned insider information against the fraternity. So the chief struck back, and his accusation of small-scale treason stung.

In 1985, when I joined the CIA, I would have given the chief the benefit of the doubt. I would have believed the Directorate of Operations had done a good job of collecting intelligence about prerevolutionary Iran's problems, and the Directorate of Intelligence, under political pressure, had downplayed or ignored the DO's information in its analysis. I would have paid little regard to the peevish antigovernment attacks and historical gerrymandering of a second-rate left-wing academic.

Not anymore. A British-accented CIA don describing the 1970s as banner intelligence years in Iran was too surreal. I walked out of the chief's office, past Rafsanjani, and the blue, yellow, green, and chartreuse doors, and into the elevator. I hurried past the small black marble bust of George Bush and the unflattering oil portraits of every CIA director. I quickly walked by the institution's "motto" from the Gospel according to St. John—AND YE SHALL KNOW THE TRUTH AND THE TRUTH SHALL MAKE YOU FREE—engraved in the entranceway marble wall and over the bald-eagle seal in the floor. As soon as I got into my car, I told myself I had to leave. Some of my more questionable impulses had found a congenial home. I'd permanently changed. If I didn't leave soon, I'd crack. I'd served long enough to see good men collapse. The lucky ones only drank too much. The unlucky ones had become instructors at the Farm or fast-track administrative assistants to senior Agency officers. I knew I had to get out before *the Angel* became one or the other.

I rose late the next morning. Hosein had waited for me. After my coffee, we were out the door. On the way down the steps, we ran into a fat chador-clad woman who exploded into a long-winded "Good morning." When she squeezed past me, she smiled and said nothing. I was about to ask Hosein about her, when he opened the door and I hit the cold and deafening streets. Tabriz looked and smelled no better than before. The traffic had already ground a light early-morning snow into black slush and splattered the sidewalks gray. Mushrooming exhaust fumes dissipated slowly over the crawling traffic. The exhaust and smell of diesel were everywhere. The sidewalks were full of men in colorless wool and leather coats; women were mostly in chadors. A teahouse down the block was already packed with smoking men who probably didn't have work. As we walked by its entrance, a blast of Azari Turkish voices came out. An old man with white facial stubble and whiskers nearly to his ears peered at me from a stool just inside the threshold. I looked up, catching sight of framed ayatollah pictures on a wall. Both Khomeini and Khameneh'i were there.

I did a quick 360 in the street. There were no security forces around, but Hosein again was off and running. He was hungry and wanted to eat before doing bazaari business. We walked several sad blocks of squat, filthy brick-and-concrete buildings before the monotony was broken by a large intersection, an open square, and a railroad station—a big white slab of a building, with virtually no one going out or in. We crossed a large avenue separating the city's center from a brick-and-cinderblock shantytown. The street's wide lanes had faster traffic but no less noise. In Iran, shifting gears requires both clutch and horn. The noise and congestion drove my attention up. Looking through a wide-angle lens at the mountains, you could almost imagine a Western tourist voluntarily visiting Tabriz.

Mercifully, it wasn't snowing. Hosein told me we'd have to leave soon for Ardabil. He didn't want to get caught in the mountain passes going or returning. He had to go to Tehran via Tabriz and not the warmer Caspian Sea roads. If snow blocked the road from Ardabil to Tabriz, we'd have to try heading east toward the sea.

I'd wanted to see the Caspian Sea for years. The English word "jungle" comes from the Persian *jangal*, the ancient word for the region's dense forests. Isolated from the rest of the country by mountains, Caspian coastlands have been softly ravaged by time. The forests, constant rain, and malarial swamps hadn't welcomed horse-mounted intruders. The Arabs and Islam had secured the region, wisely taking more than a hundred years. Turks and Mongols largely bypassed the area. Languages and dialects remained throwbacks.

Despite modernizing shahs, not all the forests and marshlands had vanished. The Persian lions, an Iranian symbol for thousands of years, were gone, but I'd heard the woods were still full of brightly colored animals and artfully clad natives. Even more alluring, the Caspian Sea people were reportedly the kindest and most honest in Iran.

Unfortunately, Hosein didn't like the idea of an alternate route. He'd lose too much money. His business interests and his friends went the other way. If we drove straight through to Tehran along the Caspian Sea, we'd have to drive through the night or sleep in the truck. Even on well-marked roads, night driving wasn't fun. It could easily be deadly.

Then again, in the open, with thousands of Iranians staring at me, Tabriz seemed deadlier. I asked Hosein about the former U.S. consulate. It wasn't far. Unlike the U.S. embassy in Tehran, it wasn't a revolutionary attraction declaring the triumph of Islam. Nobody referred to it lovingly or menacingly as a former nest of spies. Hosein hadn't thought about it in years. The only "friendly" foreign ground in Tabriz was the Turkish consulate. In an emergency, I didn't think I'd find a helping hand there. The Turks would naturally want to avoid trouble.

Suddenly the Citadel came into full view. From a distance, I saw a sandy-colored hundred-foot-high stone square with two gaping holes and a big circular bulge. The fortress looked like a giant booster rocket surrounded by a square launch tower. Time and war had dried, hollowed, and crumbled some of its form—square-toothed crenellation and iron-belted wooden doors that give castles their charm. The Ilkhanids, the Islamicized Mongols who'd built the Citadel, commissioned the most refined Persian miniatures. I saw only brute strength here. The Citadel, however, had been extensively rebuilt in the early nineteenth century. Perhaps I was looking at a modern version emphasizing utility over aesthetics. In any case, the mollahs must have used tons of TNT to blow part of it down.

I'd known the last U.S. consul in Tabriz, the only U.S. official I knew who could handle both Persian and Azari well. I remembered him once fondly describing Tabriz and the Citadel at a suburban Washington, D.C., barbecue. He'd loved Tabriz, and many Tabrizis returned the affection. Virtually alone among U.S. officials, he'd seen the revolution coming and had written so, against constant opposition from the U.S. embassy in Tehran. And, as a hostage, he sternly rebuked his captors in all his languages. Given his courage, linguistic skill, and knowledge, his captors of course considered him a spy. No one was more poorly treated. I'd heard through the grapevine he now enjoyed an endless supply of caviar from guilt-ridden Persian friends.

My historical reflections stopped as the number of Iranians around me grew. We were in the center of town. Older brick and stone structures on both sides of the street had mostly given way to concrete. The engine noise and honking from the bumper-to-bumper traffic bounced off the buildings, producing all-around sound. I started walking with my hand over my mouth, even though this identified me as a weak-lunged non-Tabrizi. As we darted across a street, Hosein pointed out the kebab joint. I went tight. Hosein, of course, told me not to worry. He'd head in first and check it out.

A minute later I followed and took a small empty wooden table with two stools. There were six men sitting and two standing at the counter with Hosein. Not knowing what to do, I took my gloves off and rubbed my hands, and resisted the urge to cover my nose. The place stank of unbathed men and years of soured frying oil.

"Where do you come from?"

The question from behind, in English, jolted me inside like a blow. My chest and throat rapidly contracted. I almost jerked my head around.

"From Europe," I slowly and softly answered in Persian.

In the Middle East, if you don't look like a native, questions inevitably arrive in English. Very few people speak French anymore. Even the least educated peasant in the worst hellhole can proudly come at you with a few well-practiced English phrases. My reaction had been natural but stupid.

"You speak Persian! By God, do you really know Persian?!" The young man shot back. He was no more than twenty, shaven, and more or less clean. Behind him at the same table, a bearded young man was listening. Behind them, a table of two middle-aged men had also locked onto the conversation.

"I speak a little," I stammered slowly.

"Where did you learn?"

"At university. I teach Iranian history in France," I said, fairly certain I had better French than anyone else in the room.

"Why have you come to Tabriz?"

He was more inquisitive than threatening. He'd politely slowed his question to match my speed. But the kebab joint was small and those close were listening.

Hosein returned to the table, slid me my food, glanced at the young men, ignored them, and started eating.

"I wanted to see it. It's a famous city. I was just curious," I answered, as I started hurriedly stuffing down my kebab.

The word "curious" exists in Persian, but the sense isn't identical to ours. It was more "nosiness" than "exploration." It suggested an ulterior motive, something gained or a loss forestalled. I probably shouldn't have used it.

"Tabriz is famous in France?"

The question came from the other leather-jacketed young man. The big smile on his face softened his beard and made him look his age.

"No, not really," I answered. "It is well known among people who love the Middle East, especially Iran."

A slight exaggeration. Isfahan, Mashhad, Tehran, even Shiraz come first to mind. Tabriz, the first or second city of Iran for almost five hundred years, didn't spark the Western or Persian imagination anymore. The 1906–11 Constitutional Revolution, Iran's first attempt to limit the power of its shahs, started in Tabriz, then the most Westernized Iranian city. It was the first revolution in the Middle East. The crushing of Grand Ayatollah Shari'at-madari of Tabriz was the city's last time in the limelight. However, with the Soviet crack-up and the independence of Soviet Azarbaijan, Tabriz might have another chance to grab everybody's attention.

"You like Iran?" the first young man interjected.

"Very much. It's a beautiful country."

"I don't," he shot back. "I'd rather live in France. People are rich in France, aren't they? French women are beautiful?"

Hosein and I had already had a long conversation on the relative beauty of women. I could tell by his chewing that he didn't really want to hear another.

"No. I think Iranian women are better-looking; that is, when you can see them."

Both young men and the two eavesdropping middle-aged ones chuckled.

"Is it hard for an Iranian to go to France?"

"I don't know," I answered. "I suspect it's very hard."

"It's not fair that you can come to my country but we cannot go to yours," the bearded one said, tightening his smile a bit.

"I agree one hundred percent," I answered.

After the hundreds, if not thousands, of Iranians I'd helped enter the States, I'd certainly deserved a visa to Iran.

"Nobody likes Iran anymore. I don't like it much either," the bearded young man added.

I turned toward Hosein, who'd already finished his kebab. He wanted to go. So did I. Quick lunches at kebab joints wouldn't cause us problems. Iranian men wanting to talk about politics and sex were natural, even in the Islamic Republic. Still, I'd not taken my eye off the door. I kept looking for armed men or former friends. I glanced at the young men, your average horny young Persians, and wondered again why I'd come to Iran. I'd definitely come too late.

Ten years earlier young men like them would have been death-wish Persians. The years 1987 or 1988 would have been ideal, 1990 at the latest. Young burned-out holy warriors with aching pink body scars would have been in every kebab joint. Now they were normal. These young men were pissed off because they were poor, their marriage possibilities were slim, and the smuggled video-and satellite-dish-delivered women were beautiful and giving.

If God played a part in their lives, it happened maybe once a month, no more than twice, at the mosque, where the best petty business deals could be made. All in all, they were healthy young men.

I wolfed down the rest of my kebab and said goodbye. Mercifully, the two of them stayed put. I made another quick 360 and did what Hosein had told me to do: walk forcefully and ignore everyone. As long as I kept my mouth shut, I wouldn't draw attention. Close up, I was obviously a foreigner, but not an attractive, rich one. I looked a little German, a little Turkish, and something else less pretty. Even if I started speaking Persian, they probably wouldn't draw the right conclusion. My accent wasn't very American, and most Iranians wouldn't in any case know American-accented Persian. A few more blocks and we'd be in the Bazaar. In its labyrinth, among friends, we'd be safe.

The Bazaar actually started before we got inside. The streets were lined with small shops and men were carrying things under their arms and on their backs. Clothes, rolled carpets, and cardboard boxes with Japanese televisions inside. A few boys were carrying folded stacks of flat bread (*nun* in Persian) on their forearms. Perhaps bazaaris had late breakfasts or early lunches. Every time someone passed by, I felt certain that they were staring at me longer than at anyone else. As we turned a corner, I froze: two men with assault rifles and one without. The armed ones were teenagers and hopping next to a propane heater. The older one occasionally looked up from popping pistachios into his mouth. They were several feet from the covered Bazaar's open arched doorway.

Hosein looked at me, I nodded, and we kept going.

For years, Rafsanjani's government had been trying to centralize and merge the country's numerous "security forces." The Shah-era National Police and the gendarmerie had never been trusted by the mollahs. However, the young toughs of the *Basij* and the *Komiteh*, the neighborhood revolutionary committees nastier than the Revolutionary Guards, had regularly gone out of control. Against the *Komiteh*, even clerics sometimes obtained no appeal. To ,guard against "counterrevolution," revolutionary excess, and massive bureaucratic overlap, the Interior Ministry decided to make a single new comprehensive security force.

However, every Iranian could still tell an old gendarme or policeman from the others. They had a certain polish and bearing. They didn't intimidate so quickly. Also, they often shaved. The men ahead were sloppy, with the obligatory stubble, the chic Holy Law minimum among the nonclerical hard core.

Just before I crossed the doorway, I glanced at the commander. I caught his eye. Several steps inside, I turned. Only an old man was behind me. Nevertheless, my heartbeat didn't relent. In the Bazaar, I wouldn't see a *Basiji* or Rev Guard until I bumped into him. I'd been wrong. In this crowd, I felt less anonymous, not more.

We were in alleys full of plastic buckets, multicolored dresses for little girls, T-shirts, underwear, pants, and socks, innumerable little stacks of Muslim skullcaps, boots, hats, cheap leather coats and bags, radios, clocks, copper spoons and pots, framed pictures of your favorite ayatollahs, and a hodgepodge of other Western and Middle Eastern trinkets and junk. Street urchins scurried about from shop to shop. Women were everywhere, though few were coupled with men. Most wore chadors. When they walked in twos down the center of the streets, men gave way, otherwise, they kept slightly to the side. Even in the cool air, men and women both left a smelly wake. So did I, probably. Occasionally, young men in brightly colored nylon coats or jackets shot through the crowds like ricocheting tracer bullets. On the back of one, I saw UCLA.

Though we were moving quickly, I could tell a few people were staring at me as they would at a stranger, but so far no teenage boys had jumped out saying in English "Mister, mister, I have leather coat, very cheap," or in Persian, "Sir, sir, I want to thank you for the visa, sir." I could remember helping a few Tabrizi bazaaris in Turkey visit the States. Because one had definitely sold rugs, among other things, I wasn't going to linger in the carpet bazaar.

We passed through an open square with new carpets on the floor.

A large black Tabrizi carpet with gold medallions was on top. It looked antique: the merchant had probably prematurely aged it in the sun. Hosein had once tried smuggling Persian carpets to Turkey, which protects its own carpet trade by strictly prohibiting the importation of Iranian rugs. He'd stopped. He didn't know carpets well, and it was too easy to get ripped off on both sides.

The rug market was dead. Too many stores and not enough people. Sitting on their carpets and kilims, the merchants just stared from their brightly lighted shops. I noticed a picture of Khomeini on a wall. Framed behind the painted green wood trim of the store's glass front and adjacent to a hung decorative prayer rug, Khomeini finally had the position he'd always craved: Archangel Gabriel, the guardian of heaven's gate. Muslims generally don't share God's grace with lesser heavenly creatures, but Gabriel is one of the few true angels sanctified by the Qur'an.

Walking through the Bazaar, I remembered the Kapalıçarsi, Istanbul's immense indoor market. I'd often scavenged there for Persian carpets and kilims, lying in wait for some tired Iranian with a rug on his shoulder. The merchandise was always second-rate. The good stuff invisibly got inside. Once, by accident, I'd run into an Isfahani rug merchant who offered me fifteen carpets for "advice" on how to travel to the States. Reluctantly, I informed him he should apply for a visa at the consulate. They couldn't be issued in the bazaar.

Tabriz's bazaar was a smaller, less glittering, far less lively version of Istanbul's. Tabriz hadn't been an imperial capital for centuries. Nonetheless, Tabriz's fifteenth-century bazaar was reportedly the most beautiful in Iran. Its small, numerous onion-shaped, intricately bricked domes dropped low over many alleys and recessed stores. Little side streets, with little stores, meandered everywhere. Small holes in the ceiling brought in the outside's grayish light. Architecturally, it was a pleasing expression of the Persian mind's intricacy and compartmentation. As soon as I walked in, I could sense the secret deals being made in the alcoves.

Moving through the Bazaar's footprinted damp streets, I realized I'd totally lost my sense of direction. If I lost Hosein, it might take me an hour to find the right door. As I was trying to count up the lefts and rights and attach them to landmarks, we stopped. We were at Hosein's friend's jewelry store. He was the family's principal money changer. I also had the impression he underwrote some of Hosein's private transport work.

Once again, I could feel in their smiles and embrace, and in the friend's hearty Western handshake, that Hosein had already told the bazaari about me. At least in his case, the introduction probably hadn't been by telephone. I was immediately asked to sit on a stool and order something to drink. I took a Coke. Again, it tasted sweet.

The shop was nearly empty of jewelry. There were a few silver necklaces and bracelets on two stands, a few more in a small glass-topped wooden case, which also had several small rows of silver rings, some with small jewels, others with polished stones. Some-where out of sight, no doubt, probably underneath the carpeted floor, was a treasure chest of precious gems, silver, and gold.

"How do you like Tabriz?" the bazaari asked in Persian. "I met a few Americans in the Bazaar two years ago. It's good to have Americans in the Bazaar again."

"I like what I've seen," I answered, wondering who the Americans had been. "I've been exceptionally well treated."

"We all miss America. Don't you believe what the mollahs say. I'm very honored you've paid me a visit."

Bazaaris, the Middle East's historic merchant middlemen, bar-gainers par excellence, had earned the reputation of being Iran's finest liars. Through the centuries, all Iranians have had to slice away little bits of their souls and give them as gifts to stronger strangers. With each slice, they have turned inward and lied more. Prime prey for both foreign and domestic predators, bazaaris have sliced, turned inward, and lied more than others. Open to the world because of commerce, closed to it because of its dangers, bazaaris have been modern Iran's finest patriots and worst scoundrels. Usually counsels of moderation and compromise, willing to trade with domestic and foreign infidels, they've frequently been among Iran's worst bigots. It's never hard to find bazaaris who loathe Christians, Jews, and especially Baha'is—merchant jealousy reinforcing an intolerant read-ing of the faith.

At the forefront of the 1906–11 Constitutional Revolution against the Qajar kings, the bazaaris bankrolled the Islamic revolution when the Shah tried to dictate their profit margins. Proud Muslims who often marry their daughters to the clergy, they happily import the VCRs and videos undermining the country's Islamic rectitude. Bazaaris I'd met outside the country had been debriefing joys. A two-hour chat session and I'd felt like I'd speed-read *War and Peace*. Only frontline holy warriors caused me more pain when I tried to figure out their rules for right and wrong. Only clerics had more interwoven and politically sensitive family trees.

"You've never been to Iran before?" he asked.

"No, this is my first time."

"You have good Persian for someone who's never been to Iran."

"I had good teachers."

"Hosein tells me you want to know about the Islamic revolution. You want to know whether anybody still believes," he said. He had an appealing deep voice. His motionless hands slightly cupped on his lap suggested he'd had a fairly conservative upbringing. His nice English tweed jacket over a brown V-neck sweater and collared white shirt suggested the upbringing had allowed a little flair.

"Yes, I'd like to know," I said, irritated *he'd* posed the questions, and *so soon*. I needed more time to learn how to spot lies and any personal grudges fueling political or religious tastes.

"No one believes."

"No one?"

"No one," he said, widening his dark brown eyes and raising his eyebrows and balding forehead.

"Not the Revolutionary Guards, the *Basij*, the Society of Combatant Clerics, Khameneh'i? No one?" I asked again, hoping he'd at least try to run.

"It's finished. We fight for Iran now, not Islam."

"Aren't they the same? Khomeini equals Islam equals Iran. Isn't that why Khomeini won?"

"Khomeini won because the Shah was weak. The Shah had forgotten both Islam and Iran. He'd sold the nation to foreigners. In 1978, we were Muslims first, Iranians second. But the mollahs have

put Islam inside their purses. We owe more to foreigners now than
we did under the Shah. With the cursed Shah, foreigners borrowed
money from Iran and I had them in my shop.

"Now Islam and Iran are equals. Soon we will be Iranians first,
Muslims second. You will see. That's why the mollahs are scared."

"What does that mean, 'Iranians first, Muslims second'? Does
that mean the clerical regime will fall?"

Persians love unhelpful catch phrases. Slicing and splicing the
Persian identity was a shell game. One moment pre-Islamic Persian,
one moment Muslim, one moment inseparably both. Iranians hate
the Arabs for conquering their country and praise them for giving
Iran the True Prophet and Only God. I'd used the Persian versus
Muslim angle to recruit Iranians, and the Azari versus Persian angle
against Azarbaijanis, but I was never sure of the volatile mix.

"Only God knows who will rule Iran," he said. "But the mollahs
won't rule Iran because they know the *Shar'iat*. They will only rule
Iran because they know how to run the country. If Iran grows richer,
they will last. If we grow poorer, they won't."

I wondered if the fellow would have been such an MBA-cum-
Marxist if he'd got onto the clerical-bazaari gravy train. If he had
Hosein as a partner, he probably operated on the fringe, without
serious clerical connections. So he had no special privileges in im-
porting foreign goods or changing Iranian money into U.S. dollars
at discount "official" rates. Contrary to their revolutionary expec-
tations, the majority of bazaaris had found the Islamic Republic a
business disaster. Corruption, a constant nuisance under the Shah,
had become a nightmare. More money to more people more often
had become the rule. Even worse, the revolutionary clerics put most
of their faith and the nation's wealth into large state-owned enter-
prises and semipublic "charitable" foundations. Only clerically well-
connected bazaaris had realized their dreams. Was Hosein's friend
a man of the people, outraged at the clerical regime's corruption
and incompetence? Or was he a jealous bazaari who hadn't married
well?

"Are Iranians becoming more nationalistic under the mollahs?" I
asked, trying to return him to church and state.

"They hate the mollahs. Some Iranians hate the mollahs because they think they're bad Muslims. I don't. It's hard to call someone who knows the Holy Law a bad Muslim. I hate them because they're bad Iranians. No one respects Iran anymore. Maybe stupid Arab fundamentalists do, but nobody else. Sometimes I find myself thinking nice things about the Shah, and the Shah was the testicle of a dog."

"So when is it going to fall?" I asked, watching Hosein step out of the shop. A bit panicked, I swiveled on my stool so only my back could be seen through the window.

"Only God knows. We are very tired. However, they will fall. Nobody respects them anymore. We used to always have mollahs for tea and listen to them explain the Holy Law and the Qur'an. Look in the Bazaar! You won't find mollahs having tea," he said, offering me another Coke before I'd finished the first.

"How will they fall?" I asked.

"Only God knows. Maybe one day they won't have enough money to pay off everyone and the Revolutionary Guards will shoot them. One thing is certain: somebody will shoot them."

"And then?"

"Only God knows. But the American consulate will open again, and I will have American customers," he said, grinning.

"You wouldn't be scared of America buying Iran like before?"

"You've learned your lesson. Khomeini made you suffer, didn't he? I've completely forgiven you. *Inshallah*, my youngest son will study in America. I would love to visit America, but I've heard they don't give many visas to Iranians."

"No, they don't," I said, immensely relieved to see Hosein once again by my side.

"Why don't they? Why doesn't America realize how much Iranians love America?"

"I don't know," I lied. A discussion of U.S. visas was too close to home.

Hosein, the bazaari, and I talked for two hours more, interrupted only once by a street-urchin messenger. Our conversation ran between local politics and business, Persian and Azari. I couldn't follow most of the town gossip. When I couldn't keep up, I looked out the window. My first impression had been wrong. There weren't many people in the streets. My nerves had amplified the numbers.

The bazaari did his best to keep us in his shop. It had been two years since he'd had an American. Finally, Hosein broke his grasp, telling him how Hazra would grow angry if he didn't run her errands. He gave Hosein several more kisses and me his hand. When we walked out, I saw the street urchin sitting by his door.

Hosein took me through several left and right turns. I doubted whether I could find the bazaari again, let alone the way out. Shop-keepers were standing by wood-framed doorways conversing with people in the streets, or just staring. You could tell Tabriz hadn't enjoyed tourists, foreign or Iranian, in years. No one leapt out ready to make deals. Blessedly, no one leapt out and said, "Sir, sir, you remember me, sir?" As we walked through narrow alleys that were barely two-men across, I reassured myself that it would be hard to recognize me from Istanbul. My diplomatic persona (suit, tie, and confidence) was gone.

Hosein stopped again. My guardian angel was still after underwear and socks. We walked into a narrow, one-room clothing shop; shirts, pants, sweaters, and coats were either front forward on hangers or stacked along the walls. Smiling and gesturing with a hand, the shopkeeper beckoned us to move closer. In Azari, Hosein stated what he was after, the shopkeeper bobbed his head, and Hosein bobbed back. The man glanced at me and shot one question more in Hosein's direction. I caught the tail end and quickly stepped forward, hoping to cut off a more truthful reply. "From Europe," I volunteered in Persian. The shopkeeper, a middle-aged, balding man with a short-cropped, thick beard, grinned broadly.

"Do you speak Persian?" he asked, in a deep voice.

"A little," I answered.

"Are you German?"

He'd probably met German tourists before. Germans, the Islamic Republic's largest trading partners, were Iran's most numerous and intrepid Western tourists. He probably knew Germans could be big and green eyed.

"No. French."

"You speak more than a little?" His question was halfway between a compliment and an inquiry. Hosein's vigorous finger-searching of stacked clothing, however, temporarily diverted him and broke his smile.

"Not really," I answered.

"I don't believe you," he said, with a renewed grin.

"Thank you, but I don't," I insisted, trying to be as politely Persian as I could be.

"You speak beautifully," returned the shopkeeper, in turn being impeccably polite.

I didn't hear an Azari accent in his Persian. He could still be Azarbaijani. I'd met dozens of Azarbaijanis who spoke perfectly accented Persian—at least to my ear.

"Did you learn in France?"

"Yes," I replied, fearing I was stuck again for the obligatory questions.

"It's splendid they teach Persian in France. Why did you study Persian?"

Without stopping his search, Hosein interjected a little humor. "Given the mollahs, it's a miracle they teach Persian anywhere."

The shopkeeper flashed an evil eye toward Hosein.

"It's a beautiful language," I replied, drawing the shopkeeper back to me. "The Middle East has always interested me, and Iran has always been the most important country in the Middle East."

His grin returned and expanded into a toothy smile. "You like Iran?"

"Very much."

"Do the French, does Europe, like Iran?" he asked earnestly.

Iranians are like Americans, and unlike Europeans: they need to be loved.

"Everyone hates us." Hosein had given up the search and rejoined the conversation. The shopkeeper winced, but didn't reprimand Hosein with his eyes.

"Not everyone," I said, trying to score a point.

"But most everyone hates us, don't they?" The shopkeeper's smile disappeared. "I haven't met someone from the West in years."

"I don't know," I said, not wanting to become a one-man arbiter for the Western world. On the other hand, I didn't want to be too kind.

"They should hate the mollahs, not us," continued the shop-keeper.

"I don't think many in the West hate the Iranian people. Though I don't think many like the mollahs."

Mollah love-hate. It's a constant of Iranian history. Persians revere them one moment, damn them the next. They can curse them collectively as Mongols, destroyers of the Iranian nation, but praise them singly as the finest Iranian patriots alive. Mollahs are deeply respected for their devotion to God's Holy Law, their historic concern for the downtrodden, and their repeated defense of the nation against foreigners and shahs too tempted by foreign ways. They are despised for their stubborn legal atavism, their dry, Arabic-based love of Islam, their derision of the softer, poetry-inspired side of the Persian character, and their easy hypocrisy with money and sex. Always a class apart, a living scholastic link to medieval Islam, mollahs *are* Persian history, for better or worse. However, with the Islamic revolution, the mollahs went too far. Now even petty merchants, once a reliable and important basis of clerical power, loathed them.

"Everyone hates us," interjected Hosein again. "The Arabs, the Turks, and the Pakistanis. Our Muslim brothers hate us. Why should Christians like us anymore?"

"The Turks and Arabs have always hated Iranians, haven't they?" I shot back.

"They hate us more now," Hosein replied, walking behind me to look at hanging brightly colored sweaters.

"The mollahs have destroyed Iran. We can barely make enough money to survive," the shopkeeper added, not wanting Hosein to have the last word.

Hosein was ready to go. He had other errands in the Bazaar. But I wanted to stay. From this cubbyhole store, I could listen to another Iranian bemoan his family's and his nation's fates and let trouble pass by the doorway. After we said our goodbyes, the shopkeeper tried to convince us to stay for tea. We politely said *"Khoda hafiz"* once more and returned to the alleys.

After doing Hazra's errands and politely brushing off a boy and a man wanting insistently to know where I came from, we left the Bazaar the same way we'd come in. The propane-heated Guardsmen had jumped someplace else. We walked back down the noisy concrete alley and took a slightly different route, past a few dirt-caked, once-regal Edwardian stone buildings and an empty sports stadium—Tabriz's only place of amusement for young men outside of private drinking or opium parties, which according to Hosein were both on the rise. The entire walk I rubbernecked, hunting for police, internal security, Rev Guards, soldiers—anyone carrying a gun. I didn't see anyone. By the time we reentered Hosein's run-down cinderblock neighborhood, my nerves were fried.

When I saw the familiar shoe rack on the sidewalk and smelled the butcher shop, I picked up speed, leaving Hosein a little behind me. As soon as we walked into the apartment, I spotted the whiskey carafe on the table. The next day, I didn't venture out. I stayed alone, played backgammon against myself, read the Qur'an and the newspaper. Hosein had got me a copy of *Resalat*, the conservative, clerical, pro-bazaari journal. In between the lines, I could see the bazaaris' frustration and anger.

How do you peer *posht-e pardeh*, behind the curtains, and separate the Truth from the Lie? How do you know when Iranians aren't lying to themselves? They don't teach that at the Farm or in the *Studies in Intelligence* journal. When in doubt, I applied the general rule of thumb I used in ferreting out the truth in operational files. Four eyewitnesses who say the same thing mean you're getting warm.

After I'd had a whiskey, I felt almost ready to go home.

7 ARDABIL

After nearly three days in the open, I loved and loathed the idea of the box. It was the only place I felt safe, but I hurt when inside. In the truck park, I hopelessly tried to find a position to save my arms and legs. Hosein had said the journey's first part wouldn't be more than two hours, depending on the morning traffic, but we were starting late—Hosein's fault, not mine. He had to drive into town to pick up a last-minute load. With the stop-and-go jolts and the horns, I wouldn't sleep. Once again, I'd feel my body go numb.

It took an hour and a half going in, forty-five minutes getting out. When we finally started to cruise, the truck slowed down. They'd hit us here if they were going to hit us at all. I couldn't hear anything clearly over engine and tire noise. I'd have to get in the box two more times: at a highway intersection where Hosein had occasionally encountered police and on the outskirts of Ardabil. After that, I wouldn't be a cripple for at least twelve hours.

I waited for Hosein to shift through the gears before screaming for permission to get out. My ears hurt from the trapped sound. I yelled again, hitting the wood with my fist. Swinging from the wrist, I couldn't thump hard. Endless minutes passed before Hosein pounded on the mattress and yelled. Turning back a fingernail, I popped the lid.

"Did you hear me yell!" I snarled, trying to rise. Again, I'd lost a leg and an arm. I grabbed my inert forearm with my good hand and put it on my lap, using my head to hold the lid.

"I heard a noise."

"Was it clear or not?" I snapped.

"Clear, but I wanted to be sure."

"I'm not getting back in that fucking box!" With my mouth, I pulled off the glove.

"Your choice," Hosein answered, not taking his eyes off the road. He'd used a polite Persian construction, making me feel like a heel.

Once again, we were flanked by snowcapped mountains and rolling plains. Hosein pointed out that the snow had dropped lower on the mountainsides. He wanted to drive away from, not toward, the cold. He didn't want to get stuck and watch the countryside suddenly go white and subzero. I didn't either, but I wanted to go to Ardabil.

Nursing my fingernail and my emotions, I quietly watched the traffic, including three army troop trucks. The drivers were the first proper soldiers I'd seen. When Hosein said "Sorry," I knew it was time. I rolled back over the seat, my tingling arm holding the lid. Only if Hosein stopped would I latch it. Once in, I realized I'd left my gloves behind. However, no one would think anything of cheap, Turkish-made black leather gloves. Had I taken anything else out of my pockets? My foreign cigarettes and fancy knife were still in my coat, I thought. I had a small bag of personal things and my little emergency telephone book, but they never left the box. Fear was again making the improbable seem likely.

Had the CIA's Soviet and Eastern European agents smuggled out of the bloc in trapped compartments felt like this—blind, maddeningly dependent, missing family desperately, and wondering if any cause had merit in the dark? I hoped they hadn't. Theirs had been a real war, not curiosity run amok. When historians finally get into the Directorate of Operations' archives and assess the clandestine service's contribution to winning the Cold War, they'll not be kind. The vast majority of its intelligence was humdrum or inaccurate—

the product of double agents, or mediocre ones. Nevertheless, the Agency had given the natives a weapon against tyranny. A double-edged weapon, of course, but I suspected most agents hadn't cared. They were willing to die to get even and to expiate their sins. To its credit, the CIA had usually done a lot to safeguard its East Bloc agents: the ones in the trapped compartments hadn't been allowed to fulfill any death wishes. Buried on their last clandestine voyage, they must have run through their entire lives. When you're alone, without light, freedom seems so abstract.

I was hidden for another thirty minutes. This time I didn't yell or knock. When I got out, the mountains were bigger, the snowless patches and rock faces were brown in color. The tallest ones, between ten thousand and fifteen thousand feet, had lengthy jagged peaks rising far above an unbroken high-rising base, which extended as far as I could see. Snow entirely covered the more eroded, rounded mountains as well as the tops of taller foothills. We were leaving behind the farmers and plowed fields that made Azarbaijan Iran's richest agricultural province. The land was slowly becoming barren. No trees, no shrubs—nothing but rock, snow, and dirt, occasionally hidden by withered grass. The rolling hills were developing valleys. I understood why Hosein didn't like driving this route in winter. In the fifteenth century, radical Shi'ism had been born up here. In the mountains, you either look down into the abyss or look up toward heaven. It's easy to dream of conquest when the horizons are so wide.

In springtime, Hosein said, driving from Tabriz to Ardabil was pretty. The rolling hills and lower mountain slopes were covered in green and the skies were sea-blue, not winter-gray. Medieval Muslim historians often divide the world into climatic belts, called in Arabic *iqlîm*. A people's character could not be properly assessed without considering the climate and topography that had nurtured or challenged it. How human character and religious inspiration develop are essentially unanswerable questions. But I thought I could see Azarbaijan's severe seasonal changes perhaps behind the appeal and triumph of radical Shi'ism under the Safavids. Moments of soft rains, lush grass, and flowers, surrounded by months of killing heat and cold. Men who are accustomed to living in hell can go wild when promised beauty they have fleetingly enjoyed.

A particularly steep turn sent my mind back to a zigzagging road that led to a fourteenth-century, mile-high Byzantine monastery nestled in the mountains above the Black Sea. There, more than in any other place, I'd felt God's pull. The sensations had been peaceful. The Sumela monastery hangs off a verdant cliff, the pine forests above and below fed by gentle mountain streams. Frescoes and mosaics of Christ, defaced long ago by Turkish peasants and more recently by Turkish tourists, cover every wall. In late spring, surrounded by fog, you feel you have ascended to heaven.

The Safavids had made it that far, to the Zigana Mountains, the farthest west they ever raided. Under the leadership of Shaykh Jonayd (d. 1460), Shah Ismail's grandfather, in 1456 they attacked the Byzantine port of Trebizond, thirty miles north of Sumela. They failed to take the city and went back to Ardabil. The next time they stormed west into Anatolia they were met by the Ottomans at Chaldiran.

The Safavids had started under Shaykh Safi ad-Din (1252–1334) as peaceful Sunni mystics. Two hundred years later, under Shaykh Jonayd, they'd become *gholat*, Shi'ite extremists who worshiped their leader as God. In the medieval Islamic world, after the coming of the Mongols, nothing seemed secure. A Mongol general sacked Baghdad in 1258 and killed the Abbasid Caliph, the spiritual sovereign, if not the ruler as his predecessors had been, of the Sunni Muslim world for five hundred years. Curious as well as savage, the Mongols experimented with Christianity, Judaism, Buddhism, shamanism, and both Sunni and Shi'ite Islam. With the Sunni Muslim status quo reeling in defeat, ordinary Muslims sought refuge in mysticism. Illiterate Turkish nomads, the Mongols' advance guard, gravitated toward Sufi mystics, who spread Allah's word orally, without reference to his restrictive Laws. Shi'ism is naturally more mystical than Sunnism. Its numerous semidivine figures, the Imams, are tailor-made for folklore's quest for magic men. With its tragic essence—Ali and his son Hosein triumphed through suffering and death—Shi'ism gained converts in the disorder; armed Shi'ism gained power.

Warring constantly against neighboring Christian kingdoms in the Caucasus Mountains, Shaykh Jonayd turned an informal body of believers into an army. With each collision, his followers, the *Qizilbash* (the Redheads) grew. The ordinary faithful looked on, alarmed. Jonayd and the Son of God Haydar (d. 1488), Ismail's father, both lost their lives to Sunni Iranian kings who'd seen the Safavid love of raiding infidels turn against their own once too often.

I looked out at windswept rock and blown snow and tried to imagine thousands of red-turbaned, mounted warriors moving in twos and threes through mountain roads. In a Persian history of Shah Tahmasp, Ismail's son, there's an account of the shah in the highlands. To demonstrate to a foreign dignitary the faith of his men, he threw a handkerchief into the air above a gorge. A warrior from his retinue leaped from his horse, caught the handkerchief, and plummeted, blessing his Master as he fell. The story could be the vision of an obsequious chronicler. I didn't think so. For a would-be martyr, jumping off a cliff at God's command is more compelling than riding a motorcycle through a minefield.

In university, I'd rarely been persuaded by the academic articles and books about religious extremism. Holy war often became more an economic than a religious mission, either an excuse to send unwanted younger sons to plunder faraway lands or a socioecological explosion of too many men on arid soil. I could never understand why a passion for God couldn't come first, and economic and political calculations second, with no contradiction between them. Thus, Shaykh Jonayd turned violent because his understanding of God had changed. Biting poverty, rich infidel knights, Christian Caucasian women easily raided for harems, the fatigue of preaching goodwill toward men, narcissism, or some childhood trauma perhaps had led Jonayd to his conversion. However, in his mind his faith was surely seamless. Muslim true believers see God undivided everywhere, in everything.

Often, at Middle Eastern studies conferences and in small colloquies with my peers, I'd heard history inverted by experts trying to be kind. Their sympathy for Islam led them to treat Muslims like children, not adults. Western civilization was too strong, Islam too weak. We shouldn't criticize Muslims as we criticized ourselves. They couldn't really defend themselves; we had to leap to their aid.

Islamic militancy and holy war were particularly touchy subjects. For these sympathetic experts, the Crusades became a reprehensible endeavor, the Muslim conquests a liberating exercise. By extension, everything else was transmuted. A progressive ahead of his times, the Prophet Muhammad primarily encouraged Muslims to wage a jihad *inside* their minds. His slaughter of the Arabian Jewish tribe, the Banu Qurayza, was therefore interpreted as a mundane power play not intrinsically connected to his message. The Holy Law division of the world into the *Dar al-Islam*, the House of Islam, and the *Dar al-Harb*, the House of War, didn't mean what it said. Similarly, contemporary fundamentalism shouldn't arouse much fear. It was a natural, if not commendable, recoiling of Muslim mores from an ever more vulgar West. Of course, fundamentalists would probably respect democracy if politically given the chance in free elections. The Ayatollah shouldn't have passed a death sentence against Salman Rushdie, but, really, Rushdie had been mean to Islam. In any case, *The Satanic Verses* was, they insisted, an awful book.

Sensitive, sympathetic, and secularized, Islam's Western friends couldn't recognize holy war as a righteous cause. Christians, Muslims, and Jews had to reinterpret it out of God's will. We couldn't praise what had become extinct in ourselves: a faith that converts violence and death into love. But martyrdom—making the ultimate sacrifice for Goodness and Truth—is a major component of radical Islam. Take it away and the *Qizilbash* who went over the edge and the Ahmads in the minefields were just deluded fools. Divine inspiration is supposed to rework a man's understanding of both the sacred and the profane.

Death-wish believers have never been a majority in Islam. Most Muslims, like most Christians and Jews, have lived peacefully with their understanding of the One True God. Muslims, however, *have* remained more susceptible than other monotheistic believers to religious militancy. Unable lawfully to separate church and state, secularized Muslims more easily give offense to their more faithful brethren. In comparison, the two older monotheisms are asleep, victims of Greek philosophy and Western man's triumph over both hell and heaven.

Of course, modern Westerners still seek transcendent inspiration—but in diluted, self-conscious forms. I'd joined the CIA to wage a cold war against the Soviet Union and Communism, as well as to pry open the Iranian mind. I'd believed passionately in the cause. The Soviet Union was Evil, perhaps not as evil as it had been under Lenin and Stalin, but evil nonetheless. It was an affront to the human spirit, an Orwellian nightmare of constantly changing encyclopedias and street signs, a vicious Western aberration intent on undermining the West. A left-winger in my youth, a right-winger by the end of college, I had the convert's desire to carry the struggle to its source. The CIA was the only institution battling inside the devil's lair. I didn't want to be a Soviet–East European ops officer in Moscow, Leningrad, Budapest, or Prague. I didn't have the proper schooling. Only in the Muslim world did I feel sufficiently at home to ask a man to commit treason. Nevertheless, I felt proud that I was a member of an institution that fought the good fight, that would give me personally the occasional opportunity to confront Soviets. For a Jewish atheist, this was far more transcendent than perfunctory reflections during High Holy Days. And the Agency gave me the chance to meet Russians head-on, to listen to them, sober, spout the Party line and, drunk, confess their youthful Komsomol love affairs and bemoan their miserable adult lives. There was little to no intelligence value in any of this, but it was a pleasant way of getting promoted. More important, it was an opportunity to witness up close the death of Communism, the West's last great faith. In my drunken Russian friends, I could smell the remnant of holy war; I could feel the sensations in myself.

In Khomeini's revolutionary speeches, I'd first caught the modern Iranian true-believer scent. His speeches were more moving than his books. A trained legal scholar before all else, Khomeini could never quite cut loose in print. Though not a prolific cleric, he had an impressive paper trail. But books on Islamic law about inheritance, no-interest loans, or the level of sin in a man fornicating with a pigeon, camel, or goat—the obligatory stuff for every ayatollah—

aren't ideal vehicles for revealing divine inspiration. In his strictly political commentary, however, I smelled it. Khomeini's master-piece, *Islamic Government*, a 1970 collection of lectures on religion and politics, is a rambling exposition of Muslim political practice and theory, but in it you can clearly see a prophet calling upon well-organized clerical cells to start the jihad.

In Khomeini's speeches, God and the vox populi thunder. It is still astonishing to remember how Khomeini caught the West off guard, even specialists and intelligence officers who were paid to keep their eyes open. As Khomeini was buckling the Pahlavi regime from his exile in France, Washington and the *New York Times* un-believably called the Ayatollah an enigma. As clearly as Hitler in *Mein Kampf*, Khomeini had told the world his intentions in *Islamic Government* and in mass-distributed cassette recordings. An eminent professor of Middle Eastern studies had tried to warn the CIA that Khomeini was not, as Senator Edward Kennedy had surmised, the George Washington of Iran. The professor translated passages of *Islamic Government* and sent them to Langley, but the CIA couldn't confirm Khomeini as the author of the book, even though the Library of Congress had the text in its stacks. In late 1978, after the Shah was finished, the CIA finally paid for a translation of *Islamic Government*—from an Arabic edition. When I arrived on the Iran desk, I found numerous unopened copies stacked along the walls.

For more than an hour, Hosein and I didn't talk. After my nervous outburst, he probably thought I was no longer the ideal companion. He perhaps even thought I was a coward. My attention diverted by a cracked fingernail and guilt, I didn't see it. Hosein's braking got my attention. A small truck had smashed into a car coming our way. Miraculously, neither had fallen off the winding road. I saw neither blood nor bodies nor an ambulance, just burnt steel and broken glass. Then I saw leather belts and holsters. One had a light beard, the other didn't. I made a quick move for the box, but Hosein already had my arm. They'd seen both of us through the window.

"Relax!" Hosein ordered, still holding my arm. "This isn't a check."

He was obviously right. But if they recognized me as a foreigner, they might ask anyway. How many foreigners use transport trucks to travel in Iran? How many foreigners go to Ardabil? All I needed was one question, "Can I see your passport?" and I'd be in trouble. "I left my passport in Tabriz" didn't seem a plausible reply. "I lost it in Tabriz and was headed back to Tehran via Ardabil" seemed the only way out. I had to see the tombs of Safi ad-Din and Shah Ismail, I'd explain; I'd studied them in school, and I'd never have the chance to come back once I was in Tehran. And, yes, I always dress like a truck driver. I'd be French, naturally—they didn't have a consulate in Tabriz—and speak just a little Persian, enough to throw myself on their mercy and express my love of Iran. To increase the noise and bother, Hosein would plead loudly for Persian generosity toward strangers.

Then the clean-shaven one came to my side of the road and looked at me. I couldn't look away, so I stared back. He couldn't possibly see the color of my eyes through the dirty glass, I morbidly told myself, and even if he did, lots of Iranians have green eyes. Then I glanced into the side-view mirror. There were three cars behind us. He was looking at them, not me.

"I think he's looking at the cars behind us," I blurted.

"*Inshallah*," Hosein mumbled, not taking his eyes off the bearded one.

We started moving again, slowly driving by the wreck, using the narrow inner shoulder that quickly ended in a near-vertical boulder rock face. The clean-shaven fellow crossed in front of us and hand-signaled Hosein to drive by more quickly. I sank back in my seat and stopped the Persian rehearsals in my mind. With each obstacle overcome, I wasn't becoming more adept. Use false documentation a few times or do a dozen clandestine meetings and you're a pro fondly remembering adrenaline rushes. I'd loved the constant jolts of walk-ins. I needed surprises to compel my attention; otherwise, I stood back and watched myself work.

Now I was overwhelmed. I'd overestimated myself. I couldn't stop shaking inside.

"You wish you'd got a visa?" Hosein grunted between gears.

He'd read my mind. A visa and a Ministry of Cultural Guidance minder to get me through the security checks. But you can't travel with a minder and expect to learn much—unless you recruit him. If the original plan had worked, I would have traveled alone and my problems wouldn't have disappeared. Visas aren't safe-conduct passes. The rules can always change on you in clerical Iran.

The Islamic Republic doesn't have one government; it has several. Neither Khameneh'i nor Rafsanjani is the Shah. Clerical networks with numerous, sometimes contradictory, allegiances penetrate every government agency, as they do every seminary school. The clergy and student mollahs in government maintain loyalties to their extended families, former teachers and classmates, *and* to their employers. Major institutions—the army, the Revolutionary Guard Corps, the Interior and Intelligence Ministries, the Foundation for the Oppressed, formerly the Pahlavi Foundation, a giant "charitable" organization that succors the poor while illicitly making millions, if not billions, for the revolutionary elite—have strong identities and, to a lesser extent, power independent of the revolutionary clergy. Simply put, Iran's government is a bureaucratic mess where a wiring diagram makes no sense and everybody gets in everybody else's business.

Though a visa to a foreigner would be cleared by Intelligence, clearances can vary. I had planned on sliding by, noticed but not flagged. At any time, of course, Intelligence could take a closer look. And the Interior Ministry, more powerful and just as curious in-country, could get involved. And further questioning would have been my undoing. An uncovered U.S. Intelligence officer in their midst would be an irresistible target. Once a spy always a spy. A visa would by no means have been safer than the box.

"Do you wish I'd got a visa?" I joked, after we were clear of the collision and security.

Hosein grinned, exhaled, and said nothing. I didn't think the accident had spooked him. Yet maybe he was getting tired of his cargo, rethinking the profit versus risk. Or maybe he'd heard a sincere question behind the joke. Persians lie, cheat, and swindle everyone but their mothers; yet they can lay down their lives for a stranger. The deception, cynicism, and mordant wit come so fast and furious it's easy to forget how sensitive Persians are, how easily a foreigner can wound them.

"If I'd got a visa, I would have seen Isfahan and Mashhad, not Maku and Marand. I can't complain," I said.

"We could make it to Isfahan and Mashhad if you wanted. You shouldn't leave Iran without seeing them."

I couldn't tell whether Hosein was serious. I'd dreamed of those two cities for nearly twenty years. Once, I had the idea of trying to reach Mashhad from the nearby Turkmen border. Even before the Soviet Union went down, you could cross over without much trouble. Surviving afterward was again the problem. However, I'd never been to Turkmenistan and I'd met only one Turkoman in my life, a KGB officer who made his Russian colleagues look genteel. Without any country experience or friends, I abandoned the idea of crossing that border. Turkey offered friends, a much easier border, and the historical route to Ardabil. When Hosein offered Isfahan and Mashhad, I didn't see their treasures. I thought of home.

"Another trip," I said, scanning the mountains and the long empty curves of road in front and behind.

"Your choice," Hosein said more warmly.

The snow was now heavier on the sides of the road. I couldn't tell whether the wind or a plow was responsible. The snow had melted and frozen again. Hosein said the snow sometimes reached five meters. Several inches would send us to the Caspian Sea and screw up our schedule. But I had to go to Ardabil, even if it was as ugly as Chaldiran. Also, Hosein had cargo. As long as it didn't snow, he'd forgive me for a day in the mountains.

Because Hosein was smoking a foul-smelling Turkish cigarette, I handed him a Marlboro. I'd stuffed several packs of Marlboros in my coat before crossing. You could get them in Iran, but they were expensive. I also had several plastic butane lighters with the Marlboro Man colorfully imprinted on them—little tokens of friendship that might help me a lot. In the old days, I always had Camels, Winstons, Marlboros, and Dunhills ready for Persians in walk-in and hotel rooms. I also had Tirs, the Iranian cigarette, to show a little native color and concern. Iranians never took Tirs.

I'd never forgotten looking up the word *tir*. It means "arrow" or, in certain contexts, as in French, "shoot." In the dictionary, I'd found: *Ura be tohmat-e jasusi tirbaran kardand*, "He was shot for being a spy." Cigarettes and dead spies became forever associated in my mind.

Hosein took the Marlboro, lit it, and ground his other cigarette out.

"Did you ever haul an Air Force pilot over the border?" I asked.

"No," Hosein answered, wrinkling his brow.

"I knew one in Istanbul who got over the border in a truck," I continued. "He'd come from some village on the Caspian Sea, not far from Ardabil. I was just wondering whether you might have helped him."

The Air Force officer had been a friend, an exile stuck in Istanbul. Every so often, we'd meet and talk for hours about Iranian military life, more often about Istanbul. In the year that I knew him, he cursed neither the clerics nor the Shah. A noble and honest man, he drank too much. Unlike most Persians, he didn't have a family telephoning, reanimating his soul. On our first meeting, he'd reluctantly asked me to help him to the States. I didn't, and he never asked again. He disappeared from Istanbul one summer, and I prayed to God that he'd made it to the Promised Land.

"No, I'm sure. Never an Air Force officer."

Hosein was sucking down the Marlboro, the ash dropping on the floor.

"Did you know many Iranian officers who fled to Turkey?" he asked, without looking at me.

Hosein had an inkling of what I'd done. Specifics and acronyms had never been discussed. They didn't need to be.

"Several. Perhaps I met one or two men you'd helped."

"Did they make it to America?"

"Legally, or illegally?" I asked, tossing the opened pack of cigarettes on the filthy, tool-covered dashboard.

"Legally," Hosein laughed.

"Some did. Most didn't. A few went to Europe. The rest got Turkish asylum or lived illegally in Turkey until they found a way to America. Why do you ask?"

"I just wonder if they're happy outside of Iran."

"What do you think?"

"I don't think we can be happy away from home."

I didn't say so, but I disagreed. Generally, expatriates did a good job of appearing content. Persians are intrepid and chameleonlike abroad. That was why the clerics had nothing to fear from the expatriate community, and why they didn't need to send Intelligence Ministry hit teams to kill them, as they often did. Expats loved Iran, had bouts of homesickness, and ran their own Persian newspapers, radio and TV channels. But they were gradually disappearing into the foreign woodwork.

"Why not?" I asked, cracking the window for fresh air.

"Only an Iranian can understand an Iranian."

Again, I couldn't fully agree. Lord Curzon, the viceroy of India, the Great Game British foreign minister par excellence, and author of *Persia and the Persian Question,* had dissected Iranians precisely. The American teacher-turned-Isfahani fruit farmer Terence O'Donnell had softly exposed the rhythms of prerevolutionary Persian life in *Garden of the Brave in War.* No Westerner has written more lovingly of the Persian soul.

"Do Iranians understand themselves?" I asked.

"No!" he shouted, popping the rim of the wheel with his hand. "But only Iranians know how messed up we are."

"Are you angry at the soldiers who left Iran?"

"No. How can I be? They were scared."

"Did you ever think about you and Hazra going to Turkey or trying for America?"

"No. I don't make much money, but Hazra and I survive. I can't imagine living someplace besides Tabriz."

"If Hazra were married?"

"No."

"Do you think things will get better in Iran?" I quickly asked, sidestepping Hazra.

"Things will get worse. The clergy will feed on us until we're bone white."

"And you want to stay?"

"I want to watch it fall apart. One of these days, we'll start to shoot the clergy. I want to be here when that happens."

I couldn't tell whether my friend had any dreams other than revenge. Revenge can easily sustain a man for a lifetime. And in Persia

a taste for revenge comes with mother's milk. Khomeini waited decades to get even with cleric-kicking Pahlavis; Hosein could wait at
least as long to get even with the mollahs. However, I still wanted
to know, if Hosein had got close to Khomeini's corpse, would he
have kissed it or spit on it. My gut told me he would have cried
and not put water to his lips for days.

"And you? Did you support the revolution?"

Hosein's question startled me. I'd never been asked my opinion
by an Iranian. It was gospel among the middle and upper classes
that "we" had. Disenchanted revolutionaries were now gradually
changing their minds—better to blame us than blame themselves.

"Why do you ask?"

"I want to know whether you made the same mistake I did."

Though I wasn't sure, I thought Hosein was directing the question to me, not me and Washington, D.C. If so, we really had
become friends.

"I thought the revolution a good idea," I lied.

Actually, I'd strictly adhered to Professor J. B. Kelly's fundamental
Middle Eastern law: every modern regime is worse than its monar-
chical predecessor. Before and during the revolution, I'd seen too
many *Mojahedin-e Khalq* student meetings in the United States and
Europe to feel good about the anti-Shah side. Listening to secularized Iranian professors grow rhapsodic as they described Khomeini's
humanity and democratic nature, I could hear the firing squads.
Given the rabid nature of the hard-core left, I'd felt sympathy for
both the Shah and the clerics.

"We all know it was a mistake," Hosein continued. "Iranians are
too proud to admit they were wrong. The mollahs still rule Iran
because we're too proud."

I was intrigued. The U.S.-clerical conspiracies, one of Hosein's
pet themes, had disappeared. Right or wrong in his analysis, he was
now consistent in his personal beliefs and political views.

"Are you saying everybody wishes the Shah still ruled Iran?"

"Yes, I think Iranians say that to themselves. I hated the Shah
and I'm glad he fell, but I wish it hadn't happened."

I wasn't sure there was an inconsistency in what Hosein was saying. It was very Persian to want something your own emotions and

actions had killed. Iranians prize honesty, yet privately deride its practitioners as fools. "Down with the Shah!" and "Wish he were still here!" could be two choruses in a new national anthem.

"You wouldn't fight to restore the monarchy?"

"Never!" Hosein snapped. "The Pahlavis were dogs!"

"But you and everybody else wishes they still ruled Iran?"

"Unless you're a mollah or one of their parasites—"

Hosein cut his response as he braked sharply and downshifted. We had a clunker of a car in front us crawling around a bend. We'd just passed through some sagging stone-and-brick villages where the only signs of life were tethered goats. I could smell something burning, a trash dump or perhaps, as in eastern Turkey, squares of dried sheep and goat shit used for home-heating fuel—an unpleasant but not awful odor. I was ready to ask Hosein, then changed my mind. "Do Azaris burn animal shit in winter to stay warm?" seemed a hopelessly offensive question to a citizen of an oil-rich nation.

"Are Iranians less proud now than before the revolution?" I asked instead.

"We are still proud. But we're ashamed of acting like Arabs. *They* should've had Khomeini, not us. Iranians are civilized. We always thought we were better than them."

"So the mollahs rule because everybody's too ashamed to admit they're *Aaaarabs*," I said in jest.

As soon as I said it, I wished I hadn't. He was sincerely trying to lay blame squarely on his shoulders, not slough it off on Arabs.

"The mollahs rule because we're too proud," Hosein continued. "When I visited my family in Turkey before the revolution, I felt pity for them. They'd been Iranian. When I go to Turkey now, I know my family pities me. I pity myself."

"Most Iranians never leave Iran. What do they care what others think?"

"We all feel it. We all know we've ruined the revolution. There's not an Iranian alive who doesn't know it. We were supposed to *lead* the Muslim world."

Hosein was slowly tightening and loosening his grip on the wheel. "One of these days, we're going to shoot the goat-fucking mollahs, or we'll make them all go live in Iraq with the dogs."

. . .

I hadn't conceived of national shame as an advantage for the clerics. Fatigue, yes. Iranians were now working around the clock to pay the bills. The more they worked, the less time they had to conspire. In the 1970s, when the Iranian economy was comparatively in much better shape, students, professors, and functionaries had more generous salaries and scholarships, making it easier both to eat and to undermine the regime.

Persians *are* proud and haughty. I'd met a number of foreigners who'd dealt face-to-face with Pahlavis and mollahs. They found them essentially unchanged: too proud for their own good. Persian pride had never smacked me in the face the way the Turkish pride had. Turks give ground to no man. As an American and *the Angel*, I always had special dispensation among Iranians. But I'd seen Iranian pride flare at others. What Hosein said made some sense. Perhaps they were truly ashamed of the mess they'd made. So ashamed that they might even, perversely, support the mollahs.

Misplaced pride had certainly helped the Agency keep going. If a C/O spends years engaged in operational exaggeration and deceit, and rises through the ranks for his achievement, it is unlikely he'll turn against himself. Most of his friends would be case officers. His wife and children would be proud of his work's secret importance. Given the poor pay, there's not much else. I'd not forgotten the overheard words of a Near East Division chief: "I like our officers thirty-five years old, with children and mortgages. They do what they're told."

When I was in the Agency—before the February 1994 arrest of the CIA officer–turned–KGB mole Aldrich Ames—all of us were proud and most of us knew we were lying. At the Farm, with cheap beer on tap, the old-timers would occasionally tell the truth. They'd talk about how much money they'd saved, and the great trips Uncle Sam had paid for. A senior Near East Division officer gladly recounted tales of the Lebanese beauties he'd banged, less enthusiastically the meaningful intelligence he'd collected. When the shells started flying, he'd bunkered down in Beirut with videos and let State security officers do the dirty work. Sober, he told how he worked the streets with a Browning semi-automatic strapped under his arm, risking his life to save others. "It's all shit," an inebriated old Vietnam-Asia hand once declared. "We're all a bunch of liars in a goddamn paper game. Just get overseas and live well. Fuck the rest." The next day, over a doughnut and coffee, the fellow was outraged that the *New York Times* had scolded the Agency. And the paper *was* wrong: it had attacked the CIA for nefarious behavior, not incompetence.

Change countries, change divisions: the lies and pride stayed the same. After work hours on the operational desks, after the division chiefs stopped calling, the minions would gather and confess. Almost always, they'd pull back before it was too late. Things were awful because this division chief or that chief of station was a vicious, incompetent cheat. No one wanted to connect the dots—the fraud in all the divisions. If you did, your hope would be gone. Also, someone senior to you might overhear your doubts. No one wanted to admit we were far from the Best and the Brightest. No one wanted to wonder why he'd got in and why he'd made it so far. So publicly you stayed proud and bristled at any outsider's criticisms. You knew the great work the DO was doing; others couldn't know because they weren't cleared.

It was late in the afternoon when I pissed the snow off a rock. With snow falling, my steaming trace would soon be gone. We'd both seen the snow-rich, thick cloud cover. The mountains were going gray in the fading light. Dreading to get back into the box, I walked up and down the road. Above and below, there wasn't a car or truck in view. We'd reached the edge of the plateau. Once over, we'd find Ardabil, a millennia-old oasis town, the cradle of Safavid power. So far, though, there were no tree-lined rivers in sight. Just slopes and mounds of brown rock, dirt, and snow. Hearing Hosein shout, I turned around, stretched my arms, back, and legs, and slowly walked to the truck. Before I got back into the box, Hosein gave me a withering look.

I heard the town before I felt it. After only a few minutes of surrounding noise, we turned off the main road. The bumps needled my shoulder and hip. The deep potholes hammered me. I hadn't thought about fashioning a cushion; neither had Hosein. Given my size and slanted angle, it would have been hard to put something in. Also, I liked having just a little wiggle room.

Mercifully, we stopped before my hip broke. We'd made it to the storehouse, so far as I could tell, without a security check. I heard Hosein's door open and shut and voices of men walking away. In the quiet darkness, my mind sped forward to the next border crossing and to how sore and cold I'd be. I expected the return crossing to take longer. The Turks would certainly want to snoop for drugs, carpets, untaxed goods, and, perhaps, undesirable Kurds, and the Iranians for unforgiven blacklisted personalities. But Hosein encouraged me: Iran to Turkey was not necessarily worse. You could get screwed horribly either way. It all depended on the truck traffic, weather, and the thoroughness, or venal whimsy, of border officials.

Once in Turkey, I'd break every fingernail to get out of the box. Once free, I'd drop and kiss the ground at the first statue of Atatürk. In eastern Turkey, he's always a soldier with a distinctly fascist mien. In the West, he's more often in bow tie and tuxedo. I wanted to see him uniformed and ramrod straight, holding Islam at bay. Then I'd get soused, and return to Ishakpasha, the ruined Ottoman palace, with mixed European, Turkish, and Iranian designs, and walk up the narrow stone steps to the roofless second floor. The two of us would be alone, and I'd thank Hosein for what he'd done, and pay him some more.

And then I'd return to Istanbul and a friend's apartment overlooking the Golden Horn. I'd go see an American film in a cinema with a bar. I'd go to the Pera Bookstore, just off Istiklal Caddesi, on the same block where the Whirling Dervishes still spin for tourists, if not themselves. The bookstore specialized in the private libraries of bankrupt Turkish diplomats; over the years, I'd done well. Then off to the Orient Express's Pera Pelas Hotel. I'd sit in the bar's big velour chairs and drink rakis, Turkish pastis. Then I'd have my Turkish friends put me to bed. I'd listen to their son, a devout Muslim, softly chant the Qur'an in the adjoining bedroom, and I'd put away my silver worry beads that had seen me through Iran.

The rear door clanked open. I bumped my head again. I listened to the footsteps, sliding skids, and several voices echoing off the ground. Periodically, I pushed the little illuminating button on my Casio watch, trying to count five-minute intervals. Each time, I pushed too soon.

I knew Hosein would have to drink tea and gossip for a bit. I waited, trying to put my mind elsewhere. Swallowing through my sore throat kept bringing me back. I didn't have the flu—Hazra's food and the day inside had helped—but I didn't feel well.

My will was in free fall. Hosein had warned that we couldn't use the truck much in Tehran. He'd get a car, but the idea terrified me. I'd have no place to hide except the trunk, an unacceptable concealment device. Tonight I'd suggest it was time to go home.

I heard Hosein's Azari voice before the truck door opened. "Hey, Mr. America!" he shouted as the bumps and potholes started pummeling me again.

I almost had the lid open by the time he thumped. It was dusk and the snow was falling more heavily than before. In the headlights, the wind twirled the snow. I was numb once again.

"If you want to see the tomb, we'd better go now," Hosein said, turning to check on me. "We are going to leave tonight, not tomorrow morning."

"I thought you said we shouldn't drive here at night."

"We shouldn't."

I thought night driving stupid. If we got stuck in Ardabil, though, I couldn't halt the trip. We'd have to go to Tehran. There would be no turning back. In Tehran's megalopolis, I had a foreboding, things would go awry.

We didn't drive long. Hosein parked somewhere on the edge of town, putting my side of the truck next to a knee-high snowdrift. When I dropped, it cracked, pushing up my pants legs. Hosein was at the rear of the truck, and over his head I could see adobe houses on slightly undulating ground, some with drooping brick walls. After I complimented him on the parking job, he scooted off on a footpath winding between mud-brick houses and stubby, leafless trees. I sniffed that slightly acrid smell. Somebody was burning dung.

Ardabil was a crumbling city of around 120,000 people, the only town in mountainous northeastern Azarbaijan. It could support such a large population because small mountain rivers crisscrossed on its desolate plateau, providing minimal sustenance for men, women, goats, and sheep. The town had also become a transit point for trucks running between the western rim of the Caspian Sea and Tabriz. Ardabil was an ancient town that survived but never prospered.

We turned onto a windswept paved road, where I saw on both sides a short row of low-rise cinderblock buildings. Next to Ardabil's sagging and cracked mud-brick houses, these buildings looked immense, strong, and foreign. At first glance, Ardabil appeared a large, densely packed village of one- and two-story buildings. Commerce seemed limited to small dimly lit street-side shops. Hosein said Ardabil had a covered bazaar: in winter, it was dead except for the shops selling winter clothing. I suspected it was the cold that packed Ardabil's houses and buildings more closely together than those in Tabriz. You wouldn't want to walk far in winter.

Winter hadn't yet killed the street life, however. Surly-looking men in dark, heavy wool coats were walking everywhere, often blocking slow cars in the streets. Every teahouse we passed was jammed solid with smoking men. As we walked by a small grocery store, two chador-clad women popped out, one of them nearly bumping into me. I excused myself; neither one smiled back. Unlike in Tabriz, you could clearly hear people talking over cars and trucks; in Ardabil, I was *positive* everyone we passed was staring at me. Hosein turned down a long alley and onto a frozen packed-earth road that ran between the back side of a row of mud-brick houses and a series of walls delimited by footpaths. When we crossed the next intersection, I spotted a dome rising just above the surrounding buildings. From the apex to the base, the dome was made of brown bricks with blue, hollow, diamond-shaped designs painted on it. I then saw the mud-brick, circular dome tower and two smaller domes: one a mix of geometric patterns in blue, white, yellow, and black, the other undecorated earthen-brown bricks. Individually, the domes were beautiful; but together they formed an awkward triptych of colliding colors and shapes.

Pilgrims in army coats, we approached the fourteenth-century mosque-mausoleum of Shaykh Safi ad-Din and Shah Ismail. The domes reminded me of a complex of astronomical observatories.

With the low-cast sky swallowing the mountains, I was on the threshold of heaven. I could see no one in the mosque's square or outside the surrounding buildings. I prayed the mausoleum was still open. Somewhere about, there had to be a watchful eye. I waited at a distance while Hosein went in. No one was near the tomb. What appeared to be a little guard stand near the mausoleum entrance was empty. Unless someone was inside, concealed by adjacent ruins, or watching us from a nearby building, we were alone. Waiting, I tried to read a band of cursive script that wrapped one of the domes.

I stopped trying when Hosein waved for me to come in. I took another long look. There had to be a guard somewhere.

He was inside with Hosein. He was kind, Hosein said: he'd give us a little time before closing. The guard was standing close to Safi ad-Din's tomb, on the other side of an ornate silver gate. He stared at me a moment and walked out. Keeping my eye on the door, I slowly turned to see all the delicate bricks and tiles, relatively few of them damaged by time. Beams of evening light came through small windows illuminating alternating geometric patterns. An unlit chandelier cast a thin shadow. Even inside it was cold enough to frost my breath, but not enough to kill the foot odor of centuries of shoeless believers. The Safavid tombs were spread throughout different chambers covered with ornate carpets. Each chamber had a heavy silver gate, and a few gates were seconded by wooden barriers. The coffins were made of carved wood with inlaid polished and precious stones.

I turned, looked upward, and said, "Allah." Before the echo faded, I said it again, and then followed more softly with "Isma'il." Hosein was standing next to me. I couldn't tell whether he understood or thought I'd lost my mind. He knew me well enough to know that I understood this wasn't how an infidel became a Muslim. I walked over to Shah Ismail's chamber and threw a coin beyond the silver door. It rolled off the coffin but stayed near. I took one more slow spin, imagining the chamber full of Redheads in long mantles draped with swords burying their *morshed-e kamel*, their Perfect Master.

For the first time in my life, I'd made a pilgrimage, a trip into

the past meant to free your soul. Years before, under the guidance
of an academic master, I'd been fascinated by Shah Ismail and the
parallels between him and Khomeini. My teacher—an atheist, a
fallen Jew of unconventional habits and passions, a linguist whose
talents reached from Beijing to Paris, and a former intelligence officer—had tried for thirty years to touch the Safavids through historical chronicles and poetry. Rare among accomplished scholars, he
was more interested in understanding people than in publishing his
work. He didn't mind my errant soul, my preference for bars over
archives, travel over study, my irregular hours. He, too, didn't like
classwork in the morning. He knew how I wanted to peel open the
Iranian mind. He sent me on my way to Langley, warning of the
profession's defects and growing death rot. Also, he warned me I
might hate Persians more and love them less by the mission's end.
My professor should have been buried in his own Safavid tomb,
covered with silk carpets and crowned by a red turban. A kind and
gentle *morshed* didn't belong in a suburban grave with infidels all
around.

"I'm finished," I said.

"Let's go. We must still see my uncle," Hosein answered, pleased
that infidels took so little time at shrines. On the way out, I didn't
see the guard. And now it was darker outside than in.

Nor did I see anywhere a clerical tribute to Ismail. Without him,
the Ayatollah would have been Sunni, and Sunnis have neither ayatollahs nor Imams. Not surprisingly, radical Sunni clerics have done
far less well trying to rouse the faithful against Westernizing re-
gimes. Sunnis don't expect an Imam or Mahdi to arrive dispensing
justice. They have rarely seen much justice in any man. Sunni rulers
don't worry as much about their religious legitimacy. That they rule
has generally been more than enough. Mohammad Reza Pahlavi was
a pussycat compared to Gamel Abdel Nasir (1918–70), the Egyptian
nationalist dictator, who developed the persecution and torture of
fundamentalists into an art. Compared to Saddam Hussein, Mohammad Reza was a human-rights activist. The Shah had no love
of the clergy, but he didn't deny them a certain reverence. Nasir or
Hussein would have killed Khomeini long before his followers called
him the Imam.

The Safavids gave Twelver Shi'ite clerics a very secure home. After conquering Iran, Ismail and his son Tahmasp imported mollahs from Shi'ite enclaves in Lebanon, Iraq, and the Persian Gulf, since there weren't enough clerics in Qom, Iran's oldest Shi'ite stronghold, to supply the state's needs. Though Ismail probably remained *ghali*, a Shi'ite radical, in his heart, he knew Shi'ite kingship over a vast newly conquered Sunni state required good administration and level heads. Traditional clerics were an indispensable part of his program to make Persia Shi'ite, Safavid, and stable. So he and his successors indulged the clergy, allowing them to establish schools and networks throughout the country. Slowly, the Safavids tried to convert the Redheads into salaried, disciplined horsemen, loyal to an emperor and not to a mystical divine guide. Eventually, the Redheads were replaced by less temperamental, musket-carrying foot soldiers and artillerymen. Respectable Islamic kings couldn't have their soldiers publicly calling them God. With clerical help, a traditional, quietist Islam reconquered the Persian soul. By the end of the sixteenth century, Iranians lay back, read Hafiz and Sa'di, and enjoyed themselves.

Safavid clerics reserved the right to criticize the emperor if he strayed too far from the Holy Law. They refused to recognize any shah as a human representative of the Hidden Imam. Centuries later, Khomeini pushed the prerogative to a logical if unexpected conclusion. He cut out the middleman between the mollahs and God.

Conquering a nation and running a state are two wholly different things. One ignites the imagination; the other calls for administration. A God-ordained revolutionary state depends by definition on imagination, the human faculty communicating the Almighty's ineffable majesty and will. Radical Islam in power must make the poor feel rich, the weary converted afresh. It must capture and hold the Prophet's magic at Mecca, where he first received God's word. Muhammad was converted and he converted others—the first holy-warrior community—through the lyrical Meccan suras, still the staple of most Muslim prayers.

Yet the clerics in power resembled more closely the Prophet at

Medina, the first city Muhammad ruled. There the revelations tended to arrive in prose, inspiration giving way to law. It's a tricky act, uniting and balancing imagination and order: cut the spark and the Holy Law becomes more a revered collection of traditions than the Divine living will. If a new and vivid inspiration arrives, the Law's sanctity will be in danger.

The clerical regime insisted on maintaining a revolutionary message—the expectation that daily life under the clerics would bring the believer closer to God and that truth and justice would soon triumph in the Middle East. The mollahs' Republic, unlike Safavid Iran, couldn't become just another Muslim state, adapting to the realities of its people's exhaustion and power. The revolutionary imagination had to stay alive and beat back the West, which was always whispering in every believer's ear.

Radical Islam was supposed to allow Muslims to dream once again, free of Western norms. In the fourteen hundred years of their history, Muslims surely could find visions to reignite their souls permanently and give them workable moral models. But when Muslims try to search their glorious past, the Western static noise, omnipresent and seductive, always brings them back. Radios, satellites, VCRs, CDs, cassettes, TVs, and the Internet, cigarette boxes, T-shirts, nylon jackets, women's underwear, and washing machines, newspapers, magazines, and contemporary books—all send Western messages.

At best, the clerics fight a rearguard action. They ineffectively scramble the Internet or force the poor, who'd pooled their money for satellite dishes, to cover their treasures with plywood boxes. Kemal Atatürk once remarked, "There is only one live civilization in the world, and this civilization is Western." Although proud of the *Ghazi* (Holy Warrior) title given him by his countrymen for saving Muslim Anatolia from invading European armies after World War I, Atatürk clearly saw the future. The Islamic and Third World have never forgiven Atatürk for telling the truth. The Third World's first hero is rarely mentioned in anti-imperialist books. But Atatürk knew the titanic struggle between Christendom and Islam, which started with the seventh-century Arab conquest of Byzantine Palestine, was over. Intellectually, if not physically, the Muslim world had been absorbed into the ever-expanding and now secularized Western mind.

Knowingly or not, Iran's revolutionary clerics and lay intellectuals massively incorporated Western themes into their militant Islamic call. The community of believers became the masses, the radical clergy the vanguard of the faithful proletariat and not the guardians of the Holy Law. Khameneh'i, Khomeini's successor, prefers the title *rahbar*, revolutionary leader, to the classically religious appellation *faqih*, Islamic jurist. IRA terrorists, Cuban revolutionaries, and Southeast Asian Communists all have honorary membership in clerical Iran's anti-imperialist mission. Though the revolutionary clergy and intellectuals loathe the West's materialism, they describe Islam's mission often in sociological, materialist prose. Everyone—mollah, intellectual, peasant, and truck driver—has become irreversibly *gharbzadeh*, "Western-struck." It's an ironic and, for faithful Muslims, a perverse situation: Islamic holy warriors advancing Western ideas and desires.

As long as Khomeini lived, the revolutionaries could pretend it wasn't so. Even an atheist could see the sacred essence in the Imam's eyes. When he died, the revolutionary war cries lost their power. You need a living charismatic spirit to survive an awful economy, clerical corruption, and, most dangerous of all, the Great Satan. Twenty-year-old men need dreams. They absolutely don't want to listen to mollahs promising new and ever-better five-year plans or TV programs dissecting the boring Holy Law. They like wearing leather jackets, dark turtlenecks, Adidas shoes, and countercultural stubble. In the modern age more than ever, you need magic, poetry, and material well-being to keep men faithful.

"The Beatles went to bloody India," a scholar of Iranian history at Tehran University once said to me. "We're not blind, you know. Wherever you go, we'll follow. You told us to look to the East for salvation, so we did. We chose Khomeini instead of some mahatma. We're Muslims, after all.

"It's your bloody fault," he added, good-naturedly casting blame. "The Islamic revolution started when you failed in Vietnam. You lost confidence, so we lost confidence in you. Iranian intellectuals, even the Shah's ministers, started writing books about the power and knowledge of the East. We started thinking the Truth was right here at home. But that was bullshit, of course. Islamic civilization hasn't produced a damn thing in hundreds of years. If you're not *gharbzadeh*, you're a deaf-mute."

Hosein and I visited his uncle's home, a two-story mud-brick house that was bare and spotless inside. Except when his wife served tea, we were alone. He was very upset that we weren't staying for dinner at least and chided Hosein every other minute for not giving him the honor of feeding a foreign guest. I was pleased to see Hosein remain steadfast. Neither one of us wanted to get stuck in the snow.

I'd firmly told Hosein to tell his uncle I was French, not American. Ardabil was too small and gossip too tempting. Sooner or later, word might get around. It appeared he'd followed my wishes. However, the uncle was polite and not inquisitive, a bad sign among Persians. Then again, older Iranians have rules. I was a foreign friend, and he spoke polite, old-fashioned Persian. Yet he knew about the border. After two teas, Hosein insisted on going. I'd risen from the tribal kilim and my pillows before he got off his knees. My boots were back on and laced before Hosein's uncle stopped pleading for us to stay.

Walking back to the truck, both of us froze. The streets had nearly emptied and I could again smell dung burning. A few boys were playing in the snow-covered streets, one of them throwing a tin can and rocks at a yelping dog. Snow was falling, a fresh four or five inches already on the ground. Mercifully, Hosein let me warm up in the truck before getting in the box. Somewhere before Tabriz, I'd tell Hosein I wanted to skip Tehran and return to Turkey.

8 TEHRAN

It kept snowing. On the main highway between Tabriz and Tehran, we finally stopped crawling. I spent most of the ride lying on top of the cot, waiting to get into the box again. Once Hosein signaled a ditched car, nothing more. Propped up on one elbow, I stared at the back of his head and thought of home. In the middle of Asia, it seemed unreachable. Once before, I'd felt this alone. I'd got sick one summer on an unair-conditioned train in southern Egypt. The train just died in the middle of nowhere. With a stomach flu in a 120-degree, smelly Third World train, you think and pray the end is near. Even hard-core stoics quietly call out to their mothers. Now, imprisoned in an Iranian transport truck, I remembered the train along the Nile.

This trip was supposed to neutralize the past. My life would have a new center, an accomplishment I could find on a map. I'd fallen in love with Persia long before I became enamored of the CIA. Once the trip was over, I'd stop viewing the Islamic revolution with a spy's eyes. I'd remember the good and forget the rest. My vices and virtues, sins and good deeds, finally would more or less balance each other out.

The farther east I went, however, the more I thought about Langley. My pitches kept replaying in my mind. You never forget a man's look when he crosses the small deadly space separating dissent from treason. The face and the hands are the first to tell you the quickening has passed and the target has realigned right and wrong. I'd known whether I'd succeeded or failed before hearing a word. Though you can never cross cultural divides altogether, a good C/O can come very close.

My venerable professor-spy had understood. Espionage should be a form of homage, in his view. I wasn't an imperialist seeking domination. I was a disbelieving pilgrim seeking God, a student trying to encourage Iranians to answer invidious questions. In the Middle East, a case officer can watch men wrestle with God, country, and man's place in between. Spying on secularized Russians, Germans, or Chinese is boring in comparison.

Curiosity, love, and guilt provoke exceptional behavior. All three had sent me across the border. Still, I was doing far less than what I'd asked others to do. I had a home and a family safe far away. My country was neither dangerous nor in danger. I didn't worry about an early-morning knock on the door. My trip to Iran was a payback for those recruitment pitches—the chance to play God. I'd let hundreds of desperate Iranians languish in Turkey. People who'd given me insights never found in books. I'd watched mothers with children drop to their knees and beg for my help. They didn't want money, just a little kindness, a visa out of their personal hell. I'd watched proud Persian men fall apart, desperate to find the Promised Land before their wives and children had to beg in the streets. I watched friends drink away their lives. Fortunately, my ancestors hadn't run into someone like me, a sympathetic man waiting in a warm room full of food, coffee, tea, alcohol, and cigarettes. A U.S. official who'd politely strip them of all their memories and every corpuscle of information and then reopen the street-side door. I confessed each day how much I'd sinned, how much I loved my work. No, my ancestors were lucky; they'd never had to visit a U.S. consulate abroad to get into America. They'd come directly by boat and only found Irish immigration officials guarding U.S. borders.

But guilt and curiosity subside quickly in adverse circumstances.

Against ever more vivid visions of Evin prison, my sins seemed less compelling than before. I'd never wanted to be a martyr. I could never commit myself fully, heart and soul, to any task. I was always outside watching, ready to tap myself on the shoulder, "That's enough now, move on." I'd always been able to cut my passion before it went too far. I'd gone to Ardabil. That was enough to make amends. I wanted to leave before my professor's warning came true. Each time I went into the box, I loved Iranians less. Tehran was too far away.

I kept listening to Hosein talking, hunting for a moment to say I couldn't go on. When he said we'd spend at least another day in Tabriz, I rolled off my elbow. I didn't need to upset him on the road. When I closed and locked the lid, it was early morning, too early for Tabriz's traffic to snag us, and internal security no longer ran many early-morning patrols. Soon Hazra would be making me breakfast. I'd broach it then, so Hosein would have enough time to plan. With luck, I'd have only one more dinner in Iran.

When I got out of the box, it was snowing lightly in Tabriz. Several trucks were pulling out of the lot, a few of them headed toward Turkey, but most toward Tehran. Those going south wouldn't have any problems. Azarbaijan and northern Kurdistan were the only two regions of Iran regularly hit with heavy snows. Once you are outside of Tabriz heading southeast along the rim of the Alborz Mountains, the temperature warms fairly quickly. By the time you reach Tehran, situated on the northern edge of Iran's central, sandy plateau, the winters more often bring rain than snow. Mercifully, Fazel was nowhere to be found, so we immediately started walking home. The light snow had taken much of the street dust and pollution out of the air. We were too early for rush-hour traffic. The outskirts of Tabriz were quiet, except for the occasional semi, car, or barking dog. The barking calmed my nerves. The revolution had empowered the age-old Islamic dislike of dogs (the Prophet Muhammad was reportedly pro-cat and anti-dog). I'd heard that Iran's cities were now canine-free. For me, a barking dog was a hopeful sign of weakening Muslim rectitude.

I spotted a couple of women in heavy coats scurrying in between roadside cinderblock houses. Hosein said most Tabrizis were up, though not out the door. They weren't like proper Persians, he said, who liked to sleep late. Azarbaijanis rose early and worked hard. They could sleep a little later today as far as I was concerned. With very few eyes around, I finally felt at ease.

Hazra was waiting for us when we arrived. After giving Hosein a hug and me a smile, she asked us whether we wanted anything to eat. We both said no and went to sleep. When I awoke, they were both gone. She'd left a key and a note on the table. I didn't touch the key until late in the afternoon, just before they were to return. My last walk in Iran, my first walk alone. For half an hour, I moved quickly through a neighborhood emptied by the cold. The winter's hibernation had begun. Men and women were milling about, but they weren't standing outside on every block gossiping in small groups, and packs of scruffy, colorfully sweatered children weren't playing soccer on the side streets or darting through traffic. I noticed a few men gathered at either end of Hosein's block. The two neighborhood teahouses had overflowed onto the sidewalks. Without coats, they weren't going to stay outside long.

As the thoroughfare in front of Hosein's apartment was clogged with trucks and cars, I turned onto a side road that led me through another row of concrete dwellings into a short stretch of open dirt road and then an "urban village." Large stones, unbaked bricks, cinderblocks—all of it stuck together with dried mud or gravity to form family dwellings. A few of these head-high houses had small goat and sheep corrals off to one side. Corrugated steel or aluminum sheets cemented onto brick corner posts kept the animals in. I suspected if it got any colder the animals were going to live inside with their owners. This neighborhood looked as poor as anything in Ardabil. I pivoted and walked out of the village.

Rested, and warm in my thermal underwear, I could have stayed out for hours. But I didn't dare go any farther. I was on the outer limits of Hosein's neighborhood. With my defective sense of direction, I could easily get lost. Whenever I went out for circuitous walks, I had to concentrate seriously on exactly where I'd been. I'd left a note giving my time of departure and return. Hosein and

Hazra would allow me a margin of error; then they'd search. Hosein would head straight for the truck and return, finding me, *inshallah,* like an idiot lost on a straight line with home.

By myself in the open, I was regaining confidence. I was probably where no case officer had ever been. I remembered reading 1950s dispatches sent from Tehran's CIA station. Dispatches were pouched, not cabled, lengthy reports on operations and events. They died out with primitive keypunch communications in the early 1970s, I'd heard. Optical readers and rapid sophisticated encoding technology had made communication between HQS and the field live-time, regardless of cable length. Accordingly, the pressure for constant production increased. C/Os wrote more but knew less. In dispatches, officers more freely ruminated about their lives.

A 1956 dispatch account of a C/O's visit to Tabriz had stuck in my mind. He'd walked the streets trying to understand Azarbaijan. I hadn't smelled in his words the usual C/O hunger for recruitments, the scalp-counting game that would eventually gut the Operations Directorate's honesty. Drawing on the commentary of both re-cruited and unrecruited Iranians, the C/O had tried to place his local cases in a larger U.S.-Soviet-Iranian context, freely admitting how much he didn't know. After reading his dispatch, I had a feel for Tabriz—the common-man, clerical, and aristocratic passions that had regularly propelled Azarbaijan into the news. Unlike Special National Intelligence Estimates, this dispatch I remembered long after I'd read it. I'd always meant to track down that C/O to see if he was still alive. The more I learned about the Agency, the more certain I was that the DO's golden age—when every C/O was from Harvard, Yale, or Princeton—was really bronze. In a closed society, fraud and mediocrity spread very quickly, regardless of anyone's ac-ademic pedigree. I'd definitely joined in the Dark Ages. Reading that C/O's contemplative dispatch made me realize the depth of our decline and the improbability of our recovery.

A senior Agency official had told me early in my career—just after giving me a recruitment award—that I should resign. The Agency that I wanted was long dead, if it had ever existed. My approach was too academic. If I wanted to stay, I had to adapt to the insti-tution's standards. A successful operations officer had to learn to, compromise. He had to ~~forgive mistakes, join the team, and not~~ engage in unhelpful criticism. Above all else, he couldn't rock the boat if he expected to rise. The Agency was a vertical organization with proper channels. You had to put your faith in your superiors.

He was right, of course, so I ignored his advice. Our respective understandings of intelligence were just too different. Too many senior officers had gone unpunished for horrendous mistakes. To respect channels in the CIA, seven times out of ten, was to be an accomplice to mediocrity or fraud.

I'd made it back to the thoroughfare, a little less than halfway between the truck park and the apartment. I had the highway, the mountains, a gas station, and a couple of distinguishable concrete buildings to guide me. Any closer to the truck park and I'd not make it back before my margin of error elapsed. Also, I was hungry. Hazra would start preparing dinner as soon as she got back. I turned and began shuffling my feet, kicking up clouds of crystalline snowflakes. I thought about dropping down and making a snow angel with my arms and legs. When a small pack of boys appeared, I changed my mind. Did children, let alone grown men, make snow angels in Iran? Someone in a truck or a car might see me, stop, and ask if I'd gone mad.

I wanted to talk to them, but we were too close to the apartment, I feared. They might hang on me for the entire walk, gaining numbers as we moved. In the Third World, poor children come out of nowhere for curiosity and money. I'd rarely spoken to Iranian children alone, listening to their kindergarten talk, the last and hardest form of language for a foreigner to learn. When do Iranians start to lie? Do their parents teach them, or do they learn in the streets? And if caught, how are children punished? Once they are punished, how long do they wait before they lie again? Helpful questions for a case officer with Iranian targets, but slightly improper for a university class on the Persian mind.

I stepped out of their way since they hadn't stepped out of mine. They were shouting in Azari. Two of them stared at me. I smiled. They continued running, glancing back. Later I smiled at a young Iranian couple walking like me on the side of the road. The man tightened his lips a bit while the woman, in an ankle-length wool coat and a scarf, smiled more. In Istanbul, I'd learned that Iranian adults would sometimes smile at you if you smiled first. Turks almost never did.

Seeing other men stomping through the snow, I tried to imitate them. Americans, more than most other people, have a recognizable gait. They walk forcefully, arms, hands, shoulders, and heads moving with their legs. Persians move their upper bodies less and take shorter steps. On the snowy walkways and streets, though, it didn't matter much. We all had diminished strides. When I caught sight of the gas station, I knew I was home. I'd successfully walked a small triangle through Tabriz without my guardian angel. As Hosein had promised, Azarbaijanis had left me alone. They just stared at me until I'd passed. Turning the last corner before the cobbler and butcher shops, I felt as if I'd traversed the Khyber Pass.

When I returned to the apartment, Hosein was waiting for me, pleased to see I'd ventured out and no doubt immensely relieved that I hadn't fucked up. We chatted briefly about the drive to Tehran before he took a nap. I realized at that moment that, imperceptibly, my walk had changed my mind. I'd come this far. I could go farther. I'd run to the center of the Iranian revolution, then run back. Hosein wasn't eager to stay long. He'd drop off and pick up a load, then return.

I'd go numb again in the box, perhaps worse than before. Hosein was thinking of making brief stops in the cities of Zanjan and Qazvin to check on his work. As Hosein would likely have to drink tea and talk, each stop could easily take two hours. And getting out and returning to the box was more painful than staying in. I could handle the dark better than the strangulation of my extremities. Even running nonstop, I'd have to stay down for long stretches.

I'd warned Hosein about his family. If he thought the visit was safe, it was his call. We wouldn't be more than a day or two, not enough time for gossip to finish either me or them. If the snow kept falling, however, I could be in trouble. Even the primary highway between Iran and Turkey might temporarily close. I poured a glass of whiskey, picked up the Qur'an, lay down on the futon, and listened to Persian radio. When I woke up, Hazra was unloading a bag of groceries. When she saw me notice the Book on the floor next to my whiskey glass, she smiled. I put it back on the stand.

There's no Islamic law saying an infidel can't read the Qur'an at home while drinking alcohol. In the Islamic Republic, infidels may drink in private if drinking is consistent with their faith. Though some revolutionaries had wanted to outlaw drinking for everyone, Khomeini the Jurist stood firm. Armenians, the best home brewers in Iran, made a killing on the black market thanks to the Ayatollah's ruling. Better to have an infidel read the Qur'an while he is drinking than not read it at all, I told myself. But I shouldn't have left the Holy Book on the floor.

I told Hosein after dinner that I was losing steam. I'd go to Tehran, but I wanted to leave quickly thereafter for Bazargan. Could he arrange a crossing soon? He wasn't surprised. He'd seen my anxiety building. I'd seen his anxiety rise. Also, he, too, was scared of the weather. The winter had started early and badly and was getting worse. We'd leave Tabriz tomorrow morning, Tehran the day after. In three days' time, weather holding, I'd see Atatürk again.

We ate lamb and rice until midnight, and talked about the times Hosein had blown tires in the middle of nowhere. Hosein called his uncle to tell him we were coming. Because they spoke in Azari, I understood little, though enough to know he'd said "friend," not "American." I was positive they'd spoken before. The conversation was too short, even for poor people watching their telephone bills. Hosein would be up at dawn; I'd rise a little later. Hazra was going to stay with me until her brother returned. I knew and she knew that we'd see each other again, one last time before the border. She knew everything, I reflected. I liked her more because of that. If she'd ever fled Iran, I would never have seen her. She would have done a one-day pit stop in Istanbul and then been on her way to Cuba, Mexico, and California. She was at least as intrepid, intelligent, and brave as her brother. I suspected she could lie twice as well. When I left late the next morning, she gave me, not Hosein, a doggie bag from the night before. She knew I wasn't going anywhere except down under.

Again, we started late. A run to Tehran could take eight hours or more. If Hosein chatted long in either Zanjan or Qazvin, we might make it to Tehran before midnight. Walking to the truck, looking toward the mountains and feeling almost safe in Tabriz's monotonous landscape of brick, concrete, and frowning faces, I grew nervous about heading farther east. In Azarbaijan, I could still feel Turkey. If Hosein dropped dead, I could perhaps buy my way back to the border. In Tehran, I'd have to pull out my little telephone book, call in a few IOUs, and beg for mercy. If I didn't land in Evin prison, it could take months to arrange my return to Dogubeyazit. Probably, I'd have to call my Turkish import-export friend Celal again and wait. Alarm bells would start going off back home. People would start asking questions. Family and friends would learn where I was. The more people in the know, the greater the risk to me and others.

Run in, run out. Hosein's planning would hold, I told myself again. Once you come on board, you don't look back. You don't reflect on the details you don't know, or why you even joined up. You take each day at a time and concentrate on the most immediate operational task. I had to keep going. I'd been studying Iran for nearly twenty years. Yet when I'd briefed senior U.S. officials or Agency analysts on the Islamic Republic, I'd felt like a poseur, only a little better than your typical CIA analyst locked away in a Head-quarters cubicle, who becomes a "country expert" after no more than a year on the job.

Walking past the gas station, I didn't feel like a total cheat any-more. I'd proved to myself some savoir faire, that years spent reading books about vanished Muslim dynasties had real-world value, that I could operate without the trappings of U.S. power. Once back in Turkey, I'd have the right to say a few words about Iran in the company of my Persian friends. Yet, except for discovering my own limitations, I still wasn't exactly sure what I was learning from my race to Tehran. I consoled myself. In most medieval accounts of Muslim pilgrimages, pilgrims rarely find en route divine insights. They discover first and foremost what the incomparable nineteenth-century British explorer Richard Burton knew as well as any man: "Travel is a portion of hell fire." A pilgrimage's worth can only be judged once the pilgrim has made it to Mecca. Personally, I didn't think the voyage was worth much unless the pilgrim returned home. With a little luck, in twelve hours I'd be in Tehran, in thirty-six hours I'd be back in Tabriz, in seventy-two, in Dogubeyazit, a day or two later, in the big cushy chairs of the Pera Palas Hotel, and I would know better what I'd learned.

At the truck park, I said my goodbyes to Fazel and barely escaped another round of tea. The fresh snow covering the lot had already been flattened by trucks. A few drivers were milling about a barrel with a fire in it. A couple of them gazed at Hosein and me as we crossed the center of the lot. Was their mean look because of curiosity about a Persian-speaking tall stranger or, perhaps, only jealousy of men who had work? Cold and frowning, we probably appeared to them just as unpleasant as they did to us.

Once in the truck, I popped the lid and rolled over. I was under a long time before Hosein yelled. I unlatched the box, stayed put, and stretched occasionally to look at the traffic, the mountains, the cleaved rocky foothills, and the brown-and-white rolling plains. I listened to Hosein tell me more about the men he'd taken out of the country. With a couple of exceptions, they wouldn't have been worthwhile intelligence sources. I'd never asked Hosein how much they'd paid him. With some, I suspected he'd done it for free. If I'd run Hosein in the old days, I could have had eyes everywhere in Iran. If a riot had exploded in Mashhad, Isfahan, or Tehran, I would have had Hosein or one of his friends quickly on the ground. Generally, the Agency had been awful at live atmospheric reporting. They were always three or four weeks behind, their reports rarely worth reading. The best official reporting always came from State, from curious consular officers with an Iranian clientele in Istanbul, Ankara, and Dubai. The very best stuff was always passed internationally between friends, by telephone, fax, and plane. Increasingly, Westernized Iranians with foreign credit cards were using the Internet for messages. Connect to a foreign access number, send, and receive. If made intelligently, such transmissions over direct-dialing lines are difficult to intercept and impossible to block. Of course, given the quality of the Iranian PTT, messages can't be long.

I wondered whether I could have recruited Hosein. My gut told me no. He'd risk his life taking men over the border, but he wouldn't rat on Iran. A long-term formal relationship with the CIA would have been too much for him to absorb. But then again, if loosely propositioned he might have bitten. Let him think at all times that he was in control, that he was doing us a favor. The outside world should know immediately when the Revolutionary Guards or the *Basij* were brutalizing his people. Only good could come if the United States knew exactly who the responsible commanders were and how many died. *If* I tried to get him regularly to accept money, I'd describe it as compensation for gas and lost transport. I'd never, ever, refer to a salary. With disappointed die-hard patriots, you always have a chance if you can gently flip right and wrong.

I was down under again and we were slowly rolling through traffic. Hosein had decided to stop in Zanjan only. What he had meant to do in Qazvin he could do by telephone from Tehran. I'd already eaten my doggie-bag lunch and I was dozing off despite the noise. I needed to take a leak, but nothing more. I was internally chilled, cramped, and scared, but my intestinal tract had mercifully shut down two days ago. Diarrhea would have been my undoing. I wasn't really upset about not seeing the small city of Zanjan, because I'd never heard anything good about it except that it had decent highway hotels. It was a charmless modern town that owed its livelihood to surrounding agriculture and the highway that ran right through the middle of it.

Zanjan is generally considered the dividing line between Azari- and Persian-speaking Iran. But that hadn't been true for years. The Azari immigration to the southern suburbs of Tehran, which started long before the Iranian revolution, had deposited Azari speakers all the way to Qom, mollah headquarters, located about a hundred kilometers south of Tehran.

Hosein was thumping hard when I woke. Almost three hours had passed.

"The box isn't that small if you can sleep in it," Hosein said as soon as the lid went up.

Again, I was holding the lid with my head. I began to wonder how many more times I could do this without causing irreparable damage.

"When I sleep, at least I don't think about you in a warm room drinking hot tea," I shot back.

"I think about you constantly when I'm outside the truck and you're in the box," Hosein replied seriously.

I was certain that was true. Blessedly, Hosein reconfirmed his intention to skip Qazvin. He'd just got more work in Zanjan. Off-handedly, he mentioned that we had hit security. He'd coasted through without even an identity check. When I was working in Turkey, Iranians were terrified of security stops. I'd known several men who'd been yanked out of their cars and beaten for no reason. Back then, a female passenger could get you seriously interrogated. If she wasn't a relative, the interrogation was usually continued in-doors. Hosein said even that was changing. Now, unless a woman had her hair provocatively popping out—bad *hijab* as the Iranians called it—the *Basij* generally left female passengers alone.

Opposition to the clerical regime no longer expressed itself through bombs and bullets. Iranians rioted more than they used to, but the clerical regime had the good sense not to strike back hard for long. The mollahs knew their countrymen were exhausted and apolitical after fifteen revolutionary years. They'd allow a little mis-behavior and a lot of public indifference, so long as no one started shooting. In their hearts, the mollahs were distraught that the com-mon faithful no longer viewed them as intermediaries to God. Phil-osophically, radical mollahs couldn't accept the revolution's end. Practically, however, they were willing to accept compromise. Better power and hypocrisy than street violence. Most Iranians, I suspected, found the arrangement acceptable. Even Hosein didn't want to start shooting mollahs. He wanted someone else to begin, then he'd join the throng.

The landscape had changed significantly. The rolling hills had turned into flat, snowless dirt fields and plains. Mud-brick hovels and villages speckled the countryside or lined the highway here and there. Filling stations and security guard posts merited concrete. Though still lim-iting the northern horizon, the snowcapped mountains seemed a lit-tle smaller. When I flopped into the seat alongside Hosein, I rolled down the window. But the cold air still rang in my ears. Though Hosein insisted the land was rich with crops in spring—a couple of river-beds and a few trees hinted at fertility—it was difficult to believe. The landscape looked dead, beyond spring's redemption. Again, I could see beauty only in contrast with the mountains.

If I'd had the time and Hosein a smaller truck, I would have explored the highland roads between Zanjan and Tehran. Somewhere up there, in the dirt and jagged-rock foothills and mountains, were Alamut and other Assassin strongholds. Originally missionaries of a medieval North African Shi'ite dynasty, the Assassins were the Islamic world's first organized terrorists. Sunni sultans, vazirs, and Crusader princes regularly fell to their knives. The word "assassin" entered the Crusaders' languages because of the novelty and efficiency of their stealthy, religiously inspired murders. The Assassins, Safavids, and Khomeiniites were centuries and sects apart, but their holy-warrior commitment was the same. When I mentioned the Assassins and their spiritual founder, Hasan-e Sabbah (1040–1124), the Old Man of the Mountains, Hosein knew them by name. He called them Muslim madmen, an uncharitable assessment perhaps, since he'd no doubt yelled *"Allahu Akbar!"*—"God is Most Great!"—on the battlefield.

Again, I was down under. We were approaching Qazvin, a capital of the Safavid empire under Shah Tahmasp, the son of Ismail. Tahmasp had abandoned Tabriz because of constant Ottoman invasions. Farther from the Ottoman-Safavid frontier and more easily defended, Qazvin enjoyed under Tahmasp a royal munificence in palaces, mosques, gardens, and bazaars. Unfortunately, Qazvin wasn't far enough away from the mountains. Earthquakes and fire regularly struck the city, ruining many of its architectural treasures.

Among Iranians, Qazvinis are not known for their faded glory; they're know for their voracious homosexual appetites. I never considered this an insightful generalization. Virtually every Iranian town is accused by its neighbors of being a den of pederasty and sodomy. What interested me about Qazvin was its riot in August 1994. It briefly shook clerical Iran. The riot started when Qazvin's chief cleric criticized the Iranian parliament for its refusal to allow Qazvin, a predominantly Persian-speaking city, to separate from predominantly Turkish-speaking Zanjan province and become its own province in order to obtain more federal aid. The cleric organized street demonstrations, which then got out of control. Young men attacked government buildings, overturned cars, and screamed, "Death to the mollahs!" The ruling clerics ordered the army to suppress the riot; the local army commander refused and the General Staff in Tehran backed him up. After two days of violence, a special Interior Ministry antiriot force from Tehran, composed of *Basijis*, restored order. The Iranian Army had made its position clear: it would not shoot Iranians in the streets, though it did stand aside and allow the Interior Ministry force to fire.

The riot and the army's reaction shocked the ruling clergy and underscored their dependence on the *Basij* and the Revolutionary Guard Corps. Hosein said Qazvin had cooled since the summer. Except for a slightly above-average number of blue uniforms about, you wouldn't know the city had experienced a major riot. I'd heard from reliable friends inside Iran that Westerners could once again visit the city without special permission. I would have liked to see the ruins of Tahmasp's palaces and asked a few young men at kebab joints about the summer violence, but I didn't want to stand out in the crowd. My information might be incomplete: visiting foreigners might quickly get reported to the police.

I stopped looking at my watch. I promised myself I wouldn't look again until Bazargan. When I was jailed at the Farm as part of my Agency training, I'd taped a small wristwatch to my groin. During the incarceration, I occasionally stole a look. Each time I did, I felt renewed. Now knowing the minutes was torture. I couldn't stop pushing the glow button and watching time slow down.

I was wired and going numb. Repeatedly, I tried throwing my mind back into history and toward home; it kept returning to the box. We were stopping and going too much for the tire noise to lull me into sleep. Perhaps Hosein had changed his mind. "Skipping Qazvin" in Persian might really mean several hours drinking tea with friends. I opened and shut my eyes over and over again, trying to see differences in darkness. With my eyes shut, it wasn't as black. When Hosein thumped, I was slowly counting down from ten thousand.

The traffic had picked up. It would be less than an hour before we hit Tehran's ever-expanding limits. We were going to a part of south Tehran where Azaris perhaps outnumbered proper Persians. I wasn't going to see Shah Mohammad Reza Pahlavi's city, the 1960s and 1970s Tehran of tree-lined, four- and six-lane boulevards and avenues, with Middle Eastern skyscrapers twenty-five stories tall, and large, smoothly poured concrete, stone and stucco houses, some of them with marbled indoor swimming pools, belonging to members of the Iranian and diplomatic elites. I wasn't going to walk under the *Shahyad*, now *Azadi* (Freedom) Arch, which is as high as St. Louis's Gateway Arch along the banks of the Mississippi. I wasn't going to see the Persian Crown Jewels, before oil the guarantee of the Iranian currency, buried in the vault of the National Bank, or Tehran's large public gardens.

I was going south to where the boulevards and avenues dead-ended into an ever-growing maze of dirt streets, many of which have no name. I was going close to the Paradise of Zahra cemetery, where the martyrs against the Shah and Saddam Hussein are buried. Here skyscrapers are three- and four-story brick and cinderblock houses, and goats and lambs have their throats slit in the streets during religious holidays. We were headed toward the desert, which begins not too far south of Tehran. On the southern outskirts of the city, when the wind blew, Hosein said, you usually got sand, as well as pollution, in your mouth.

We were entering a city of awful car and factory pollution. The smog was so bad in Tehran that the entire Alborz range would sometimes disappear. The central and southern districts, the most densely populated, were probably the most polluted.

Adrenaline pumping and eyes wide open, I thought about the past. I'd sent others to Tehran; now I'd sent myself. I wasn't going to walk into an official building, read classified documents, and send secret messages back to Langley. Hiding in a truck was the limit of my courage. But I'd kept my word. I was going to the city quarter that had made my one-legged friend Ahmad, and the hundreds of other south Tehranis I'd known in Turkey. And, with any luck, I wouldn't meet them.

Hosein's uncle, half Azari, half Persian, had a little house in an Azari ghetto. He was a conservative Muslim, a retired professional soldier, an NCO who'd backed Khomeini. He'd locked horns with Hazra years before because he'd found her too outgoing. He'd supported the revolution because the Shah had become a bad Muslim who'd sold the fatherland to the West. However, he hadn't liked seeing mollahs and women with guns on their shoulders. According to Hosein, he was very pleased to meet me; he hadn't seen an American in years. We'd park fairly close to his house, about an hour's walk from the truck park. Hosein's uncle and aunt would have dinner ready when we arrived.

I could tell by the traffic and the density of roadside shadows and lights that we'd entered Greater Tehran. The outskirts were a big sprawling mess of buildings, cars darting in and out, and bewildered peasants occasionally on the roadside. Crisscrossing streams of red and white lights surrounded us. When Hosein finally gave me the word, I didn't want to get under. I wanted to smell noxious exhaust and factory fumes. I didn't love the Middle East only for its mausoleums and citadels, poetry and chronicles, sultans, caliphs, and shahs. The merciless collision between East and West—the unstoppable, often ugly bulldozer of Western civilization—interested me as much as the past. I was fascinated by the seeming inability of the Islamic Middle East to construct a single attractive modern building.

I went under, knowing I'd made the right decision. Just a taste of Tehran's modernity, just a glimpse of its jungle, was more than enough payback for tracking the mollahs from afar. I'd almost made it to Tehran in 1979 as a student. Khomeini's hostage-taking "students" canceled my plans. If I'd got here then, I probably wouldn't have come by truck later. I might have hated it, the way I did Cairo in the beginning. Back then, I hadn't loved the Middle East as much as I came to love it later. My curiosity might have turned to disgust at some ugly anti-American incident. It takes time to translate urban mess into the beauty of societal struggle.

There's nothing worse than studying something and never consummating the devotion. For years, I'd had a Persian map of Tehran on the wall, memorizing its different numbered districts. Just one day would give me sensations for a lifetime.

I'd almost counted down again from ten thousand by the time

Hosein thumped and yelled. We were turning into a small truck park with its own filling station. Not far from the pumps, truckers had lit a fire inside an oil drum and were leaning over it, rubbing their hands. There was no friendly attendant here, so we wouldn't have to drink tea in the cold. After checking the locks on the trailer doors, we set out down a deserted dirt street wet from a light rain. With weak legs, I struggled to run across a busy intersection. On the other side were two- and three-story buildings. Most of the windows were dark. The lit ones had a dim white glow, one bulb, maybe two. I looked north toward the mountains, but I couldn't see them through the clouds.

In the early 1950s, when Tehran's population was under one million, there was little development in the northern hills. Prime real estate was in central Tehran, near the American and British embassies. According to Hosein, if you had money you definitely wouldn't live there now. The pollution and traffic congestion were unbearable. Central Tehran had in effect joined the south, the Tehran of peasants who'd fled the countryside. As elsewhere in the Middle East, Iranian peasant flight had started before World War II and gradually gained momentum until the 1970s, when it exploded. The 1971 oil-price hike, largely engineered by Shah Mohammad Reza Pahlavi and Libya's Muammar Qaddafi, significantly increased Iran's wealth. The 1973 Arab boycott and resulting trebling of oil prices gave the Shah seemingly limitless funds to industrialize. The population of Iran's major cities daily added hundreds—and Tehran thousands—as city wealth, work, and dreams overwhelmed the countryside. With urbanization came Westernization and the sins, inequities, aspirations, and freedom that drove the radical clergy into rebellion. After the Shah's fall, Iran's urban population continued growing even faster than before. A traditional people with modern appetites, Iranians kept having children while pursuing their material dreams. Also, the mollahs encouraged the faithful to multiply. In under fifteen years, Iran's population had almost doubled, from thirty-five million to over sixty million. With the possible exception of Cairo, Tehran had become the largest city in the Middle East, with a population between ten million and fifteen million.

I looked northward again toward the mountains I couldn't see. I saw a bright crease of light where I imagined the foothills met Tehran's flat plain. Those lights were perhaps north Tehran, or maybe the glow of lights in central, even south Tehran. In the dark, on flat land, across a city with the area of Los Angeles, it was hard to tell. I suspected the revolutionary clergy who'd moved into houses abandoned by north Tehran's Westernized elite could perhaps look down through the pollution clouds. If so, they probably felt the same way their predecessors had. Anxious.

Though it was almost 11 P.M. the streets were full of people: chador-clad women amazingly balancing children on their hips and large sacks in their hands, small groups of older men chatting and smoking, some in drooping peasant trousers. And everywhere young men, alone or in groups, walking through the streets, leaning on filthy cars, or sitting on boxes on the dirt. A few seemed to be working. One young man had a stack of books under each arm. Everyone was talking. I also spotted sheep and goats, tethered and on the loose.

We walked past a recently built mosque with loudspeakers on the minarets. The horizontal dark tile strips on the minarets made the unfinished stuccoed concrete dome look particularly modern and ugly. While traveling in the Middle East, I'd only occasionally seen muezzins in minarets making the call to prayer. Even in small villages, I'd found tape machines rigged to timers. Loudspeakers allowed God's call to reach farther; tape machines allowed muezzins to avoid early-morning climbs up narrow staircases.

No one was going in or out of the mosque. Even for the devout, it was too late for prayers. The two teahouses we'd passed, however, were full. Through floor-to-ceiling windows, I saw bearded men sitting and smoking at green bench tables. The Middle East's historic entertainment, teahouses, had been greatly aided by the Islamic revolution. Nothing in the Qur'an or Muslim tradition prohibited men from sitting day and night, drinking tea or coffee, gossiping, smoking, and staring. Given the paucity of work and much-protected female virtue, there wasn't much else men licitly could do to pass the time.

South Tehran wasn't at all like the ghettos of Cairo, in which poor people lived however they could, stuffed into small rooms or in the open air. Cairo had seemed like a seething ants' nest. My first impression here was of space somewhat thinning humanity. Brick and cinderblock apartments and houses weren't endlessly squeezed one against the other. There were open spaces. If you'd had five or ten Iranians to a room with a gas or coal heater, windows would have been fogged, but those that were lit were clear. Also, the masonry looked solid. I'd spent many nights walking Cairo's poorer streets. Not once did I feel I could hide. Here the streets were full of people, yet there were innumerable empty corners, side roads, and alleys. I didn't know what south Tehran looked like under the Pahlavi shahs, but it was obvious the clerics had been spending money. Most of the neighborhood was not more than twenty years old—parts of it had been built, literally, yesterday—yet I saw as many paved roads as dirt ones. Buildings, if not streets, had electricity. There was very little garbage on the ground. Almost every window had glass, and very few windows were broken. People looked dirty and poor, cars rusted and old. Yet the poverty didn't seem pulverizing, at least at night. Much more than Cairo and even Tabriz, Tehran was part of the modern world, with asphalt, electricity, and some kind of indoor plumbing. Looking north toward Mohammad Reza Pahlavi's Tehran, I could understand why revolutionaries once had had hope. Progress was everywhere; a much better life seemed within sight. The collision of Islam, modernity, and Iran's oil wealth had made Khomeini God's representative on earth. Unfortunately for his successors, south Tehran was still growing. The peasant exurbs continued far to the south of where I was standing. People had started to move away from Tehran's rivers and build on the desert. I doubted whether south Tehran's young men thought they lived in a Promised Land.

We'd been walking for more than an hour, through short streets of small brick houses. A recent rain had stimulated neighborhood odors. Wet dirt mixed with animal and human leftovers. It wasn't overpowering, just a little annoying if you breathed in too deeply. Hosein pointed out a door in a head-high brick wall. We walked inside a small courtyard full of car parts, tin cans, and stacked wooden planks. Hosein knocked on a door and Hosein's uncle ushered us in.

The first thing I noticed was his smile and the short white hair on his head and face. After taking off our shoes, we followed him into a small living room with a couch, a coffee table, two wooden chairs, and several tribal kilims. The plastered walls were unadorned.

"Please, please sit," insisted the uncle, pointing to the couch. "I'm honored to have an American in my home."

I took the couch and they the chairs.

"Hosein has told me of the problems you had at the border. I'm very sorry you were treated poorly."

"It was the only time. Everyone else has been very kind," I said, wondering whether the uncle was lying. Did he know I wasn't leaving via the airport? Before coming to Tehran, I'd been very serious with Hosein about telling the truth to his family. He'd suggested meeting, not only his uncle and aunt, but a couple of Tehrani cousins as well. I absolutely refused. I intended to stay only one day and not push my luck. Gossip could spread rapidly: I felt certain I was the only American in south Tehran. I kept imagining loud knocking on the door and bearded, wild-eyed Revolutionary Guards barging in, their assault rifles flipped off safety. No, I'd pushed it as far as I could. My little voice kept whispering, "Go home now!" Hosein would have to deal with any neighborhood and family echoes of my visit; I'd warned him several times. We could have slept in the truck, as I'd advised.

Hosein's aunt entered and began to serve a multi-dish dinner of vegetable stew, chicken and rice, cucumbers and yogurt. She was veiled by a scarf concealing all her hair. Her robelike dress touched the floor. She had a very round face that looked pleasant when her yellowing, stained teeth didn't show. She stayed with us when she wasn't serving.

After asking a few questions about my Persian, faith, family, and profession, Hosein's family chitchatted about the cold, wet weather and Hazra's cooking. Over honey cakes and tea, difficult questions began again.

"You like Iran, don't you?" the uncle asked as I sipped my tea.

"Yes, the border guards didn't change that," I answered, thinking he was still worried about the rudeness at the border.

"Hosein told me you love Iran."

I hesitated. Iran had consumed much of my life. It had given me immense pleasure, frustration, and anger. Before Iran, I'd certainly had a very abstract understanding of sin. If I had a soul, Iran had helped forge it. Yet the question stopped me. Confessing my love of Iran to a Persian seemed insincere and wrong. Iranians are supposed to say, "I love America." Americans, particularly former government officials, aren't supposed to say, "I love Iran."

"Yes," I said, watching the old man's smile spread.

"You don't hate us for what happened?"

"I never have."

"Do you think Iran and America will be friends again?"

"I would love to see diplomatic relations restored," I replied. Even in the best of circumstances, it's hard for a Muslim and a powerful Western country to be friends.

"Then you should tell America to strike the mollahs," said the old man firmly, his brown eyes moist with earnestness.

Again, I had the feeling that Hosein had told his uncle more than he should have. However, Iranians often talk to all Americans as if they were U.S. officials. The reflex certainly contradicted one of the mollahs' favorite refrains: "We don't hate the American people; we hate the American government." In Iranian eyes, we were all agents of U.S. influence. Naturally, some of us were more satanic than others.

"Strike them how?" I asked.

"Shoot them. Bomb them."

Hosein was grinning in agreement between bites of cake. His aunt was alternately looking at me and staring at the floor.

"Do you want U.S. intervention again?" I asked.

"The Shah was a tyrant. America shouldn't support tyrants. When I was young, I once trained with American soldiers in Iran. They were very knowledgeable. We all liked the Americans more than we liked our own officers. None of us understood how the Americans could have allowed the Shah to oppress his people.

"But the mollahs are worse. Just like the Shah, they send the nation's wealth abroad. Our prisons are still full of innocent people. His *Imperial Majesty*," he said, pronouncing the title with precise derision, "was a bad Muslim and a bad Iranian. But the mollahs are awful Muslims and worse Iranians. They preach Islam and steal from the poor. If America destroyed the mollahs, we'd forgive you for the Shah."

I stared at the old man, sifting his words for any real contradictions. Like most Iranians I'd known, he didn't *really* object to the principle of U.S. interference. Everyone interferes in everyone else's business—that's a given in Persian society. A proud Muslim patriot, he wanted the America of his youth—the polite, specially trained, and culturally sensitized U.S. military instructors' America—to come back and aid his country and his faith. That America would pose no threat to Iran and Islam. Of course, that America wasn't real. The real America was Khomeini's America, an engine of uncontrollable change encouraging women to shed their clothes. Fortunately, the mollahs had more or less wiped this memory clean. Thanks to the *akhunds*, perhaps America and Iran could again be friends.

"I don't think America is going to bomb anybody," I said, hoping the old man wasn't insulted.

Hosein's uncle nodded in disappointment. Mercifully, Hosein didn't jump in with another theory of U.S.-clerical conspiracy. We went back to drinking tea, eating sweets, and talking about the weather.

In the Agency, I'd heard only one lecture on the Persian mind. At a CIA conference on Iran, one bright analyst had tried to squeeze the subject into a broader discussion of Iranian nuclear research, explaining the Iranian patronage system with finesse and subtlety. He was the Directorate of Intelligence's only first-rate Iran analyst. He'd been informally tutored by a professor who'd been in the CIA in 1953, when the Agency helped topple Mosaddeq.

The analyst's twenty-five-minute lecture drew applause, albeit few questions. Later he and I talked together. Not long before, he'd had the misfortune of briefing senior case officers on Iranian terrorism. He was shocked at how dull-witted they were. The Directorate of Intelligence was in horrible shape, with first-rate bureaucrats and second-rate analysts rising to the top. Still, you could occasionally find sharp cookies, even in senior positions. The Directorate of Operations was, however, a "wasteland," he said, "a Mecca for know-nothing men."

.   .   .

"Saudi Arabia is going to go Protestant, I tell you," said the young, hard-charging case officer. "It's only a matter of time. Islam is such a stupid religion. One day even the Saudis are going to realize it's a no-go."

"I don't want them to go Christian. Muslims are easier to recruit," replied another C/O, who'd recently targeted Europeans. "It's much easier to get ahead quickly in NE [Near East] or AF [Africa] Divisions. My classmates who've only worked in NE and AF are already one or two grades ahead of me."

"On my last NE tour," interjected another, "I just kept a wad of money in my pocket. Shit, in six months I had a half-dozen recruitments. I love NE. I could be a senior officer before I'm forty-five."

Six of NE's finest young case officers were drinking around a table. I wasn't talking much. I'd never liked team sports or fraternities. Unlike my colleagues, I chased Iranians alone.

"I like working against Arabs more than against Iranians," said another C/O. "They like Americans more. If it weren't for the goddamn Israelis, everyone in the Middle East would still be our friends."

"Including Iran?" I asked, trying to join the crowd as devil's advocate.

"Damned Persians. They'd probably like us more, too."

"I like Iranians," cut in the hard-charging C/O. "They often give me caviar."

The other turned to me. "You really like Iranians, don't you?"

I ignored the question at first. I was listening to an operational story across the table, curious to hear how my colleagues approached their prey, whether they preferred appeals to patriotism, money, or varnished coercion. That Iranians fascinated me was no secret. However, I didn't realize I'd revealed so much affection. My corridor reputation was that I was a good C/O with an academic streak in Islamic studies. I hadn't intentionally hidden my interest. As with my Jewish background, I just didn't discuss it at work.

"You've studied Iran, haven't you?" he asked, moving his eyes to the more raucous side of the table.

"They have their good moments," I answered.

"So you like them," he said, glancing at the Persian newspapers in front of me.

Reading Persian newspapers was a sure sign of questionable target love. I remembered the comment of a Harvard-educated C/O, a rare breed in the 1980s CIA. He'd wryly remarked that most C/Os view books as recognition signals for clandestine meetings and not as something to read.

"Do you like them?" I asked.

"A couple. Most of them I hate. They're such goddamn liars."

"Do they lie any more than we do?"

Then the hard-charging C/O barged in. "Do you know what I learned in my last meeting? I think it's first-rate ops-intel, if not a full intelligence report. It's such a great case. I think it's one of the best we have."

I nodded for him to continue.

"Did you know that the Revolutionary Guard Corps doesn't have military ranks? They just call each other 'brother.' A whole army of brothers. It must get very confusing."

I raised my eyebrows and smiled. Reliable rumors were already flowing out of Tehran about Rafsanjani's imminent (and ultimately unsuccessful) plan to integrate the Revolutionary Guard Corps into the regular army. As a preliminary, Rafsanjani had introduced military ranks into the Guards. Their practice of addressing one another as "brothers," begun in the early revolutionary days, had already changed.

Later, the C/O told his boss the discovery. The chief thought Washington "consumers" would want to know. "This is such a great job," the C/O exclaimed in triumph, returning to his desk.

He was right, of course. That was the pity. (And the problem.)

Hosein and I slept in the same bed and rose together at the crack of dawn. He had to make a few telephone calls and run some errands. He'd be back before noon. Then we'd go to the truck, pick up the load, and head for Tabriz. If I wanted to see Khomeini's tomb before leaving, he'd borrow a car. My idea of visiting the Revolutionary Guard bookstore next to the former U.S. embassy I'd abandoned long ago. Even Hosein thought that a bit insane. Still revved from the night before, I told Hosein to get the car.

For two hours I stayed in bed looking at a collection of army photos hung on the wall and feeling my courage wane. In Tabriz it took half a day for me to get out the door. I didn't have that luxury here. What seemed easy at sunrise was difficult now. I'd visited the Turkish-Iranian border before crossing. I'd almost called off the trip, imagining sequences of horrible events. Every quarter of Tehran had its local *Basiji* and ex-*Komiteh* snoops. They weren't nearly as active as they had been, but they weren't gone. I couldn't hide my gait. I couldn't hide my size. Seeing a few tall Iranians hadn't comforted me much. All I needed was a lingering glance. Still, the odds were in my favor, I told myself; no one was expecting an American in south Tehran. I was big, but dirty. I'd blend in.

I got up and put on my clothes. Hosein's aunt intercepted me with breakfast: tea, white cheese, and bread. She kept replenishing the food, only speaking to ask if I wanted more. After several rounds, I told her I'd be back in no more than an hour.

The street was alive and more colorful in daylight. The surrounding two- and three-story houses were mostly made out of brown mud-brick, and there was a big pile of garbage fifty feet down on the other side of the road. Two mangy yellow dogs were sticking their snouts into the refuse. Because there were no proper sidewalks, the two-lane street had a steady stream of people, most of them young men and boys. A chador-clad woman walked by with two little girls in knee-high dresses and loose dark pants underneath. One girl was uncovered; the other had a blue-speckled white head scarf tied under her chin, leaving ringlets of brown hair on her forehead. The mother and children stared at me as I passed. I smiled; the mother, whose face was open, smiled back. Joining the crowd, I walked down the middle of the street, trying not to return stares or get hit by a car. Feeling surrounded, I stepped off the street onto an empty side road, which led me to another busy intersection of dirt and paved roads. Because the land was absolutely flat, I couldn't see over any of the buildings. I could, however, see over everybody's black-haired head. I definitely felt much too tall and a little too pale.

As the street blocks were short, I'd have to keep turning right or left. With the mountains, which were visible on the horizon, I couldn't lose the primary directions. I could easily go too far, however. I'd got lost in Denver once on a CIA training exercise. I'd had north, south, east, west, and a map, but I barely made it to my "clandestine" meeting.

Across an open dirt square, I could see medium-sized concrete high-rises. Next to shorter buildings, they looked like turrets on a fortified wall. I'd heard the clerics were encouraging suburban urban planning. After the countryside's hovels, they no doubt looked good: one step closer to modernity. I wondered who lived in them—the shrinking Iranian middle class or the poor with good connections.

I followed the rim of the sandy dirt field and turned inward toward more light-brown brick buildings. I'd run into another makeshift street market, set up on tables and carts. I scanned for blue uniforms and guns. I saw leather, filthy sheepskin, wool, and army coats, black and gray pants, blue jeans, brightly colored nylon coats, and tennis shoes. I was certain the *Basijis* were somewhere. I unwisely stood still and searched. People were speaking both Azari and Persian. Long Persian vowels rose above the Turkish monotone. I heard someone say *"akhund."*

I spotted a small pack of boys coming my way from the open field. I turned away from the street market. Once again, I was positive everybody was staring at me. In the morning rush hour, I was quickly losing courage.

I walked past the boys, not smiling as before. They all looked at me but kept going. I retraced my path, almost breaking into a run. When a car honked from behind, I nearly dove off the road. I pivoted, hunting for markers: a light-brown brick home with a full clothesline strung from an unfinished second floor, an unpainted wooden gate, and a tethered goat. I returned home via a slightly different route. When Hosein came back with a car, I told him I wasn't going. I'd be stuck in a mass of Iranians with no place to hide. Khomeini's tomb would have security. I didn't want to study the Imam close up anymore. He was dead and I wanted to go home.

Hosein understood. We'd take the car to the truck park and leave it. I didn't want to walk the streets again. On the periphery of the city, the car would be safe to use. There were just too many people. We said our goodbyes to Hosein's aunt and uncle. The old man begged me one more time to strike the mollahs. I quickly shook his hand and got into the car. I looked at Hosein the entire ride, thinking he was an absolute idiot to have agreed to this trip. Hosein drove through several blocks of congested streets, honking madly like the rest of them. Women in chadors appeared to outnumber men, making the roadsides and sidewalks look like laundry lines hung with billowing black sheets. Suddenly I saw a long white banner with red-lettered *nastaliq* hanging on an unfinished concrete building. We drove by too quickly for me to read it. I made out only *"Allah,"* *"sakhteman"* (construction), and *"shahdari"* (city government). Whatever it was, it was the first sign I'd seen touching on God and government.

The early years of revolution had produced some of the most colorful, ingenious poster work, blending medieval miniature techniques and symbolism with larger-than-life, muscular Stalinesque art. Most of it damned the United States and Iraq in bloodred detail. I hadn't seen many pro-government messages on buildings or walls. In poor neighborhoods, images of Khomeini and Khameneh'i seemed limited to carpet shops, teahouses, and tin shacks in truck lots.

I liked traveling by car more than walking. No one noticed my height. People couldn't stare too long. But I kept searching for a police control. By the time we reached the truck, my right hand was glued to the side of my face. In the truck's side-view mirror, my wrinkles and receding hairline stood out. In five days and seven hundred miles, I'd aged ten years.

When Hosein gave the word, I rolled over the seat and lifted the lid. I lay back and locked it. Regardless of numbness and traffic noise, I'd sleep now. Images of home went through my mind—family, friends, and places I just might see again. Before I went to sleep, I remembered my grandmother, who'd died a year earlier. More than anyone else, she'd taught me about joy and courage. She'd always understood how a Midwestern boy could fall in love with Iran. To her alone I'd confessed all my sins. In the box, I lifted my invisible hand and made the sign she'd taught me as a child. "One for all, all for one."

An hour and a half into the traffic, I conked out. I woke when the trailer doors opened. I didn't hear another word until Hosein was yelling and banging. Five days of fear were rushing out of my body. I pulled myself over the seat, fell back on the cot, and stared quietly at the back of Hosein's head until I fell asleep.

9 THE RETURN

Tehran–Istanbul

Except for a road check on the outskirts of Qazvin, we drove non-stop. An hour from Tabriz, we ran into a blizzard. Eastern Anatolia had been getting hit hard for two days. If I didn't get stuck in Iran, Hosein could get stuck in Turkey. Fearful for his work and truck, he suggested stopping for a few days. He and Hazra would have the time to host me properly: bigger meals, with more family and friends. We could revisit the Bazaar. He didn't want me to leave fearing his countrymen.

Hosein's irrepressible concern convinced me I had to go. Self-confidence can thin one's luck. I could warn him until Judgment Day about expanding the circle. If we drove slowly, we wouldn't drive off the road. Tabriz to Bazargan was less dangerous than the road to Ardabil. The storm was far less dangerous than staying in Tabriz. Hosein had been able to arrange a small load, so we wouldn't cross empty. We'd be able to start by late morning, getting through customs and security perhaps by midnight.

Hazra had food on the table when we arrived. We ate, talked a little, and went to bed. In the quiet, I lay awake listening for west-bound trucks and to Hazra and Hosein through the door. I wanted to know what they thought of me. Had I hurt Hazra with any of my questions? Did they believe a hundred percent that I was a spy? Did I fall short in their eyes? If I offered Hosein more money, would he take it? When he opened the door, I feigned sleep. I was still listening for traffic when the muezzin made his first morning call.

They woke up not long after. She had work; he had errands. Before leaving, Hazra made us breakfast and gave us doggie bags. I gave her my U.S. and Istanbul address and telephone number. Hosein already had them, but I wanted personally to show my thanks. Westerners aren't as hospitable as Persians, I told her, but she should give my family and friends a chance.

I wanted to kiss her on the cheek, but refrained. I'd so kissed a couple of my agents' wives and ill-starred young women seeking the Promised Land. They'd been awkward encounters. She thanked me and wished me luck. With Hosein, I said, I wouldn't need it. She kept smiling until she shut the door.

Hosein left soon after. I made more hot tea and counted trucks. I estimated a foot of fresh snow on a flat-roofed building across the street. The highway would probably still be covered. Turkey–Iran traffic wasn't heavy this time of year. Iranian snowplows might not have moved quickly into action. For a couple of hours, I just stared out the window, fearful that some neighborhood *Basiji* snoop had uncovered me and called the Guard.

Hypersensitive to hallway sounds, I heard Hosein shut the street-side door. He was ready to go. Adrenaline pumping, dreaming of home, I walked just ahead of him to the truck and eagerly jumped into the box. Neither sleeping nor counting down from ten thousand, I stared into the dark. When Hosein thumped, I quickly pulled my body out and over the seat. The highway already had paths driven through the snow. At almost sixty kilometers an hour, we'd reach the border in about six hours. For the first time in the trip, Hosein didn't do most of the talking. Chattering like a rug merchant with silk-priced fleece carpets, I didn't notice the stopped vehicles and cars. Hosein did, and I quickly went under. Before I'd pushed the watch's glow button once, we were moving. Only Hosein's voice had penetrated the box.

In five hours, we were at the border. With a big gulp of fresh air and a long look at the mountains, I opened the lid. Locked tight and reinforced with hands and knees, I counted the downshifts. When the cabin door slammed shut, I listened to my breathing and started counting down from ten thousand. Mercifully, no curses pierced the box. Except when the trailer doors opened, I heard no one, just a few trucks and a bus. Adrenaline eventually gave way to darkness, silence, and fatigue. I turned inward and started thinking about me and Iran. But I, again, hit a wall, going neither forward nor backward in time. Scared, numb, and blind, I wanted a light sleep, allowing me to hear voices but compressing time.

As the hours passed, I realized we'd escaped a cabin inspection. Hosein was probably again locked in some bureaucratic battle with corrupt border officials. Finally, darkness won. When the engine ground on, I woke. Four hours. A few minutes later, we stopped again. Turkish customs and security! "I'm out!" I shouted silently several times. My body shivered, evacuating the fear and guilt. Evin prison would get neither Hosein nor me. Nor Hazra, nor the uncles or aunts. Since we'd begun the trip in Istanbul, I'd learned my wife was pregnant with our first child. Ever tolerant of my odd behavior and passions, my wife would forgive me for what I'd done. Iran would be as it was before, and the pilgrimage over, I could get on with my life.

The cabin door opened, closed, and several minutes later opened again. At least two Turks were alongside. If they found me, I'd be okay. They'd perhaps even leave Hosein alone if I yelled enough. The Turks were fairly tolerant of intrusions on their national sovereignty so long as Turks weren't hurt or targeted. Though Ankara and Tehran had proper diplomatic relations, they loved to stick it to each other behind the scenes. The Turks might think they'd uncovered a CIA operation. If so, they'd definitely leave Hosein alone. They'd interrogate us, listen to the CIA deny all knowledge, and let us go. We'd probably both be able to visit Turkey again within a few months.

Given the lack of danger, I didn't notice the hours pass. Only my body reminded me I had to get out sooner rather than later. We'd barely started rolling when Hosein thumped and yelled. As my entire left side was numb, I popped the lid and stayed put. A few miles down the road, Hosein hauled me out. In the headlights, Turkey was black and white.

Dogubeyazit, a rough and wild frontier town, was buried and quiet. Hosein spotted a row of parked trucks on the outskirts of town. We fell in line. Hosein had me by the arm again before I reached the running board. When my left leg gave way, he pulled me through a roadside drift. We walked arm in arm down the center of the principal street. Parked cars were piled with snow. Paths had been shoveled to most buildings, making Dogubeyazit's one-street downtown look like a network of waist-high trenches. A snow-free, empty police car was guarding the parking lot of our hotel. After a few seconds of banging and buzzing, we saw a frowning night clerk come to the door. Though I didn't have my passport, he let me check in. I briefly protested the posted prices, gave up, and took the keys. We finally had separate rooms.

I told Hosein to wake me before noon. He smiled and bet I'd gladly be up early for the first time in a week: fear wouldn't keep me in bed. Outside my room, I shook his hand, shut the door, and headed for the bathroom. I bathed for an hour, browsing through a Turkish newspaper. It was too late to call Istanbul and the outside world, so I celebrated by stretching my body to the bed's four corners. Twenty years dreaming, a few years preparing and planning, and nearly a week in Iran, yet I didn't feel much joy. Though warmed, clean, and safe, I felt electrified but numb, incapable of concentrating on anything more complicated than the newspaper's bare-breasted women. Hours passed before I relaxed and shut my eyes.

When Hosein knocked, I was already awake. We had an early breakfast. Given the snow, we weren't driving up the valley road to Ishakpasha. Anything off the main highway was impossible. Hosein had checked the road gossip and weather forecast. I told him to do as he pleased; I could make it to Erzurum or Van by myself. From either city, I could fly back to Istanbul.

By lunch, he'd decided to make the Erzurum delivery and turn right around. He'd spend the night in Dogubeyazit or cross the border and sleep in the truck. We left after eating.

Plowed, the highway was tricky but passable. Traffic from Dogubeyazit and Van had also cut paths. As we cruised on an endless rolling white sea, my eyes started to hurt. If we'd had bright sunlight, I would've gone blind.

Knowing that for the last hour the end was near, we hardly talked. Neither of us wanted a long goodbye. When Hosein stopped the truck near the city center, I shook his hand and thanked him. I gave him the rest of the money we'd agreed on and added several hundred more. He didn't count it: the final gesture of mutual trust. He thanked me and wished me luck, then reprimanded me for not staying longer. I shook his hand again, touched his shoulder, and dropped down to the running board. He again wished me luck and hoped I'd call. It's a small world, I told him: we'd stay in touch. On the ground, I heard him shout, "Death to America!"

"Death to the mollahs!" I yelled back, and he smiled and drove on.

According to the Agency, a good agent is an asset who follows orders and shows initiative by providing hard-copy intelligence easily and in reams. Such agents are very rare. Ratting orally on your country is one thing; providing internal classified documentation, another. I'd been as eager as any spy to find such men. However, I preferred the opposite: agents who'd never follow your debriefing notes. I liked proud men who betrayed their country according to their own terms. Men who always messed up polygraphs.

Hosein had pumped my adrenaline like no agent before. He'd proved again that the best agents always lead their C/Os to the Promised Land. They're the masters; you're the disciple. My clandestine voyage into Iran fortified the impressions I'd had for years. Hosein, his family, his friends, and others I'd met intensely expressed the truth about the revolution. It was finished, and they felt cheated and angry that radical Islam's promises had devolved into cheap rhetoric aiding clerical graft.

My trip hadn't given me any insights into the timing of clerical collapse. I was still certain it was going to give way one of these days, probably in a violent Götterdämmerung. In the Muslim Middle East's take-no-prisoners politics, you're an idiot to give up power voluntarily. Given the extent of the anger and dry rot in Iran, the Islamic Republic's post-Khomeini history would probably be measured in years, not decades. Another riot would start, in Qazvin, Tehran, Tabriz, Isfahan, or Mashhad, I thought, and this time the army—or maybe even disgruntled and disgusted units of the Revolutionary Guard Corps—wouldn't allow the Interior Ministry to shoot poor Iranians in the streets. A chain reaction would follow, and the wise and lucky mollahs would beat a retreat to their turquoise-tiled mosques and seminaries and pray for a flowering of the soft, forgiving side of the Persian soul.

The degeneration of Islamic radicalism, not the date, was important. Elsewhere in the Muslim world, Sunni radicals were already trying to distance themselves philosophically from the Iranian experience. Shi'ites had always been cursed creatures, destined to fail. But behind the sectarian invective was an apprehension that Islam didn't have all the answers. The reunification of church and state might not make Muslims better able to handle Western challenges.

Radical Islam in power was perversely advancing the secularization of the Muslim mind. Except for the death edict against Salman Rushdie—an outrageous and successful intimidation of the West—Iran's Islamic revolutionaries had lost everywhere. In Afghanistan, Central Asia, the Caucasus, the Gulf, and even in the Shi'ite strongholds of Lebanon, they'd been isolated or ejected. Among themselves, Iranians were meaner, more hypocritical and duplicitous than they'd been before. They prayed less often and far less hopefully. Persians no longer thought they had a mandate from God. Worst of all, sixteen years after the revolution, America was more idealized than before.

The voyage had taken me deeper into the Persian mind. I slid less in its twists and turns. Hosein had also given me a pleasure I'd never had before. He'd taken me into a forbidden land and reversed our roles. For the first time, I'd actually fallen in love with my agent-cum-case officer. When he drove away, I hurt inside.

"Was it worth it?" Celal asked as I sat in his Istanbul office. The return trip from eastern Anatolia had been easy and anticlimactic. "It was a short trip for so much money."

"Money well spent," I said.

"So, are the mollahs going to fall? I lost a lot of money in Iran and I'd like it back."

"One day, *inshallah*."

"If the CIA paid for this trip, they're not getting their money's worth."

"I paid for it. I don't work for them anymore."

I'd told Celal several times that I'd left the Agency. He just couldn't believe I'd resigned from what he considered the world's most powerful organization.

"You're crazy."

"Not anymore."

"So, what did you learn?" Celal asked, pouring me a small raki.

"I learned how much I like alcohol and hate trucks."

"So you now like Turks more than Iranians?" Celal asked with a grin, raising his chin and wrinkling his brow.

"I still prefer Iranians."

"To hell with you, then! You haven't changed."

We had dinner together that evening. When I took the waiter aside to pay the bill, I discovered Celal had beaten me. Though I'd done him significant favors, I still remained hopelessly indebted. Being a gentleman, he would never ask to be repaid.

Standing before my consulate's pea-green walls, I looked at the visa section's Iranian bulletin board. Some of my old Persian handiwork was still posted. Straightforward, innocent information to help applicants visit or immigrate to the States. It was after hours: no Americans at the windows, no Iranians waiting in line. So far as I knew, there were no more *Angels*. I was the first and last of my kind. The clerics had run television programs and even made a film, I was told, warning their countrymen of the dangers waiting in U.S. consulates. Telling Iranians, or any Middle Easterner, that there were spies in foreign embassies and consulates was hardly news. The British in particular had always preferred consular cover for their spies in the Middle East. In consulates, spies, or as the British sometimes called them, "information officers," could get closer to the people. I'd asked Iranians regularly about the programs. They all said the same thing: the best pro-American publicity they'd seen in years. The mollahs had confirmed the Great Satan's reach and power. No matter how they tried, the mollahs kept achieving the opposite of their intentions.

I walked across the street to the Pera Palas, had two rakis in a big cushy chair, and then visited my favorite bookstore. No Turkish diplomats of any erudition had recently gone bankrupt or died. I walked inside a nearby green wooden mosque. It was off-hours and empty. The neighboring Sufi house of the Whirling Dervishes was closed; the turbaned headstones of minor Ottoman nobility and religious shaykhs stood guard outside. I went to see a big-budget Hollywood film in a cinema with a bar.

Afterward, I slowly made my way home through Beyoğlu's hilly, winding streets. As I unlocked the door, my friends' son greeted me in Arabic. "Peace be upon you," he said. I replied in kind. Together we watched Turkish fundamentalists on TV reading the Qur'an in one of Istanbul's great mosques. Superimposed on the Qur'an readers were immense transparent flowers, grass fields, and running water—a computer-generated paradise to animate God's words.

Tired, I bid the young man good night, exchanged blessings with him, and went to bed. Through a window, I looked out at the Golden Horn and an illuminated Hagia Sophia, the greatest domed church in Christendom, and the Süleymaniye, the Ottoman Sultan Suleiman the Magnificent's many-domed mosque. An empty *vapur*, a shallow-keel, smokestack Bosporus passenger boat, was crossing from Asia to Europe. Lit from bow to stern, the *vapur* looked on fire.

Here in the 717 naval battle of Constantinople, Christianity had been saved. From the city's seawalls and ships, Byzantines pumped "Greek fire," the ancient world's napalm, on tens of thousands of Muslim holy warriors. For days, men and vessels burned. Scorched, afflicted with plague, the Arabs eventually withdrew. This Christian victory, not the victory of Charles Martel at Poitiers in 732, saved a vulnerable Europe from Islam. When the Ottomans finally took Constantinople in 1453, the West had recovered culturally and militarily from the collapse of Rome. With the Ottoman defeat at Vienna in 1683, Austrians and Poles buried forever the holy warriors' hope that the House of Islam would one day rule the world.

Khomeini hadn't changed Vienna's outcome. Under the mollahs, Iranians were as dependent on the West as ever. Against their neighbors, they were far weaker. The Islamic revolution was a guerrilla action against the inevitable separation of church and state in the Muslim mind. It was a male scream against the gradual, irreversible liberation of women and the Westernization of the Muslim home. The Iranian revolution was dead, and even Turkish fundamentalists with their high-tech television shows were committing suicide in slow motion. Radical Muslims might worship the Prophet's and early caliphs' golden age, but they were hooked on progress, too. And progress inevitably leads you to the Great Satan and a world more or less on his terms.

A highly evolved parasite, *the Angel* had stayed alive feeding off the dreams and frustrations of young Iranians. Yet he wasn't all lies and deception. He'd always wanted to help Iran while advancing his own country's interests. Incapable of faith, he'd needed Iranians to lead him to the white light, the ineffable divine essence for which Khomeini, too, had searched. He'd wanted to feel the warmth and fraternity of Muslim men losing their identities in collective prayer. Not unlike the holy warriors he hunted, *the Angel* wanted at least for a while to turn off America's static noise.

Before I fell asleep, I thanked my private god, the only one I could believe in, that I hadn't really suffered for my curiosity and my sins. I swore that when I left Istanbul I'd leave *the Angel* behind. I'd have enough time before my flight, however, to visit my old stamping grounds again and perhaps make a new friend.

ACKNOWLEDGMENTS

In Persian conversation, it is common to hear Iranians offering to sacrifice themselves for one another. A Westerner unfamiliar with Iran's age-old, demanding *politesse* might conclude that Ayatollah Khomeini's revolution successfully created a nation of fanatical, fraternal true-believers. That is emphatically not the case. Eighteen years after the Islamic revolution, most Iranians are neither fanatical nor fraternal.

I have been fortunate in my Persian friends. I have found Iranians in whom politeness, kindness, and sacrifice are living morals, not lingering reflexes of an ancient order. I owe this book to such Iranians. Their ministrations, often far more constant over the years than my concern for them, have allowed me privileged access to things Persian, and kept me repeatedly out of harm's way, especially on my journey to Tehran. I will always be indebted to them.

My debt to my Turkish friends is only slightly less. Living and working in Istanbul, arguably the most seductive city in both the Western and the Muslim worlds, ignited my curiosity about the oldest and most passionate clash of civilizations. Through innumerable Turkish coffees and apple teas, head-splitting Turkish vodka and wine, sweet chicken pudding and baqlava, I gained self-confidence. Without Istanbul and *Istanbulus* behind me, I would never have gone farther east.

Because the Middle East is not a nice place and association with the CIA is not always a compliment, I have camouflaged my friends throughout this book, changing certain details of time, place, and personality. I have, however, tried to render people and places as accurately as possible.

Beyond Iranians and Turks, I am indebted to many others for their contributions to *Know Thine Enemy*. I will not try to name them all. Given my past, I suspect many would prefer to remain anonymous. Not everyone who helped me over the years with Iran and Islam knew I was, or had been, a case officer in the CIA. Ruining their ignorance or cover is a worse offense than failing to mention their help. There are some people I will mention, however.

To my mother, who has always known how to encourage and to cheer me, I owe all. Without her, and her mother, I never would have ventured far from home.

My father engendered in me a lasting fondness for things foreign and surreal. His writings about motorcycling overseas inspired me and provided a model. I have never met a more provocative man.

To Harold, an incomparable voyager in Islamic lands, I am indebted for his encouragement, criticism, insight, and his inexhaustible capacity to listen. Setting aside his skepticism about intelligence officers, he had the kindness to judge me in person. My life has never been the same.

To the Professor, I owe my eyes. Through conversations over late-night whiskies, essays, and books, he taught me how the study of medieval Islamic history remains an indispensable guide to the contemporary Muslim world. He also convincingly demonstrated that such history is a pretty good primer for espionage.

I must thank Oliver, an unrivaled boon companion. Rarely does one have the chance to be in the presence of a brilliant mind with such staying power. I drank deeply, absorbing history, philosophy, and religion with every drop.

Constance and Leigh showed me endless hospitality during my long peregrinations that gave birth to this book. Night owls, they indulged my penchant for early-morning conversations about medieval and modern holy war. More tolerant friends cannot be found.

I must thank Robert and Rita for their constant support. Immensely knowledgeable about the pitfalls of writing and publishing, they lovingly provided sharp-eyed editing, encouragement, and a tropical hideaway.

I cannot possibly repay Eddie for his essential early help with this book, and his sage advice, always generously given, thereafter.

My superb lawyer, Mr. Joseph Oneck of Crowell & Moring, is my guardian angel. Every spy should have one, particularly ex-spies who write.

My literary agent, Henry Dunow, believed in me long before *Know Thine Enemy* took shape, and my two indefatigable editors at Farrar, Straus and Giroux, Paul Elie and Jonathan Galassi, very gently took an inexperienced, stubborn writer through the hoops of turning a manuscript into a book. I am deeply indebted to them all.

My wife kept me sane and social while I wrote and rewrote the manuscript. In difficult circumstances, she daily proved herself a devoted reader, a very demanding editor, a supportive and loving wife, and a dedicated mother. I did not nearly thank her enough through the ordeal, so I thank her a thousand and one times now.

Last but not least, I must thank my *faux*, but very real, *frère*, Antoine. But I do not know how. I owe him so much, but, most of all, I owe him my freedom.

Needless to say, none of the above is responsible for any of my errors, peccadilloes, or sins that appear in these pages.